WOODLAND MANAGEMENT

A PRACTICAL GUIDE

Chris Starr

The Crowood Press

First published in 2005 by
The Crowood Press Ltd
Ramsbury, Marlborough
Wiltshire SN8 2HR

www.crowood.com

British Library Cataloguing-in-Publication Data
A catalogue record for this book is available from the British Library.

ISBN 1 86126 789 4

Dedication
To Hannah and Becky.

'We all travel the Milky Way together,
trees and men.'
John Muir, *The Mountains of California*

Disclaimer
Chainsaws and all other tools and equipment used in woodland management
should be used in strict accordance with both the current health and safety
regulations and the manufacturer's instructions. The author and the publisher
do not accept any responsibility in any manner whatsoever for any error or
omission, or any loss, damage, injury, adverse outcome, or liability of any kind
incurred as a result of the use of any of the information contained in this
book, or reliance upon it. If in doubt about any area of woodland management
readers are advised to seek professional advice.

All photographs by the author, except where indicated otherwise.
Line-drawings by Keith Field.

Typeface used: Bembo

Edited and designed by OutHouse Publishing Services,
Shalbourne, Marlborough, Wiltshire SN8 3QJ

Printed and bound in Great Britain by The Cromwell Press Ltd,
Trowbridge, Wiltshire

Contents

Acknowledgements

This book could not have been completed without the help of family, friends and colleagues, and although I did not always heed their advice and thoughtful criticism I am very grateful for it.

I should like to take this opportunity to thank the following owners who kindly allowed me to use their woodlands as case studies. Toby Coke at Weasenham New Wood, Jim Ralph at Knapp Coppice, Maggie Gordon and Bob Lee at Barfil Farm, and Graham and Sarah Chaplin-Bryce at Low Bridge End Farm, generously gave me their support and encouragement. I hope the case studies manage to do justice to their hard work and vision.

I am grateful to those who kindly let me use their photographs, woodland sites and drawings, including Ted Wilson, Hans Morsbach, Jim Ralph, Chris Seymour, Edward Mills, Rebecca Oaks, Neville Elstone, Tom Kent, Nigel Williams, Martin Clark, Colin Blanchard and Malcolm Riding. Simon and Jacqueline Stone at Robin Forest Surveys and John O'Keefe at the Harvard Forest were very helpful in responding to my last-minute pleas for material.

Bob Watson, Mike Jones, Ted Wilson, Eva Casson-du-Mont and Dorothy Parry commented on various drafts of the text while my employers, the University of Central Lancashire, funded my sabbatical leave. The staff at The Crowood Press always responded quickly to my requests for help and advice, and Keith Field has done a great job of turning rough sketches into excellent diagrams.

Finally to my parents, Audrey and Richard, for supporting me in my choice of career, and to my wife Helen, who kept me fed and watered in the shed and occasionally steered visitors away as the manuscript deadline approached – thank you!

Introduction

I have read many definitions of what is a conservationist, and written not a few myself, but I suspect that the best one is written not with a pen, but with an axe. A conservationist is one who is humbly aware that with each stroke he is writing his signature on the face of his land. Signatures of course differ, whether written with an axe or pen, and this is as it should be.

Aldo Leopold
A Sand County Almanac, 1949

While writing this book I spoke to many woodland owners, and the more I talked to them the more I came to realize the diversity of reasons that people have for owning, buying or wishing to buy woodland. This has meant that I have, of necessity, had to cover a very wide range of material and had to think about this from the perspective of those who often know little or nothing about woodland history, silviculture or wildlife management. This is more of a problem in Britain than in many European countries, since Britain lost much of its rich woodland culture when the rural population moved to the cities during the industrial revolution. Perhaps the increasing interest we see in woodland today is part of a migration back to the countryside, at least in spirit, and a reawakening of a long-dormant woodland culture, once so rich here and evident in our woodland heritage.

Increasingly, woodlands are being purchased by individuals seeking a stronger link with their natural heritage. Others buy woodland for a wide range of objectives including, among many others, financial return, investment, sporting and recreation, lifestyle change, and habitat and wildlife conservation. Some acquire it simply for its own sake – because it is a pleasure to own. For those not in a position to actually own a woodland, membership of charities concerned with the conservation of Britain's woodland heritage enables people to make a contribution through voluntary work.

Woodlands are not static, and their extent, composition and structures have changed considerably over time. They are surprisingly resilient and, although many have been cleared to make way for farming and urban development, others have survived and continue to provide a strong link with the past. Where land is left idle, woodlands return with great vigour to reclaim the space, often forming complex and interesting new habitats. Even in hostile urban environments, woodlands flourish on the most degraded sites, improving the soils and microclimate.

The terms 'woodland' and 'forest' can have different meanings. In the past, the distinctions that existed were based upon land ownership and use; more recently forests have come to be seen as places for timber production. However, the New Forest in Hampshire, itself a woodland set aside originally as a royal hunting reserve and later extended through planting, has recently been designated a national park with protected status. Suffice it to say that such distinctions, while of interest to historians and academics, are not central to the purpose of this

This heart-shaped woodland grows on the side of Blease Fell in Cumbria and was planted by a local farmer. It is seen every day by thousands of motorists travelling along the M6 near Tebay, and by rail passengers going north on the West Coast line from London to Glasgow: look out of the right-hand side window shortly after leaving Oxenholme.

book. Woodland is used throughout this book as a general term to mean land covered with trees and managed for a wide variety of objectives, but excluding large-scale commercial forests.

There is no right way to manage woodland, but there are some wrong ways and there are some guiding principles. An understanding of how different trees respond to such things as soil, light and competition is important if cause and effect are to be understood. The choice of a particular species might be dictated by personal preference, by the history of the site, by the end use of the timber or by the needs of a particular habitat or animal.

This is not a book for the professional forester, but rather an introductory text aimed at those with an interest in owning and caring for woodlands, whatever their particular objectives. I have tried to keep jargon to a minimum, and have used technical terms only when absolutely necessary. The common names of tree species will be used throughout, but in some cases the scientific name is also added. This is not to confuse, but to add another dimension to an understanding of trees and woodland. The scientific, or Latin, name often describes a species better than the common name, and is recognized throughout the world. In some cases, woodland types are described by their scientific names rather than by the common ones.

Although many of the technical principles and species described in this book apply

equally to woodland throughout temperate Europe, the cultural, social and legislative framework of England, Scotland and Wales is sometimes woodland specific. In addition, the impact of devolution on, for example, woodland grants and policies has led to a divergence of approach between the three countries. (I was also asked to consider including Northern Ireland and the Republic of Ireland, but they, too, have quite different legislative and land-use structures and priorities, although much of the book applies equally to them.) For these reasons, the practical management of woodlands in Britain – meaning England, Scotland and Wales – is the subject of this book.

A glossary of technical terms will be found at the end of the book and, for the reader interested in finding out more, a list of sources of further information and guidance is included, together with a list of technical publications and more advanced reading.

The history of woodland management is partly one of keen amateurs and landowners experimenting with new species, approaches and techniques. Many woodlands are now in better hands than they have been for years, and the success of new initiatives bodes well for future generations. It is too easy to be despondent in the face of the great global concerns facing the natural world. Local actions in local woods may help to put these concerns into perspective, and thereby enrich local lives, local landscapes and local wildlife.

CHAPTER 1

Woodlands: Past, Present and Future

In the absence of people, Britain and, indeed, many other countries throughout the world, would be substantially covered in woodland. The highest mountains and the estuaries aside, woodland would stretch from sea level to above 600m, forming what is often referred to as 'mixed oak forest'. In reality, this would have been a complex mosaic, consisting mainly of broadleaved species, with open spaces and, in places, grazed pasture woodland. Only in the more northerly regions and on some of the poorer soils in the south would Scots pine have flourished. The species composition of this mosaic would have varied in response to the local climate, soils and the degree of exposure. Although Britain is a small island, it exhibits a wide range of microclimates, and the woodland would have reflected this.

The Wildwood

Oliver Rackham, the eminent woodland historian, evocatively refers to our prehistoric forests as the 'wildwood', reflecting the diverse nature and primitive hold they have on us. We have a strong affinity with this wildwood and it is reflected in our fables, our literature and in our deepest desires and fears. It is easy to forget that not so long ago large mammals roamed our woodlands. The wild boar, wolf, beaver and elk all lived in Britain's woodland before hunting drove them to extinction. The last wolf was killed in Scotland as recently as 1743. The only large mammals now found wild are deer. Today, the reintroduction of some of these mammals is under serious consideration, particularly in the more remote parts of Britain. A private landowner is currently considering plans to convert some 10,000 hectares of land in the Highlands of Scotland into a reserve stocked with long-extinct mammals such as the bison, wolf and lynx as part of an ecological restoration project.

Forest Types

On a broad scale, Britain lies within what is known as the deciduous summer or temperate forest. This stretches across Europe and into Asia, covering vast areas as far north as Scandinavia and as far south as the Mediterranean. Although primarily made up of broadleaved species, it also contains some conifers, particularly at higher altitudes. Across much of Europe the climate is continental, exhibiting greater extremes of temperature with warmer summers and colder winters than our own.

In Britain, by contrast, the effects of the close proximity to the sea are felt everywhere and this is why even at quite high altitudes broadleaves grow well here. Only in the far north do British woodlands merge into another large-scale forest type, the northern or boreal coniferous forest that stretches across Scandinavia and Russia; in fact, most

Ancient westerly 'Atlantic' oak woodland growing on steep-sided valley slopes at Culbone in north Somerset, bordering the Bristol Channel and Exmoor. This represents something approaching the natural woodland that would have covered parts of the region in the past. The woodland has been worked for tan bark and coppice, so oak is probably more common than it would have been. The effects of wind and salt spray cause the trees to become stunted towards the shoreline.

of Siberia is conifer forest. These are the native pinewoods dominated by Scots pine, and sometimes referred to as the Caledonian Forest. Now restricted to the Highlands of Scotland, often in quite isolated groups, considerable effort is under way to regenerate these pinewoods, using local seedlings protected from the effects of grazing.

Native Tree Species

Native tree species are those that colonized Britain naturally after the last ice age and before the formation of the English Channel some 8,000 years ago. These native species gradually moved back from mainland Europe as the climate warmed and the ice retreated. It is possible that one or two might have survived during the ice age in isolated refugia, but we cannot be sure of this.

These native tree species – of which there are about thirty-three – are listed in Table 1. In the past, they made up the complex woodland cover of Britain and are of the utmost importance for nature conservation and the maintenance of our remaining semi-natural woodlands. Today, they are supplemented by species introduced at various stages over the last 8,000 or so years, including some that would have arrived naturally had the Channel not prevented them.

Table 1 lists the native species in the generally accepted order of arrival – the wind-pollinated pioneer species followed by those with heavier seed. As they arrived, they migrated northwards, colonizing regions where the climate and soils were suitable. Some of the later arrivals, notably beech, reached only as far as the south of Britain naturally. Note that nearly all the species are broadleaved, a clear indication of our place within the temperate forest ecosystem of the northern hemisphere.

Wood Pasture and High Forest

In recent years the Dutch ecologist Hans Vera has challenged some of our notions of what the natural forest in Britain and much of Europe would have looked like after the last ice age. Rather than being dense high forest, he proposes that some of it was more like wood pasture, with widely spaced trees browsed by larger mammals. He suggests that as the ice melted, the larger grazing mammals, including the now extinct wild ox, together with the wild cattle and the wild horse, moved into Britain ahead of the trees. These ungulates had a major effect on the spread and regeneration of the woodland, resulting in more of the light-demanding species such as oak and hazel being present (a fact observed from the pollen record).

Table 1: The native tree species of Britain

Common name	Botanical name	Notes
Common juniper	*Juniperus communis*	Now restricted to small isolated upland and heathland sites
Downy birch	*Betula pubescens*	Typical pioneer species, with local adaptations to site
Silver birch	*Betula pendula*	Typical pioneer species, with local adaptations to site
Aspen	*Populus tremula*	
Scots pine	*Pinus sylvestris*	Once native in southern England when the climate was cooler than it is today
Bay willow	*Salix pentandra*	Native willows important for insects
Common alder	*Alnus glutinosa*	
Hazel	*Corylus avellana*	
Small-leaved lime	*Tilia cordata*	
Bird cherry	*Prunus padus*	
Goat willow	*Salix caprea*	
Wych elm	*Ulmus glabra*	
Rowan	*Sorbus aucuparia*	
Sessile oak	*Quercus petraea*	Important for insects and lichens
Ash	*Fraxinus excelsior*	
Holly	*Ilex aquifolium*	
English oak	*Quercus robur*	
Hawthorn	*Crataegus monogyna*	
Crack willow	*Salix fragilis*	
Black poplar	*Populus nigra* var. *betulifolia*	Quite rare. Not to be confused with the introduced hybrid black poplars
Yew	*Taxus baccata*	Poor for wildlife but of high cultural value
Whitebeam	*Sorbus aria*	
Midland thorn	*Crataegus laevigata*	
Crab apple	*Malus sylvestris*	
Wild cherry (Gean)	*Prunus avium*	
Strawberry tree	*Arbutus unedo*	
White willow	*Salix alba*	

(continued overleaf)

Table 1: The native tree species of Britain *(continued)*		
Field maple	*Acer campestre*	
Wild service tree	*Sorbus torminalis*	
Large-leaved lime	*Tilia platyphyllos*	
Beech	*Fagus sylvatica*	
Hornbeam	*Carpinus betulus*	
Box	*Buxus sempervirens*	Restricted to southern England, this was the last tree to cross from Europe before the English Channel formed

The woodlands that developed did so with more open pasture woodlands forming a mosaic of grazed grassland and scrub, and areas of more closed woodland composed primarily of light-demanding species. In many ways, these would have looked much like parkland. These wooded pastures, which have been well documented in England for over 1,000 years, would have been rich in a range of different habitats including deadwood, natural pollards and grassland.

Research is currently under way to assess the sorts of grazing regimes, animal density and tree responses to grazing under conditions likely to have been found in the past. While we are still unsure of quite what the wildwood would have looked like, and the variations that might have occurred across Britain, it is likely that the role played by large grazing mammals in our woodland history and development has been understated.

The Changing Face of Woodland

Following the retreat of the ice sheet after the last ice age, the climate gradually warmed up and plants gradually returned, culminating in woodland. As the climate changed, so the species composition changed, with the pioneer species such as alder and birch giving way to the longer-lived, large seed-bearing trees such as the oaks, beech and hornbeam. The woodland that is composed of these longer-lived species is sometimes called the climax vegetation.

Initially, the human impact on the natural woodland would have been minimal. As hunter-gatherers, the Mesolithic population would have been scattered, with the forest home to small numbers of families. Only later, once settled communities grew, did forest clearance take place, and so began the transformation of the landscape into one we would recognize today.

The pattern of clearance varied considerably in different parts and regions of Britain. While the Lowlands of Scotland were cleared quite early on for grazing, and were substantially cleared by the Middle Ages, the Highlands retained their woodland well into the 18th century. By contrast, the South Downs in Sussex were cleared of large swathes of woodland by Neolithic times, and then saw a return to woodland during the so-called Dark Ages. Even with flint axes, Neolithic man was able to clear large areas of wooded land quite quickly. Helped along by fire, grazing and the ringbarking of standing trees, substantial inroads were made into the natural woodland cover.

Clearance of Woodland for Farming

In Britain, the clearance of woodland started on the lighter chalky soils and the sandy heaths where it was relatively easy to clear the tree stumps and to till the land. In response to the development of settled communities, the clearance for agriculture gathered pace

Most of the uplands of Britain are now bare of trees, with the result that erosion is a major factor in management and restoration.

BELOW: *Woodland cover in Britain from the last ice age to the present day. The reversal of large-scale woodland clearance in modern times is almost unprecedented.*

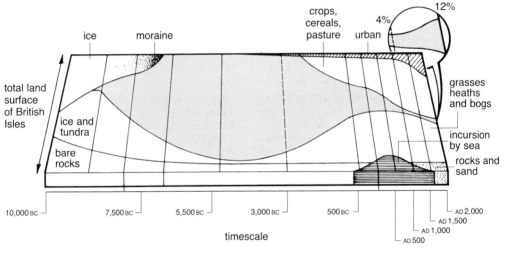

and the population of Britain increased. Since the earliest human settlements, wood has played a key role in the development of wealth and power. As a primary natural resource, easily worked and with a multitude of uses, wood has played a part in the development of every civilization from the ancient Mesopotamians in the Fertile Crescent to the people of today and the ongoing exploitation of the tropical rainforests.

Britain has a maritime or oceanic climate, with nowhere more than 110km from the sea, and is ideally suited to a pastoral farming system. The clearance of woodland for grass-

land and grazing was the foundation upon which agriculture developed.

The clearance and, much later, management of the major woodland tree species served to build our transport infrastructure, to house the growing population, to defend our shores and to build a trading nation and, later, the Empire. The 'noble hardwoods', among them the oak, ash and hornbeam, contributed immensely to wealth creation and employment, and were the 'hearts of oak' on which naval power was built.

Britain was substantially cleared of much of its primary forest or wildwood by the time

11

the Romans arrived. The historical low point at the start of the 20th century led directly to the formation of the Forestry Commission in 1919 and the subsequent rise in the area of land planted with introduced conifers. What is not generally recognized, however, is that there has been a considerable increase in the area covered by broadleaved woodland, which in England currently stands at its highest for many centuries.

Uses of Wood

The varied structure found within woodland and the different growth rates of trees allowed a variety of types of building material to be grown on the same site. For example, trees that need a lot of light grow to form the upper storey of a woodland canopy, and these may provide the large timber; the more shade-bearing species such as hazel grow beneath the canopy as smaller-diameter material, forming what used to be referred to as the underwood. This material was more easily worked and harvested.

The methods of management used also reflected the technology available. With simple hand tools, it was small-sized produce, easily cut and shaped, that was preferred. The advent of metal tools, and later of power tools, enabled larger material to be transported long distances and to be manufactured off-site.

Species Preferences

Our woodland trees are extremely versatile. From the earliest times, it became apparent that certain species grew better than others, that some were more demanding of soils and exposure, and that some regenerated with less effort than others. Similarly, certain timbers were better suited to specific situations, and the trees could be manipulated while they were growing to meet specific local needs.

For these and other reasons, certain trees were preferred to other species, and were either planted or regenerated in greater numbers. This meant that the composition of the natural woodland altered in favour of certain species that had greater utility. For example, beech was favoured for chair making (bodging), particularly in the

Broadleaved woodland and farmland on the Sussex Downs. Note the clear boundaries between the farmland (on easily cultivated chalk) and the woodland.

Chilterns, while in parts of the Weald of Kent and the Lake District, oak was managed for charcoal.

After many centuries of use and management, the woodlands reflected both the local climatic conditions and the uses the inhabitants made of them. Since we were, initially at least, woodland dwellers, then sites also tend to retain artefacts, dwellings and archaeological remnants of settlements. In many cases, woodlands remain one of the few places in which a strong link with the past is retained. Even when the trees are removed, the underlying soil tells a story in the accumulation of pollen built up in layers over a long period. It is for this reason that many of our ancient trees and woodlands are at least as important as ancient buildings in defining who we are and where we have come from.

Ancient or Veteran Trees

Recently, there has been renewed interest in what are termed ancient or veteran trees. Often found isolated in fields or hedgerows, they represent a link with a more wooded landscape and, in their shape and location, tend to reflect past management practices.

Types of Management

Historically, woodland was managed in a number of different ways, depending upon the type of material to be harvested, the species of tree being managed, and the availability of tools and the necessary skills. As technology developed so the ability to fell and to utilize larger-diameter timber grew. This necessitated new approaches to management and the evolution of a range of different silvicultural techniques and systems (*see* Chapter 10).

A more scientific approach to woodland management became evident in England with the publication in 1664 of John Evelyn's classic account of woodland management and plantation silviculture, *Sylva*. Woodland

owners also became more interested in managing their trees and in experimenting with new species and methods of establishment. The increase in area of privately owned plantations during the 17th century was a direct result of many of the landed gentry indulging in their new-found hobby of 'forestry'.

Coppice

The earliest form of management, coppicing relies on the ability of many, mostly broad-leaved, species to regenerate from a cut stump or 'stool'. This technique produces small-diameter material ideally suited to hand working. Most of our native broadleaves coppice, and the time between successive cutting periods – the coppice cycle – may vary considerably between species.

An ancient yew, certainly well over 1,000 years old, in the Borrowdale Valley, Lake District, England. Shortly after this picture was taken a larger part of the tree was destroyed in the gales that swept Cumbria in January 2005.

Woodsman cutting oak bark for tanning leather in coppice woodland in Sussex in about 1890. Note the other produce in the background and the landscape, which is recognizable today. Oak bark is still cut for tanning, although on a much reduced scale.

Coppice with Standards

This allowed the production of both small-diameter material and larger sawlogs by growing a proportion of mature trees among the coppice. In some cases, the same species were used for both while, in others, notably hazel coppice with oak standards, the different species were used for specific markets.

Overstood Coppice

Now very common with the demise of the coppice industry, overstood or neglected coppice has been left past its traditional cutting cycle. Many of these woodlands are now in desperate need of management, which might entail a resumption of coppicing or conversion to another system.

High Forest

This is another traditional approach where trees are allowed to grow straight and tall and form a closed canopy. Usually having a number of levels or strata, the dominant trees may be a single species, or a number of different species, sometimes chosen to make the best use of the differing light levels found within the woodland. High forest can be managed in many different ways and with varying degrees of complexity.

Neglected coppice is sometimes converted to high forest, by 'singling' the multiple stems that arise from a cut stool. In cases where the neglect has been pronounced, the coppice may have already grown tall enough to form a closed canopy, but might be quite unstable and prone to wind damage.

ABOVE: *A profile through a broadleaved high forest of oak, ash and hazel, showing the structure typical of temperate woodland in Britain.*

RIGHT: *An ash pollard recently cut to promote new growth and maintain vigour. St Johns-in-the-Vale, Cumbria.*

Pollards

This is a specialized type of coppice designed to keep the young shoots away from grazing animals, particularly cattle. Often seen as isolated trees in fields or in hedgerows, most pollards tend to be long-lived and often ancient. In addition to pollarding, other specialized forms of management, still quite common in some European countries, included pleaching, shredding and suckering.

Wood Pasture

This is a form of 'agro-forestry', where stock graze between widely spaced large trees grown for both shelter and timber. Many wood pastures are now neglected and suffering from a lack of active management. Some historians believe that wood pasture was far more common than is often supposed.

Plantations

Plantations are usually established with the primary purpose of growing timber. They may be planted on bare land, or converted from existing woodland by felling and replanting with other species. They make up a large proportion of the woodland cover in Britain.

Past Management Practices and Ancient Woodlands

When managing woodland it is important to appreciate how past management affects the options for the future. Just as a 'listed' building needs protecting and conserving, so, too, do certain types of woodland. Table 2 summarizes the key features of the designated types and the commonly accepted terms used in designating woodland. We will see later how these designations may affect the options for future management.

To the best of our knowledge, all the natural woodland in Britain has been altered in some way. Even in the more remote regions, the vegetation will have been changed either by man's activities or by the actions of domesticated or feral stock. Even in mainland Europe only small remnants of truly natural woodland remain in the more isolated regions of countries such as Poland, Finland and Romania.

Designations

During the late 1980s, it became apparent that many ancient woodlands were still being cleared for farming and development. In response to these threats, an Ancient Woodland Inventory (AWI) was completed for England and Wales on a county-by-county basis. This was followed in the late 1990s by one for Scotland.

Many of these designations might at first appear confusing or even arbitrary. In fact, in some cases the distinctions are either difficult or even impossible to make on the ground. Woodlands are in a continual, albeit long-term, state of change.

Many of our oldest woodlands, despite being irreplaceable, still lack any formal statutory protection. At the time of writing, fewer than 15 per cent of ASNW sites are formally protected, and PAWS woodlands have even less formal protection.

Each of the designations is explained in a little more detail below.

Ancient Semi-natural (ASNW)

This term reflects the fact that even the oldest of our woodlands have been altered at some stage in the past. However, these woodlands retain a strong historical link with the natural landscape, and are defined as having been wooded continuously since at least 1600 (prior to 1750 in Scotland) and being composed of species native to the particular site. These dates correspond approximately to the period when large-scale new woodland planting became more common, particularly on private estates. In conservation terms, they are of immense importance, and are the direct descendants of our once extensive and complex post-glacial woodland.

The term 'semi-natural' implies the regeneration of locally native species by either seedling or vegetative reproduction, rather than by planting. In the case of coppice, this

Table 2: Woodland designations affecting management

Designation	Age	Management features	Importance
Ancient Semi-Natural (ASNW)	Pre-1600 England and Wales Pre-1750 Scotland	Composed of species native to the site. Not planted but regenerates naturally. Indicator plants present	Rarest type. Highest conservation value
Plantations on Ancient Woodland Sites (PAWS)	Originated pre-1600, but planting at any time since	Often support species characteristic of ASNW. Soils often maintain seed bank and archaeological features	Formerly semi-natural but since planted with conifers, broadleaves or mixtures
Recent Semi-natural	Post-1600	Regeneration of locally native or naturalized species. Secondary succession	May be valuable habitats, species mixes and structure
Recent Plantation	Post-1600	Often single species. Many established from the 19th century onwards	Very varied: from pure commercial to high amenity and parkland

Scots pine growing near the natural tree line in the Highlands of Scotland at Rothiemurcus. The altitude here is 550m and grades into a sub-alpine tundra above the sparse woodland cover. (Photo: Ted Wilson)

might include 'layering'. The woodland would therefore regenerate itself in clearings or following wind damage. One of the positive outcomes of the 1987 hurricane that hit the south-east of England was the opportunity to monitor the regeneration of woodlands following a large-scale natural disturbance. Rather than clearing all the fallen trees and replanting, areas were left untouched. The succession of plants, the competition between them and the woodland structures resulting from this, are all now being monitored.

The structure and species composition of every woodland differs considerably, and reflects the local soils and climate as well as past management practices. Many of these woodlands would have existed prior to the large-scale changes brought about by agriculture, and therefore retain a link with the pre-industrial landscape. They are now often isolated and fragmented, and one of the real challenges in future is to connect them with new and more recent plantings, and thereby increase their size. The conservation value of these woodlands, from both an ecological and cultural perspective, increases with size. Small woodlands have a proportionately longer 'edge' than larger ones, and the microclimate effects and susceptibility to wind and exposure are more pronounced.

Plantations on Ancient Woodland Sites (PAWS)

In contrast to agricultural practices that tend to entail complete disturbance of the soil, the replanting of an ancient semi-natural woodland with another tree species will not destroy many of the important historical features of the site. For example, the soil and the seed bank will remain substantially intact, and the archaeological features may remain undisturbed in many cases. With careful management and financial support these Plantations on Ancient Woodland Sites (PAWS) may be restored.

Ancient Plantations

This sub-category includes plantations established pre-1600 using native species (as, for example, on a large private estate for the production of oak timber, or conifer plantations using introduced species established on ancient sites). These sites will vary greatly in their importance for conservation, and in many cases it will be difficult to distinguish them from the ASNW above, particularly if planted with native species.

Recent Semi-natural Woodland

This category includes a wide range of woodland types, but all are characterized by the regeneration of locally native species, often on heathland or moorland. Many woodlands on disturbed industrial sites such as old quarries or disused railway lines, together with areas of birch scrub, will come into this category.

Younger woodlands will be composed predominantly of pioneer species, while the older post-1600 woodlands might include species such as ash, oak and beech. In some cases, these woodlands will include native species regenerating outside their natural range, such as beech in the north of England.

Farmland left under set-aside schemes may well revert to this type of woodland, particularly if it is adjacent to existing woodland and if grazing pressures have been reduced.

Recent Plantation

This is a large category and includes all the plantations established by the Forestry Commission since 1919 and private forestry companies since the 1960s. In addition, it includes extensive plantations established by private landowners during the 20th century. Many of these plantations are composed of species introduced by the great Victorian plant hunters of the 19th century, including Douglas fir and Sitka spruce.

This category also includes many of the great landscaped parklands of the 18th century, together with smaller woodlands planted in the lowlands for shelter and game.

Many recent plantations are of very high landscape or amenity value and, increasingly, they are seen as important for wildlife, too. In some cases, these plantations will not be felled when the timber is ready, but will be left to grow on to ecological maturity. In some regions of Britain, plantations are reserves for the native red squirrel, and play host to wildlife as diverse as the osprey and the wild cat.

Woodlands on the March

There is a commonly held view that the area of woodland in Britain is decreasing, and that there is an urgent need to 'do something about it'. While there are real concerns about the decline of specific woodland types, notably ancient woodland, and of individual ancient trees, the reality, at least in the temperate regions, is a little different.

Whether we are talking about Britain, Europe or North America, both the area of woodland and the volume of timber is increasing year on year. In fact, the area of woodland in Europe is currently at its highest for many centuries, while in North America far less than the annual new growth (increment) is felled for timber each year. In Britain, woodland has increased from some 9.2 per cent of the land area in 1980 to 11.6 per cent at the time of the last census carried out by the Forestry Commission in 1998; in Scotland the figure is even higher, with some 17 per cent of the country now under woodland.

Simply put, woodlands are in general better managed, used more efficiently and carefully, and are growing faster, than at any time within recent history. The reasons for this include:

- The timber that is felled is used more efficiently in modern mills, and technological advances enable smaller-diameter material to be utilized.
- Advances in measurement and mapping, and the development of computer-based information, has ensured that the resource is better used.
- The development of systems for certifying the good management of forests has resulted in more woodlands being carefully managed rather than exploited.
- Advances in tree breeding and methods of selection ensure that the species chosen for new planting schemes are better suited to the site.
- The warming of the climate over the last few hundred years and, in particular, the increasing levels of CO_2 in the atmosphere, mean that trees are actually growing faster than they have in the past.
- Changes to agricultural practices, particularly in the uplands, have resulted in new woodland creation, sometimes as a result of natural regeneration.
- The enlargement of the European Union has brought in countries with extensive areas of woodland, many of which have been under careful management for centuries, but under-utilized in their previously stagnant economies.
- Increasing concern for, and interest in, the environment has resulted in an increase in the number of woodland owners.
- Charities for the conservation of woodlands, specifically the Woodland Trust in Britain, have prospered. They have been successful in promoting both new woodland planting and buying and managing existing, primarily broadleaved, sites.
- There is increasing interest in wood as a sustainable and renewable natural resource with very little 'embedded energy' used in its production. Architects are increasingly specifying wood for use in new buildings, and research is currently under way in identifying appropriate construction techniques for timber-framed buildings suitable for the damp British climate.

The plight of many of the natural forests in the tropics is a serious cause for concern, but somewhat outside the scope of this book. However, by better managing, utilizing and expanding our own woodlands, the pressures on some of the natural tropical forest resource may be partially reduced.

CHAPTER 2

Getting to Know Trees and Woodlands

Woodlands and forests cover nearly four billion hectares of the Earth's surface, over 30 per cent of the total land area. Within them live some of the largest, heaviest, oldest and tallest living things on the planet: trees. The trees in turn support myriad other plants and animals to create distinct woodland ecosystems.

Over many millions of years trees have evolved the ability to grow in many different climates, ranging from the Arctic Circle to the Equatorial swamps. Some are survivors from before the dinosaurs roamed the Earth, little changed in structure or shape (the conifers), while others have evolved into more complex forms (the broadleaves).

This chapter is designed as an introduction to how trees grow, how wood is formed, how they live together in woodlands and how we can recognize the types of woodland we see all around us. Finally, we will look at some of the ways in which we control the growth and development of woodlands, through the use of silviculture.

As time and space is limited, we will consider only those trees and woodlands from

The biggest tree in the world. The 'General Sherman' is a giant sequoia growing in the Sierra Nevada mountains of California. Weighing an estimated 6,000 tons it stands over 87m (285ft) tall, and is 24m (79ft) in girth. The author can just be seen by the fence to the left. (Photo: Hannah Starr)

the northern temperate zone, and more specifically from Europe and Britain. Many tropical and subtropical trees and forests adopt quite different strategies for survival and reproduction, and their ecology is complex in ways sometimes quite different from our own trees and woodlands. By understanding these things better, we will be able to appreciate how and why woodlands are managed today.

What is a Tree?

The definition varies, but often a tree is defined as a woody perennial with the capacity to grow a single stem of at least 6m in height. Not very inspiring! However, this definition clearly distinguishes a tree from a shrub or other flowering plant, although some trees may also be shrublike if conditions allow.

It is this ability to grow a straight stem, capable in some species of reaching over 100m in height, that leads to the complex ecosystems we call forests and woodlands. Growing from this stem are many different structural elements designed to capture sunlight, provide shade, absorb oxygen and expel other gases.

The main parts of a tree are:

Above Ground
- *Leaves* These convert energy from sunlight into carbohydrates (sugars and starch).
- *Reproductive structures* Male and female reproductive structures can be present on the same tree, or on separate trees, depending on the species.
- *Branches* These support leaves and reproductive structures.
- *Stem* This provides support for the tree crown, and transports water and minerals from the roots to the leaves, and sugars from the leaves to the roots.

Below Ground
- *Structural roots* These give stability, transport water and mineral nutrients, and are also used for the storage of starch.

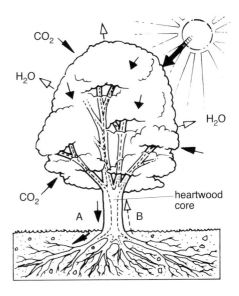

Simplified diagram showing the movement of carbohydrates, water and mineral nutrients. Carbohydrates formed in the leaves descend to the roots (A); water and mineral nutrients move up from the roots (B). The leaves take carbon dioxide from the air and 'fix' the carbon, releasing oxygen in the process.

- *Fine roots* These facillitate the uptake of water and mineral nutrients.
- *Mycorrhizae* A fungus–tree partnership that enhances the uptake of water and certain mineral nutrients.

How Does It Grow?

This is quite a complex subject. A number of different things occur in a number of specialized cells and structures.

- The cambium, a thin layer of cells, actively divides both outwards and inwards.
- The cambium forms a sheath inside the bark of every shoot, branch, stem and structural root of the tree.
- Cells divide outwards to form the phloem tissue (inner bark or bast), which transports sugars around the tree.

21

- Cambium cells dividing inwards form xylem cells, which we more commonly call wood. The wood is organized as a network of sieves, tubes and pipes for conducting water and mineral nutrients coming up from the roots.
- Once growth of, say, a shoot has stopped, a process called 'secondary thickening' occurs. This process, which creates the annual ring, gives trees their immense strength and the ability to grow to a great height.

Some of the bristlecone pines found in California have been accurately dated to over 6,000 years old, but it is only their cambium and a few layers of xylem that are still alive, surrounding a skeleton of long-dead wood. Similarly, the veteran trees found in many parts of Britain (such as that shown in the photograph on page 13) are often hollow as the wood itself has decayed. As long as enough wood is left to maintain strength and structure they will stay upright.

Differences: Conifers and Broadleaves

Conifer

In evolutionary terms, conifers are less advanced than the broadleaves. Botanists know the conifers as gymnosperms, meaning 'naked seeds', a reference to the relatively primitive reproductive structures – the cones – that distinguish this group of woody plants. A conifer has leaves that are either needles or scales; the leaves of most conifers remain on the tree from two to six years and continue growing throughout the year, except when the conditions are too cold for active growth. Conifers are also called 'softwoods', a general term that does not apply to the wood structure of all coniferous species.

Broadleaf

Broadleaved trees come into leaf every spring from a bud at the end of a shoot. The leaf is made up of a stalk (petiole) and a broad, flat blade, hence the name. Botanically, they are called angiosperms, meaning 'seeds in a case'. An acorn or a beech nut is a case containing a seed. Most broadleaves seen in Britain are deciduous, meaning they lose their leaves in autumn and become dormant over the winter. Confusingly, they are called 'hardwoods'. but again this is a generalized term that does not apply to all species in the group.

What is Wood?

Wood is one of the most remarkable of natural materials. Flexible, durable and strong, it is composed of layers of xylem cells laid down in annual rings. Each year a new ring is formed. These rings are relatively wide in youth, but later in life they become increasingly narrow, reflecting the work the tree has to do just to stay alive. If you look at the growth rings closely, you will notice that they sometimes differ from year to year; such differences occur because of drought or some other environmental factor.

Wood is composed of a number of different types of cell. The majority of xylem cells, known as tracheids, are thin and narrow. They are the only types of water-conducting cell in conifers. In the case of broadleaves, wider cells called vessels are also found. This leads to the creation of two different types of wood: ring porous (like oak) and diffuse porous (beech). The different structures affect both the grain of the wood and the way it behaves when cut or split. Lovers of fine furniture soon appreciate the differences between the species.

Another distinctive feature of wood is the presence of heartwood and sapwood. Heartwood is older wood, which is primarily structural, often dark coloured and contains chemicals making it resistant to decay. Yew, for example, is especially noted for the beautiful, deep-red colour of its heartwood. Sapwood, by contrast, is the outer wood in which the sap is still flowing. This may be more susceptible to decay. These differences are important when considering the uses of timber for such things as fencing and stakes in contact with the ground.

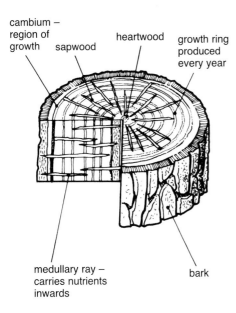

cambium –
region of
growth   sapwood   heartwood   growth ring
                                   produced
                                   every year

medullary ray –   bark
carries nutrients
inwards

Cross-section through the trunk, showing the major conducting tissues, bark and growth rings.

Once a living tree is felled, the timber starts to change, going through a process known as seasoning in which water is lost to the surrounding air. When freshly felled, the wood is 'green'; it is timber in this state that it is used for green woodworking.

Do Trees Grow Differently in Woodland?

The simple answer is yes, although things are a little more complicated than that.

If a tree is left to grow on its own in the open, it will spread out to maximize the amount of light collected by the leaves. Depending upon the species, it will form a large crown, with a short woody stem or trunk and spreading branches. Underground, the roots will also spread out and, without competition from other trees, will radiate in all directions, seeking out moisture and mineral nutrients.

In a woodland, however, each tree will be competing with its neighbour, which may be the same species or an entirely different species. Competition for light takes place above ground, while roots must fight it out with neighbours for the mineral nutrients and water in the soil. As a result, woodland trees tend to be taller than those grown in the open, often with deeper roots, and less heavily branched.

Some species are better adapted to growing in a woodland situation, while others prefer more space. When managing woodland it is important to understand how different species grow and interact, and how their responses can be used to meet the objectives of the woodland owner. The terms pioneer and climax are used to classify species on the basis of their responses to light and shade:

- Pioneer species, such as birch, alder and pine, like a lot of light, grow quickly on the right sites, improve the soil and have wind-pollinated seeds. They literally 'pioneer' the way for the next group of trees.
- Climax species, such as beech and yew, are happier in woodland conditions, with slower rates of growth and heavier seeds. They form the canopy of woodlands that have developed over many years.

A more useful distinction when managing woodland is one based upon the ability of different species to withstand shade. Table 3 (*see* overleaf) indicates the tolerance to shade of some of the more common woodland trees. The use of this distinction is discussed in more detail in Chapter 10.

Succession

If you bought a field, fenced it to prevent animals such as sheep and deer from getting in, shut the gate and walked away, what would happen? Over time it would gradually revert to scrub. Seed from the pioneer tree species would blow in, followed by that of the larger seeded trees, carried by birds and mammals. In most parts of Britain, it

open grown   woodland grown

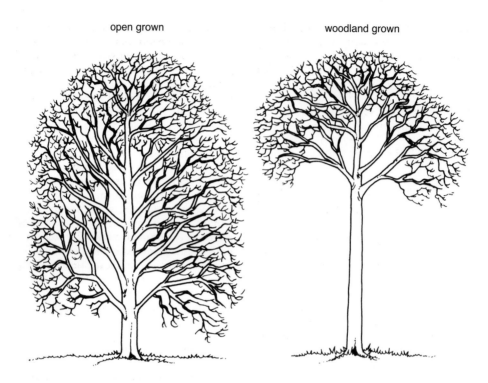

An open-grown and woodland-grown oak tree illustrating the large differences in form and habit. When oak was grown for naval use in the past, the open-grown shape was preferred for some timber as it enabled complex shapes to be sawn more easily.

Table 3: The shade tolerance of some common woodland trees

Light-demanders	Moderate shade-bearers	Shade-bearers
Alder	Ash (only when young)	Beech
Ash	Hazel	Hornbeam
Birch	Lime	Western hemlock
Oak	Sycamore	Noble fir
Poplar	Lawson's cypress	Western red cedar
Sweet chestnut	Douglas fir (only when young)	Yew
Willow	Coast redwood	
Larch (all three)		
Corsican pine		
Scots pine		

would eventually turn into broadleaved woodland, and the canopy trees would vary depending upon the soils, climate and local factors, including the presence of other woodlands in the area.

This process of dynamic change in the vegetation is called a succession, with the final stage being the natural community or climax vegetation. The process is shown diagrammatically below.

Differences: Native, Naturalized and Exotic Tree Species

Britain is unusual in having a limited number of what are termed 'native' species (listed in their order of arrival in Table 1, *see* page 9). Our native flora is restricted to some thirty-three tree species, nearly all of which are broadleaved. Later introductions are classed as either naturalized or exotic species.

Naturalized species reproduce freely and behave like native species, regenerating naturally from seed, colonizing sites and forming woodland. They include, among many others, the sycamore, sweet chestnut, European larch and Norway spruce.

Exotic or introduced species have been imported at various times from other countries. Many of the introductions occurred during the 19th century when the great plant hunters and collectors brought back tree species from both the Old and New Worlds. Such species include the cedars, southern beeches and the monkey puzzle.

Britain is fortunate in having a climate well suited to a very wide range of tree species. Many of our tree collections, called arboreta, contain rare and tender plants from throughout the world and are well worth visiting. The oceanic nature of Britain where winters are mild compared with continental climates, combined with the different microclimates created by landform and the proximity to the sea, means that relatively frost-tender species from the Mediterranean and the subtropics survive alongside species from much more northerly latitudes.

Classifying Woodland

Woodlands may be classified in a number of ways, depending upon the particular interests or organizations involved. Different specialists

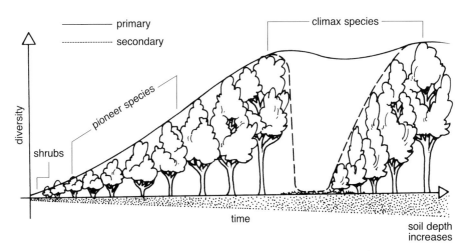

A primary succession from bare ground to climax woodland, illustrating the colonization by pioneer species and the equally important development of the soil structure over time. A secondary succession occurs following clearance of previously wooded land.

Even a Mediterranean species such as the cork oak (Quercus suber) *is, owing to the warming influence of the Gulf Stream, able to grow in some westerly areas of Britain. This example is the Gosforth cork oak in Cumbria. (Photo: Ted Wilson)*

see woodlands in different ways. A woodland ecologist will observe quite different features and plant associations from those seen by a timber-harvesting specialist. There are also regional and national disparities in what constitutes woodland, and the relative importance attributed to such things as landscape, recreation and cultural values. An understanding of the different types of woodland that may be found in Britain will help when thinking about the management objectives and options open to a woodland owner.

There are three main ways in which woodland may be classified:

• By its structure.
• By the major tree species present and the ways in which these have been managed (the Silvicultural System).

• By the ecology of the woodland and the plant associations found there.

The Structure of the Woodland

Woodlands differ considerably, both in structure and in size. In some they are composed of many species of different ages, while in others they are predominantly one species, perhaps planted at the same time. However, in all cases they are composed of strata much as a cityscape might be. This vertical stratification tends to be less complex in the more northerly boreal woodlands than in the temperate ones. Interestingly, it appears that one of the reasons people find woodland so attractive is this element of diversity in structure.

Woodland is composed essentially of four different layers:

1. Tree or canopy layer. The canopy of the woodland formed by the crowns of the mature trees.
2. Shrub layer. The taller shrubs and smaller trees.
3. Field layer. The taller flowering plants and ferns.
4. Ground layer. This is composed of the very small plants, including mosses.

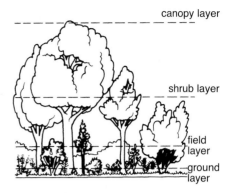

The strata or layers in a woodland, with trees and shrubs occupying particular positions in relation to the amount of light filtering through the canopy.

When walking through a woodland it is helpful to consider it in terms of these layers, as they can give clues to the past and current management. Not all woodlands contain every layer and, in some cases, it can be difficult to distinguish the layers that are present; for example, is that young tree part of the shrub layer or of the tree layer?

Different types of woodland will also exhibit different proportions of each layer. For example, ash allows a lot of light to penetrate the canopy, thereby helping the lower levels to develop, whereas pure beech may dominate woodland, allowing minimal growth in the shrub and field layers. Coppice woodland, briefly described in Chapter 1, looks quite different structurally from a plantation of Sitka spruce.

The Tree (or Canopy) Layer
As well as naming the different layers, it is necessary to distinguish between the different classes of trees within the canopy. This will become important when we consider how to manage the trees for particular objectives of management.

The canopy of a woodland is not uniform, but is a complex jigsaw of leaves, branches and crowns, all seeking out the optimum amount of light or shade for their own needs. In some woodland the canopy might be composed only of one or two species, while in others many species will jostle and compete for their preferred position. The trees within this layer are named with reference to their relative positions in the canopy:

• Dominant. These trees form the upper canopy and are usually the tallest and broadest. The species concerned usually gives its name to the type of woodland, e.g., beech or oak.
• Co-dominant. These are often the same species as the dominant trees.
• Intermediate.
• Suppressed.
• Wolves and whips.
• Dead and dying.

Each of these classes (illustrated overleaf) is important for different reasons, and the relative abundance of each will be dictated by the objectives of management. In a primarily timber-producing woodland, the aim is to concentrate on the dominant and co-dominant classes, while in a woodland managed primarily for nature conservation, as many classes as possible will be preferred, with deadwood habitats being actively encouraged.

Beneath the canopy might be an 'understorey' of trees. Some of these may be of similar age to those in the canopy, while others might vary in age and size quite considerably. When managing woodland for diversity it is often this layer that is actively promoted. These trees can rapidly respond to fill in gaps created when the canopy trees are blown down or harvested.

This understorey can be quite complex in structure and might be composed of the

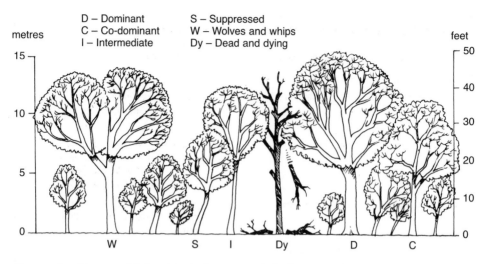

D – Dominant   S – Suppressed
C – Co-dominant   W – Wolves and whips
I – Intermediate   Dy – Dead and dying

Trees are classed in terms of their position in the canopy, with the dominant and sub-dominant trees forming the upper strata.

same species as the canopy, with younger trees waiting to emerge as light levels allow, or it may be composed of species unable to compete with the dominant trees.

Mixed broadleaved woodland might, for example, have a canopy of oak or ash, with an understorey of field maple, wild cherry or holly. In the event of clearance of the canopy, younger ash or oak will emerge to replace the mature trees while the understorey remains in place.

The Shrub Layer

This layer is usually between 2m and 5m tall; in some woodlands it will be very well developed while in others it will be absent. Typical larger species include hazel and hawthorn, together with young saplings of the canopy trees. Smaller shrubs include dogwood, guelder rose and honeysuckle. Tree saplings might be quite common, particularly after good seed years and, in the case of shade-bearing species, may grow quite slowly until released by openings in the canopy.

A feature of many trees is their ability to change from relative shade bearers when young to more light-demanding species when older (*see* Table 3, page 24). For exam-

ple, mixed conifer woodland with Douglas fir might have a lot of regeneration among the shrub layer, but this will grow into the canopy only when light conditions are right. Ash is another species that is often abundant in the shrub layer, particularly if soil conditions are suitable for seed germination.

One shrub species that often causes problems in woodland is rhododendron, introduced from southern Europe originally as cover for pheasants. This species is quite capable of smothering the shrub layer, particularly on acid soils. Clearance can be a major problem and its control is discussed in Chapter 9.

The Field Layer

This often develops into two distinct layers where the larger herbs such as bracken or bramble grow above the smaller herbs such as bluebell or dog's mercury. In older woodlands, this layer is often very complex, particularly on deep, fertile soils, and might include such species as bugle, wild primrose and ramsons.

Many species of the field layer are valuable indicators of ancient semi-natural woodland (some of these are noted in Table 4). Care must be taken, however, in the use of these

Table 4: Some possible indicator species of ancient woodland

Common name	Botanical name	Comments
Wood anemone	*Anemone nemorosa*	
Dog's mercury	*Mercurialis perennis*	Neutral to calcareous soils throughout Britain, except northern Scotland
Bluebell	*Hyacinthoides non-scripta*	The leaves appear in January or February and then wait until soil warms to flower. Very susceptible to harvesting damage before flowering
Wood sorrell	*Oxalis acetosella*	Moist acidic conditions. Leaves contain oxalic acid preventing grazing
Sanicle	*Sanicula europaea*	
Ramsons or Wild garlic	*Allium orsinum*	
Oxlip	*Primula elatior*	Traditional coppice flora species
Herb-paris	*Paris quadrifolia*	
Pendulous sedge	*Carex pendula*	
Remote sedge	*Carex remota*	

indicator species. There are large regional differences in them, and in practice they are often used to confirm ancient woodland sites following other survey information, including maps, archaeological features and archive records. Many of these woodland indicator species rely on woodland shade for survival and migrate very slowly, if at all, to other more recent woodland.

The field layer is generally found growing up to about 2m tall and, where light is plentiful, may be quite dominant and impenetrable. Where woodland is managed primarily for timber production, this layer will tend to be found only in openings in the canopy, or alongside the ride edges. However, when the timber is felled the field layer may develop very quickly and cause problems with the establishment of the next crop.

A feature of many woodland plants is the ability of the seed to lie dormant in the soil

Wood anemone growing under oak and hazel in Sussex. The woodland plants flower first, followed by the hazel; the canopy trees come into leaf last.

for many years. This seed bank is particularly valuable when restoring woodland sites that have been planted with species that are no longer required, as it allows the original flora of the site to develop quite quickly.

The Ground Layer

Although often neglected when managing woodland, the ground layer, which is found growing up to 10cm tall, has great value in its own right. It provides some of the most vital functions in a healthy woodland ecosystem and acts as the link between the above-ground plants and the soil below. This layer also includes the seedlings of the taller plants together with the shoots of any coppice species present. In addition, fungi are often present although they are only apparent during fruiting in autumn. In many predominantly coniferous woodlands managed for timber, fungi are common and may even be gathered as a cash crop.

The presence of mosses – and there are over 600 species growing in Britain alone – indicates damp and shady conditions. They are seen most frequently in the west of Britain. Ancient oak woodlands in the western parts of Britain often have a very well-developed moss flora.

The importance of the deadwood habitat for nature conservation is now recognized, and this is often found within the ground layer. The key role played by the invertebrates and fungi in the ecology of woodlands, particularly in nutrient cycling, means that attention should always be given to minimizing disturbance of the ground layer during woodland operations.

The Silvicultural System

Many woodlands in Britain have been substantially altered by human activities. In some cases, this has involved the wholesale clearance of locally native trees and their replacement with introduced timber species. In other cases, there has been a gradual shift in favour of one species over another, usually because a certain species or its timber had greater utility.

Silviculture is the branch of forestry concerned with the control of regeneration, development and growth of forest stands. Silvicultural systems comprise one or more planned interventions that alter the stand structure. There are two broad classes of woodland where silvicultural systems are applied: high forest and coppice systems.

High Forest

This term is usually applied to woodland in which the canopy is composed of trees regenerated from seedlings. This term spans a very wide range of stand structures, from single-species and single-age class stands to

Coed Dolbebin, Wales: an upland 'Atlantic' sessile oak woodland with a ground flora of mosses typical of the oceanic west coast of Britain. The soils here are acidic, and the oak grows with birch. (See NVC W17 in Table 6.)

Management of conifer woodland on continuous cover principles.

multiple-species and multiple-age class stands. These structures result from stand history, species interactions and management objectives.

Even-aged woodlands These are surprisingly common in nature, especially in the boreal regions where large-scale forest fires, which are a common feature of the ecology, destroy the previous stand. Planted woodlands are favoured commercially due to the ease of management, straightforward operations and economies of scale. These woodlands may comprise a single species, or more than one may be present, particularly when another species has been planted to protect or nurse the main species.

The time between planting and final felling is called the rotation, and this may vary from as little as fifteen years in the case of fast-growing poplar clones to in excess of 160 years for high-quality oak.

Even-aged plantations are not confined to commercial conifers and may be seen in a wide range of broadleaved species. For example, in the Chilterns many of the beech woodlands established for furniture manufacture are even-aged.

Plantations are usually thinned on a regular cycle but, in some cases, they may be left un-thinned if timber quality is not a priority. Thinning is designed to remove the poorer and misshapen trees, to allow more light into the plantation, to concentrate growth on the better trees and to provide access. Thinning may be done manually or with purpose-built machines, or even with chemicals in situations where the value may be low. Declining prices for small-diameter material, especially conifers, has meant that many early thinnings are now uneconomic. However, if these are not carried out future revenues may be compromised. Thinning has important implications for biodiversity. Gaps in the canopy allow light to reach the woodland floor, stimulating growth of the ground flora and encouraging insects and mammals.

This type of system best suits light-demanding species, although it may also be used with shade-bearers if a suitable nurse species is used.

Uneven-aged woodlands Continuous Cover Forestry (CCF) is a recent term used to describe silvicultural systems in which the canopy remains fairly closed at all times. Another common term for CCF is 'low impact silvicultural system' (LISS). Such approaches are now actively promoted as part of a shift towards management solutions that draw more on natural patterns of development and change in woodland ecosystems.

In order to maintain a continuous canopy, such a woodland will be composed of trees of varying ages and may possibly also contain a number of different species. It might have been deliberately planted or regenerated at different times, or it might

31

have developed as a result of changing management practices.

The main types of uneven-aged systems likely to be seen in Britain are:

1. Shelterwood, including uniform, group and irregular variants.
2. Group selection.
3. Single tree selection.

Many even-aged woodlands are now being managed with the aim of transforming them into continuous cover systems. This is a complex and time-consuming technique and specialist advice should be sought.

A detailed description and explanation of the management of CCF systems is outside the scope of this book. However, a number of useful guides and booklets are available from the Forestry Commission, and more advanced textbooks on the subject may be borrowed from public libraries.

A good example of an uneven-aged system (group selection) is described in the case study on Weasenham New Wood in Chapter 5.

Coppice

Coppice systems are believed to be the oldest silvicultural systems known, and were certainly used by the early Greeks and Romans. Once very common throughout Europe, many former coppice woodlands have been converted to high forest or replaced with other species to meet the needs of modern industrial processes.

This system relies on the fact that many of our native broadleaves send up shoots from a cut stump or 'stool'. This also applies to many introduced broadleaved species, notably the sweet chestnut. A few conifers will also coppice, including the coast redwood. The coppice is cut on a regular cycle related to the end use of the produce. This may vary from as little as six years in the case of hazel to a maximum of thirty years for oak. At the end of each cycle, the coppice is completely felled from the area or 'cant' and then allowed to regrow. Little management is required apart from maintaining the number of coppice stools, protecting the site from grazing and replacing moribund stools by layering or planting.

This illustration is intended to convey the structure of a woodland managed on a group selection system, similar to the photograph on the previous page and in Chapter 5. All ages and sizes are present in a relatively small area.

The high habitat value of coppice is related to the short cycle of cutting, the longevity of the coppice woodland and to the high light levels found under the coppice in the early stages. This favours the vernal or spring plants such as bluebell so typical of many lowland woodlands in Britain.

Coppice with standards A variation on the coppice system is known as 'coppice with standards'. This traditional form of management was once quite common in Britain. The understorey of coppice provides small-diameter material, while the 'standards' are managed to produce larger timber. The standards, often light-demanding species such as oak or sweet chestnut, are usually widely spaced across the woodland. Because they grow in quite open conditions, they tend to form larger and deeper crowns, and

Old sweet chestnut 'cant' marker. The area to be cut on a regular cycle would have been marked by these living 'mini-pollards' along the boundaries.

to be more heavily branched than those grown more closely together.

In a well-managed coppice with standards woodland, the ages of the standards will be a multiple of the rotation of the coppice. For example, in a hazel coppice on a rotation of eight years there should be standards of all ages from eight, sixteen, twenty-four, etc., through to the age at which the standards would be felled for timber.

Today, something less than 1 per cent of British woodland is categorized as coppice, or coppice with standards, but much of this has a high historic value. Bradfield Woods in West Suffolk is a good example of managed woodland with a history of coppicing stretching back to at least the 13th century. Although the commercial value of coppice is quite low, interest is now focused on:

- Maintaining existing coppice for nature conservation.
- Managing coppice woodland for greenwood crafts and added-value produce.
- Promoting landscape diversity.
- Developing low-carbon approaches to sustainable production.

As a result, grant aid may be available to actively manage these woodlands to meet certain clear objectives.

Short Rotation Coppice (SRC) One other woodland type that is becoming increasingly common in the lowlands is SRC, sometimes referred to as 'biomass forestry' or as 'energy crops'. SRC has more in common with high-input farming systems than with traditional woodlands, but it does provide an important habitat in its own right.

SRC is planted at high density with fast-growing clones of willow or poplar and harvested after two to four years, usually with mechanized harvesters. The resulting biomass is then chipped and burnt to produce heat and power, ideally within an integrated Combined Heat and Power (CHP) system.

These woodlands afford short-term habitats, and contribute to landscape diversity. Game species including partridge, pheasant and deer make good use of these woodlands for shelter, while aphids on the willow provide food for a wide variety of other insects and woodland birds. The use of the crop is carbon neutral; that is to say, the carbon fixed in the plants is then burnt with no net increase in the amount of carbon emitted.

Ecology of the Woodland

One of the great challenges for a woodland owner is in knowing which species to plant and which silvicultural systems to adopt. A number of tools have been developed in recent years to help classify woodland based on vegetation or ecological conditions.

During the 1980s a systematic assessment was made of the vegetation of Britain which is now referred to as the National Vegetation Classification (NVC). This is based upon the

plant species present rather than the structure or past management. The plant communities present on the site are usually related to underlying features such as soils, nutrient status, moisture conditions and location.

Each community is designated by a number and a name and, in some cases, may contain closely related sub-communities. The NVC system is now accepted as the standard classification for vegetation in Britain.

Woodland NVC Types

Within the NVC are eighteen main woodland types, five scrubland types, and two representing woodland-edge habitats. These are further subdivided into a total of seventy-three separate units or sub-communities. The woodland NVC is based on a large sample of both recent and ancient woods throughout

Table 5: Summary of the structure and regeneration of the common silvicultural systems found in Britain

System	Stand structure	Regeneration
High forest		
Clear fell	Even-aged, with one or more species	Planting
Seed tree	Even-aged, with one or more species	Natural regeneration
Uniform shelterwood	Substantially even-aged, usually one species	Natural regeneration, supplemented by planting if required
Group shelterwood	Two or more age classes, one or more species	Natural regeneration, planting or both
Group selection	Many age or size classes, usually two or more species	Natural regeneration, planting or both
Single-tree selection	Many age or size classes, two or more species	Natural regeneration, planting or both
Coppice		
Coppice	Even-aged single species	Vegetative
Coppice with standards	Varied age classes with one or two species	Vegetative and planting
Short-rotation coppice	Even-aged, single species or clone	Vegetative

Britain. It is still incomplete and additions are likely to be made over the coming years, yet it remains the most complete ecological classification in current use.

Each of the major types, listed in Table 6 below, may be recognized by the distinctive mix of trees, shrubs, flowering plants, mosses and lichens present. In the table, the first name belongs to the main tree canopy species while the second denotes the indicator species for the ground flora. Even with this system, major differences may still be found between two woodlands having the same classification, and this may be due to structure, management or past history.

While the NVC may be too complex for many day-to-day woodland management tasks, it is increasingly used to inform decisions on what to plant where, and as an aid in classifying ancient semi-natural woodland.

Table 6: NVC woodland communities

No.	Name of community	Major tree species and ground flora
W1	*Salix cinerea – Galium palustre*	Grey willow with marsh bedstraw
W2	*Salix cinerea – Betula pubescens*	Grey willow and downy birch
W3	*Salix pentandra – Carex rostrata*	Bay willow with bottle sedge
W4	*Betula pubescens – Molinia caerulea*	Downy birch with purple moor grass
W5	*Alnus glutinosa – Carex paniculata*	Alder with greater tussock sedge
W6	*Alnus glutinosa – Urtica dioica*	Alder with nettles
W7	*Alnus glutinosa – Fraxinus excelsior – Lysimachia nemorum*	Alder and ash with wood pimpernel
W8	*Fraxinus excelsior – Acer campestre – Mercurialis perennis*	Ash and field maple with dog's mercury
W9	*Fraxinus excelsior – Sorbus aucuparia – Mercurialis perennis*	Ash and mountain ash (rowan) with dog's mercury
W10	*Quercus robur – Pteridium aquilinum – Rubus fruticosus*	Pedunculate oak with bracken and bramble
W11	*Quercus petraea – Betula pubescens – Oxalis acetosella*	Sessile oak and downy birch with wood sorrel
W12	*Fagus sylvatica – Mercurialis perennis*	Beech with dog's mercury
W13	*Taxus baccata*	Yew
W14	*Fagus sylvatica – Rubus fruticosus*	Beech with bramble
W15	*Fagus sylvatica – Deschampsia flexuosa*	Beech with wavy hair grass
W16	*Quercus* spp. *– Betula* spp. *– Deschampsia flexuosa*	Oak and birch with wavy hair grass
W17	*Quercus petraea – Betula pubescens – Dicranum majus*	Sessile oak and downy birch with a moss community (*D. majus*)
W18	*Pinus sylvestris – Hylocomium splendens*	Scots pine with a moss community (*H. splendens*)

Uses of the Woodland NVC
When applying for grant aid, the NVC may be taken into account when assessing the management proposed in existing wood-land, and the choice of species in some new plantings. For many woodland owners, the ecology of the site is often more important than other features, and there is considerable scope for amateur botanists and ecologists to add their observations to the knowledge base of woodland ecology.

Semi-natural Woodlands
In Chapter 1 the importance of semi-natural woodland was explained from the perspec-tive of woodland history. Depending upon the location of the woodland and such factors as soils and exposure, there may be many different species present, or just one or two dominant species. In general, they will tend to be more complex than other more recent local woodlands, and some or even all of the following features will be evident:

- A wide range of ages and sizes, including moribund trees and deadwood habitats.
- Evidence of regeneration where gaps occur in the canopy.
- Well-developed layers.
- Rich associations of shrubs and wood-land indicator plants.
- Evidence of long-term use in the form of banks and ditches.
- Locally native tree and shrub species.
- High biological diversity.

Ancient Semi-natural Woodlands (ASNW)
The ecological complexity of these wood-lands, together with the impact made on them by their long history of management, means that they do not fit easily into the NVC system.

They have been assigned eight woodland types on the basis of their history, regional and ecological character and future man-agement requirements:

- Lowland acid beech and oak woods (NVC types W15, W16).
- Lowland beech–ash woods (NVC W12, W13, W14).
- Lowland mixed broadleaved woods (NVC W8 a–d, W10).
- Upland mixed ashwoods (NVC W8 e–g, W9).
- Upland oakwoods (NVC W11, W17 – oak dominated).
- Upland birchwoods (NVC W11, W17 – birch dominated).
- Native pinewoods (NVC W18, W19).
- Wet woodlands (NVC W1–W7).

Habitat Action Plans (HAP)
These are UK-wide plans for habitats defined under the UK Biodiversity Action Plan (BAP). In the case of woodlands, they aim to conserve, restore and, where possible, expand the range of natural woodland types present across the UK.

The BAP sets government targets in line with international agreements, and thus informs policy and strategy, in particular with respect to both regional and national forestry strategies. They contain quantita-tive targets for identified habitats (HAPs), and these are more likely to attract grant aid – both for existing woodland and for new planting.

CHAPTER 3

The Broadleaves

Left to nature, broadleaved trees would form temperate woodland throughout Britain and much of Europe. Temperate woodlands encircle the northern hemisphere where they extend across much of the eastern seaboard of the USA, forming vast tracts of oak, ash, walnut and maple forest, and are also found throughout Asia. They are not limited to the lowlands, and in the European Alps may be found at altitudes of 2,000m in sheltered valleys. However, in Britain, the altitudinal limit is somewhat lower, at around 600m. This means that in the absence of grazing pressure, primarily from sheep and deer, most of our uplands would be covered in mixed broadleaved woodland.

The Keskadale oaks, growing near the natural tree line in the Lake District. The altitude here, at the upper limit of the woodland, is 450m. This oak woodland was probably coppiced in the past and is now suffering pressure from sheep grazing.

The limits to the spread of broadleaves are primarily climatic. In the northerly latitudes, broadleaved forest gives way to conifer when the growing season becomes short and the number of days where the soil temperature reaches above 6°C decreases below a certain level. The southern limits are set by a lack of summer rainfall. Here, the temperate woodland merges with the Mediterranean forest species; these show adaptations such as waxy leaves, designed to reduce drought stress and ensure their survival.

Distinguishing Features

As the name implies, the broadleaves are distinguished from the conifers, or needle-bearing trees, by their broad leaves. These are usually, but not always, deciduous and function for only one season, being discarded in the autumn. The tree stores its reserves of energy and nutrients in the roots and branches ready for the following spring. They have the capacity to form wide-spreading crowns and to put out branches from different parts of the stem. In many cases, they are able to reproduce from cut stumps and by layering. The ability to form wide-spreading crowns, and to be able to respond to changing conditions of light and space, make them very adaptable.

Many broadleaved trees are long-lived and, in some cases, go through a prolonged period of senescence, or gradual decay, while still putting on new growth. In fact, there is an old saying that the oak grows for 300 years, stays the same for another 300 years and then slowly declines for another 300 years!

Very old or veteran trees are sometimes found in ancient woodland, where individuals may pre-date the younger trees by many centuries. Large differences in longevity are also apparent between different species: while

Common beech, probably over 250 years old, showing extensive signs of decay. The tree is now a valuable ecological resource and would ideally be left to decay naturally, providing a rich deadwood habitat.

a 100-year-old birch is unusual, a 400-year-old oak is not uncommon.

Table 7 below lists some of the key features of our more common broadleaved trees. It highlights the variation in such things as height, age and the preferences for different soil types. Much of the variation within a particular species is due to the site it is growing on, with exposure and soil depth having a major effect on growth. Even moving a short distance, perhaps from the bottom of a sheltered valley to the upper

Table 7: Some key features of the common broadleaved trees found in British woodland

Common name	Native or naturalized	Height range (metres)	Silvicultural characteristics	Preferred soils and sites	Age range and typical timber rotation (years)
Ash	Native	20–35	Light demanding	Fertile and freely draining	120–200, 60
Common beech	Native in SE, otherwise naturalized	20–40	Shade bearing	Freely draining	150–220, 120
Silver birch	Native	18–26	Light demanding	Sandy soils and mountain regions	40–80, 35
Pedunculate or English oak	Native	20-40	Light demanding	Heavier soils in S. and E.	200–300+, 120
Sessile oak	Native	25–45	Light demanding More erect growth than pedunculate	More westerly, moister uplands	200–300+, 120
Sycamore	Naturalized	20–35	Moderate shade bearer	Best on fertile neutral soils	150–400, 70
Sweet chestnut	Naturalized	20–35	Light demanding	Well-drained acid soils	150–400, 120
Downy or white birch	Native	10–24	Light demanding	Heathland and well-drained valleys	40–100, 35

NOTE: The figures for height and age exclude the largest and oldest trees, many of which exceed these figures considerably. The optimum age for timber production may, for certain species, be higher or lower than that given above. The figures are for guidance only. Trees in urban areas often grow quite differently from those in woodlands.

slope, may have a surprisingly large impact on growth or even survival.

The Common Native Broadleaves

The Oaks (*Quercus* spp.)

The most common broadleaved tree found in British woodland, the oak is in fact two closely related species. These species are distinguished by a number of features and are often found in distinct regions. To confuse matters further, the two species hybridize, particularly where their populations overlap. Although in many respects they are generally similar, and up until quite recently were classified as one species, the woodlands they form are often quite different and each will be dealt with separately.

Pedunculate or English Oak (Q. robur)
Distinguished from the sessile oak by the acorns that hang on stalks or 'peduncles', this is primarily a species of the lowlands. It grows best on deep, fertile soils but is very tolerant of poor sites. This is the traditional species used for coppicing and, in the past, for tan bark. It is now in demand for high-quality construction, either as seasoned timber or as 'green' oak, and for furniture-making. Depending upon the type of management adopted, the form of any individual tree will vary from a narrow crown with a straight bole to a wide-spreading crown with a short trunk.

This is an important species for nature conservation, and the key to the survival of certain invertebrates. Large areas of neglected coppice remain, and options for these include the conversion to 'high forest' or the restoration of a coppice cycle.

Sessile Oak (Q. petraea)
In many ways similar to the pedunculate oak, the sessile oak thrives better in upland areas, on the shallower and more acidic soils. Less susceptible to frost, it also maintains a better 'form' and is the preferred species for high-quality timber production.

Acorns of the pedunculate oak, showing the stalks on which the acorns hang. These distinguish the species from the sessile oak in which the acorns 'sit' on the twig.

Mature sessile oak showing the form preferred for timber production. This species tends to have lighter branching and a more compact crown than the English oak.

40

Sessile oak woodlands are found throughout the western uplands where they are of considerable importance for nature conservation. In places, they contain remnants of the natural upland forest type, either dominated by oak or in mixture with birch, rowan and, on more fertile sites, hazel.

Common Beech (*Fagus sylvatica*)

There are some ten species of beech found in the temperate woodland of the northern hemisphere, although only one is native to Britain.

Beech has a native range restricted to the south-east of England, but it is found naturalized throughout the country, where it has been planted and managed for centuries. In semi-natural woodlands, it is often found growing with either ash or oak. It casts a dense shade and, as a result, the ground flora tends to be quite poor. The bark is smooth, thin and a silvery grey, although variations caused by soil and exposure are common, and individual cells in the bark may remain alive for up to one hundred years.

Beech is a shade bearer, with a thin bark susceptible to sun scorch and frost crack. In some areas, it is subject to severe damage by grey squirrels, and the nuts are sought-after by many mammals and birds. It will grow on a wide range of soils apart from heavy clay and peat.

Common Ash (*Fraxinus excelsior*)

Found throughout Britain, ash grows best on the deeper calcareous soils, often on land in demand for farming. Capable of producing very fine timber, it requires careful management to reach its full potential. It is common as coppice woodland and, in the past, was much sought-after for firewood. Ash casts a light shade on account of its pinnate leaves and is one of the last of our native species to come into leaf.

Ash is a good species for conservation but suffers from deer, rabbit and hare damage when young. It is the food plant for the privet hawk moth. It is rarely damaged by squirrels and is an increasingly good choice for planting in the lowlands. A shallow rooting species, many mature trees are suffering from the effects of intensive agriculture and cultivation. Unlike many of our larger native trees, ash is relatively short-lived, rarely exceeding 200 years of age, even on the best sites.

The leaves of the common beech are able to withstand shade and will 'flush' under the canopy of other trees. When young the leaves are very tender and may be used in salads.

41

Ash flowers and the black buds typical of the species.

BELOW: *The bark of silver birch changes with age, starting off quite smooth and eventually becoming deeply fissured.*

Birch (*Betula* spp.)

There are two different species of birch: the silver birch (*B. pendula*) and the downy or white birch (*B. pubescens*). In many respects, they are very similar, being typical pioneer species, and were some of the earliest arrivals after the last ice age. They set seed freely and invade woodland sites after felling or clearance. Birch tends to be fast growing but short-lived, trees over eighty years of age being uncommon. Downy birch usually lives longer and attains a larger size than silver birch.

Birch are locally adapted to site and are difficult to establish on new land. Of high conservation value, the extensive seed production favours many bird species. Silver birch prefers the lighter soils in drier regions while downy birch favours wetter, more acidic sites.

Wych Elm (*Ulmus glabra*)

The only elm native to Britain, this is the tree Constable painted to evoke and reflect the quintessential landscape of lowland England. One of his more famous paintings is entitled *Trunk of an elm tree*. Now severely depleted by the ravages of Dutch elm disease, the

Wych elm is occasionally seen in isolated pockets in England but is still quite common in parts of Scotland.

Research and breeding programmes have identified some promising species/cultivars that are worth planting on a small scale, and the tendency to send up suckers means that in many parts of the country the elm is regenerating. An Elm Map of Britain is currently being put together by volunteers; the project can be found at the Ramblers Association website (*see* Useful Addresses).

The Common Non-native Broadleaves

Sycamore (*Acer pseudoplatanus*)
Plane in Scotland

A tree that arouses a great deal of passion, the sycamore has been much maligned in recent years, often for little or no reason. A native across much of central Europe, it is thought to have been introduced to Britain around the time of the Tudors. Now naturalized, it thrives in many regions and sets seed freely. It supports a high biomass of insects which, in turn, are good for birds. It is an important tree in urban areas, withstanding airborne pollution better than most species.

Much sought-after for its timber, particularly for high-value veneer, sycamore grows well in both plantations and semi-natural woodland. It grows well on a range of sites, although it requires well-drained soils, and is tolerant of exposure.

Sweet Chestnut (*Castanea sativa*)

Common throughout the south-east of England, where it is most often found as coppice, sweet chestnut also occurs as a tree in most regions of Britain. Most probably introduced by the Romans, it requires well-drained and warm soils. Since it comes into leaf quite late, it is unlikely to be affected by frost, except in the more northerly latitudes. It rarely sets fertile seed and natural regeneration is uncommon. Coppice is usually propagated vegetatively by bending young shoots over and pegging them into the ground.

A fine timber plantation of sycamore, about fifty years old, with a nurse of larch (which has since been removed).

Highly valued in the past as small-diameter coppice produce for fencing on account of its durability, many woodlands are now neglected. In France, it is used for flooring and furniture and is similar in appearance to English oak. It is sometimes found growing with other species, notably oak, as coppice with standards. Some neglected woodlands have the potential to be converted to 'high forest'.

The traditional coppice cycle, together with the continuity of management of some of the chestnut woodlands, has resulted in areas of very high conservation value, particularly where a number of other species are present in the understorey and canopy.

The possibility of warmer summers in future might herald a renaissance for this

ABOVE: *The leaves and fruit of sweet chestnut. The fruit seldom ripens in Britain although, when it was introduced by the Romans, it was planted for the chestnuts, which were either eaten or used to make flour (as is still the case in northern Italy today).*

LEFT: *Alder catkins. The male catkins shown here shed pollen in late summer. The fruit turns from green to brown, resembling a cone.*

species, which is native to Italy and parts of southern Europe.

Other Native Broadleaves

Common Alder (*Alnus glutinosa*)

The alder is a fast-growing tree found on river and stream margins, and as the major component of alder carr woodlands. A pioneer and light-demanding species, it is able to grow on a very wide range of soils. On infertile sites, its ability to fix nitrogen through root nodules makes it particularly suitable for land reclamation. It grows rapidly and may be planted in mixture with species such as oak and ash, where it acts as a 'nurse', improving the growth of these species.

It is often planted in the new urban forests being established on 'brownfield' sites, pioneering the way for the more demanding species. It sets seed easily, and regenerates from the floating seeds in the mud of streamsides. It is an important seed source for the siskin and redpoll.

The wood was previously used to make clogs and is suitable for charcoal production. In Sweden, it has recently been used to make high-quality furniture and is particularly suitable for turning.

Aspen (*Populus tremula*)

The aspen is often found with a bushy habit on poor soils. It sends suckers up freely and is a useful pioneer species on heavy clay soils. The suckering habit leads to clumps of identical shoots forming, all of which are clones of the parent tree. The leaf has a flattened stalk (petiole) causing the leaves to flutter or 'quake' in the slightest wind.

A valuable species for wildlife, it is used by deer for browsing and, if planted, may help reduce damage to other tree species. It is an important food plant for many moth species.

In the past, aspen would usually have been found in nearly all woodland types apart from lowland beech and yew woods, but is now uncommon in some regions.

Box (*Buxus sempervirens*)

Although a common garden plant, box is also found growing naturally as a tree in a few counties of southern England, where it thrives best on chalk and limestone. It often grows with two of the native conifers, yew and juniper, where it forms quite dense thickets. It is also found growing in beech woodland, where it forms an understorey. It has been widely planted on sporting estates in southern England as game cover.

The best-known population in England grows, not surprisingly, on Box Hill in Surrey. Box is now nationally scarce and

Aspen leaf showing the flattened stalk, which causes the tree to 'tremble' in the slightest wind (hence its species name, P. tremula*).*

efforts are underway to protect the remaining habitats.

Wild Cherry, Mazzard or Gean (*Prunus avium*)

A common tree of woodland edges and hedgerows, wild cherry can grow to 30m tall, though it is usually much smaller. Fast growing on a wide range of sites, including heavy clays, it is often planted for its blossom. Unusually among the cherries, the wild cherry may be very long-lived. Old specimens may well indicate continuity of woodland cover. It should be planted in small groups to ensure cross-pollination and fruit production.

Although this tree is capable of producing excellent and valuable timber, it is difficult to grow unless time can be devoted to its management. One of the first broadleaves in Britain to be subjected to rigorous genetic selection, improved planting stock is now marketed under the 'Wildstar' label. A lot of supposed wild cherry planted in Britain is actually poor-quality imported material.

An open-grown tree showing the broad domed crown and short trunk typical of wild cherry found on the edge of a woodland.

BELOW: *Fruit and leaves of the hawthorn in late summer.*

Bird Cherry (*Prunus padus*)

A small tree, bird cherry is mainly found in cooler and moister regions, often at altitude and on exposed sites. It is one of the species targeted under the habitat action plans. It is locally uncommon, though it may be found in nearly all upland woodland types.

Bird cherry is often found in more open woodland and along field edges, and it grows best on shallow and neutral soils.

Hawthorn, May or Quickthorn (*Crataegus monogyna*)

The hawthorn is one of our more common small native trees. A pioneer, it is found in hedgerows, woodland edges and old coppice throughout Britain. It grows on a wide variety of sites and may reach up to 15m tall. The dull maroon fruit is an important food source for many bird species and it can be made into a jelly.

Midland Thorn (*Crataegus laevigata*)

Nationally scarce, the Midland thorn grows mainly on heavy soils in southern England. It is usually found within woodland as it

prefers shade. Its presence in or on the edge of woodland may indicate ancient semi-natural woodland. It sometimes forms hybrids with the common hawthorn.

Hazel (*Corylus avellana*)
Usually found growing as a large shrub, the hazel may occasionally be seen as a small tree growing to 10m or more. An important component of many woodlands, it has been managed in the past for coppice, and in some parts of the country is undergoing a resurgence as the demand for hazel hurdles and other traditional crafts develops.

It is an important habitat for nesting birds and for the endangered hazel dormouse.

Common Holly (*Ilex aquifolium*)
Found as a large shrub or small tree, the common holly is an evergreen broadleaved species. It will regenerate under the shade of other trees, and provides valuable shelter in winter. The food plant for the holly blue butterfly, it grows well on a wide range of different soil types. It does not transplant well, and either container-grown or root-balled

stock should be used for successful establishment. The leaves may be very spiny, particularly on the lower parts of the tree, where browsing may occur. This is a good example of an adaptation designed to prevent damage to the tree.

In the past holly. was seen as vital to woodland regeneration, protecting seedlings from grazing damage. In the New Forest laws were enacted in the 18th century to protect the holly from human interference.

Hornbeam (*Carpinus betulus*)
The name is derived from two Saxon words, 'beam' meaning 'tree' and 'horn' meaning 'hard'. Traditionally grown for butchers' blocks, wooden cogs and gears, it is often found as coppice or pollards. Often mistaken for beech, the leaves are more serrated and the bark fluted.

There is evidence that hornbeam was quite common in the wildwood, and would have been an important 'high forest' tree in the south of England in Neolithic times. It is resistant to the grey squirrel and an important food source for hawfinches.

The female flowers of the hazel open a few days after the male catkins shed their pollen. In Britain this usually occurs from late January onwards but may be even earlier in milder regions.

Holly leaves and berries in autumn.

The Limes (*Tilia* spp.)

Small-leaved Lime (T. cordata)
Once very common throughout England, this tree is now nationally rare and its presence in woodland may well indicate long-term continuity of management. However, the tree needs warm summers for the seed to germinate and regenerate naturally, and for this reason it is only a reliable indicator species in southern England.

It is often found growing as coppice, and some lime stools are amongst our oldest surviving examples of woodland management. Limes in general produce excellent white timber and the nectar is favoured by bees.

Large-leaved Lime (T. platyphyllos)
Capable of growing to over 30m tall, this tree is now rare in Britain. It grows best on fertile soils in lowland deciduous woodland. The sap or honey-dew from the leaves is an excellent food source for aphids.

Field Maple (*Acer campestre*)

This is the only maple native to England and Wales, and is found on lime-rich soils. It provides good autumn colour and is often planted alongside woodland edges. It tends to produce its best leaf colour on heavier soils.

Wild or Common Pear (*Pyrus communis*)

The wild pear is what is termed a 'doubtful native' but it has certainly been naturalized in southern England for some considerable time. It is usually found along the edges of woodlands, often as isolated specimens.

Once common in lowland mixed broad-leaved woodland, the wild pear is now nationally scarce and a target for conservation and restoration under habitat action plans.

The Poplars (*Populus* spp.)

Only two of the many poplars seen in Britain are definitely native. The aspen is referred to above. The white poplar may be native, too, and has certainly been here since ancient times, while the grey poplar is a hybrid between the white poplar and the aspen.

Black Poplar (P. nigra *var.* betulifolia)
Now nationally quite rare, this native poplar is a tree of floodplains and river valleys rather than woodlands. However, there is a great deal

OPPOSITE PAGE: *Mature hornbeam showing the fluted bark that distinguishes this tree from the common beech.*

ABOVE: *This massive lime stool is at least 1,000 years old and grows in the National Arboretum at Westonbirt, Gloucestershire.*

of interest in promoting the planting and management of a tree that once occupied an important place in the landscape of lowland England. Recognizable by its massive, leaning trunk, often heavily burred, the tree regularly reaches over 30m in height.

During the Middle Ages, this was one of the commonest trees in Suffolk and Essex. Habitat action plans target the restoration of the native black poplar in wet woodlands.

Rowan or Mountain Ash
(*Sorbus aucuparia*)

This is a common native tree found growing from sea level up to 600m. It is short-lived and thrives on a wide range of different soils, including acidic sandy soils. Particularly attractive in an upland setting, it is an important component in many managed woodlands for its contribution to conservation. The berries are an important food source and are eaten by thrushes.

Strawberry Tree (*Arbutus unedo*)

Native to an area around Killarney in the far south-west of Ireland, the strawberry tree is an evergreen, related to the Pacific madrone,

and planted for its bell-shaped white flowers and distinctive fruit. A relict from the last ice age, it is thought that it survived in Killarney beyond the reach of the ice sheet. It is often planted in parks and gardens, and is susceptible to frost damage in many parts of Britain.

Rowan fruit in autumn. (Photo: Ted Wilson)

BELOW: *The white, bell-shaped flowers of the strawberry tree open in October and November when the previous year's fruit colours to deep scarlet. The fruit is edible but unpleasant (the species name, unedo, means 'I eat one').*

Wild service leaves showing the similarity to the maples. In autumn they turn reddish brown.

BELOW: *The underside of the young leaves of the whitebeam is covered in a white 'down' when young.*

Wild Service or Wayfaring Tree (*Sorbus torminalis*)

Once common in the south of England, this tree is now used as a possible indicator of ancient woodland. It may reach over 15m in height and is also found as a hedgerow tree. It grows well on thin, dry soils. It is often mistaken for a maple. In the past, the berries were used to make jam and the alternative name of 'chequer' is still in use in the names of public houses, particularly in southern England.

Whitebeam (*Sorbus aria*)

The whitebeam is closely related to the mountain ash, with similar fruit and flowers, but looks very different, with entire leaves and a broader, more dense crown. A very wind-resistant tree, it is quite common on some chalk and limestone sites in southern Britain, where it may grow to over 12m in height.

It is found throughout Britain and is a species associated with upland mixed ash woods. Locally rare native forms of hybrids with the wild service tree grow in isolated pockets in, for example, the Avon Gorge, the Wye Valley and along the coast of Somerset near Exmoor (*see* the photograph on page 8).

The Willows (*Salix* spp.)

This is a large group of trees, numbering over 200 species and varieties in Britain alone, and remarkable for the range of uses to which they have been put in the past. Interestingly, they are found nearer the North Pole than any other shrubby plants. Most are able to withstand waterlogged conditions and they regenerate easily from cuttings. Their fast growth and site tolerance make them especially useful on degraded soils. Apart from the native species listed below, there are many other useful species, including a number of clones selected for energy crops.

Bay Willow (S. pentandra)
The bay willow is native north of the Midlands and in north Wales, and is similar to the crack willow.

Crack Willow (S. fragilis)
The name derives from the brittleness of the branches. The sapwood and sap both turn from white to a salmon-pink colour when exposed to air. In the past, the roots were used to make a purple-red dye.

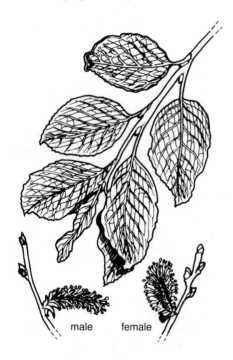

The goat willow has a broader leaf than many of the other willows, some of which are quite narrow.

Goat Willow (S. caprea)
Saugh Tree in Scotland
The goat willow is commonly found as coppice and in hedges, with purplish-brown branches and large broad leaves, wavy at the edge. It is found throughout Britain apart from the Outer Hebrides. It is a valuable understorey species and an important food plant for moths.

White Willow (S. alba)
A native over most of Britain, the white willow is common alongside rivers in the lowlands. On fertile, moist sites this is a very vigorous tree, reaching over 25m in height. The leaves are blue-grey above and silky beneath.

Producing one of the better-known timbers in the English-speaking world, the cricket-bat willow (*S. alba* Coerulea), is probably a hybrid originating in East Anglia. A specialized growing regime involving high pruning and intensive care, mainly in Suffolk and Essex, produces this valuable timber. The English growers are now competing with growers in China, India and Australia.

Other Non-native Broadleaves

Britain is home to an outstanding collection of broadleaves from all over the world. Many of these are found in parklands, arboreta and private gardens. Occasionally, some are found in woodland, either as introductions or self-sown. In some cases, they may have been planted experimentally with a view to assessing their potential for timber production, or simply out of interest.

Although the list below is not intended to be exhaustive, it does give some indication of the potential range available to the woodland owner interested in creating species diversity or considering other species in the light of concerns over climate change.

The Eucalypts or Gums
(*Eucalyptus* spp.)
A very large genus, most of which are too tender to survive in Britain, they are capable

of very rapid growth. Experimental plantings by the Forestry Commission indicate
that a number have the potential to succeed,
and recent re-evaluations suggest that they
may form an important, albeit restricted,
component of future woodland expansion.

The blue gum, originally from Tasmania,
is widely used in plantations throughout the
tropics, where trees may reach heights of over
30m in eight years!

Norway Maple (*Acer platanoides*)

A fast-growing tree, the Norway maple is
capable of reaching a height of over 25m on
good, freely draining sites. It roots deeply and
will withstand a moderate amount of shade.
Quite long-lived, this introduced species is
common throughout Europe, extending up
into southern Sweden.

Southern Beeches (*Nothofagus* spp.)

Native to the southern hemisphere, southern
beeches are quite similar to the beeches found
in Europe, and actually belong to the same
family, the Fagaceae. They are capable of fast
growth and do not cast as dense a shade as
the common beech. They are light demanding and have the potential to grow well in
Britain. More research is needed on suitable
provenances, but plantations of the Roble
(*N. obliqua*) and the Rauli (*N. procera*) have
grown well in Britain.

They are capable of producing quite high
volumes of timber. Some of the best plantations in Britain have been raised from seed
collected in Chile and Argentina.

The Poplars (*Populus* spp.)

A large genus of trees well known for their
prodigious uptake of water, and in urban
areas for the spread of their roots, the newer
cultivars of poplar show promise for their
fast rates of growth. Traditionally used for
peeled veneer, poplars produce clean, white
pulp and have the potential to be used as
energy crops. Poplar growing is specialized,
and owners should seek advice from experts before attempting to cultivate them.
Poplars should never be planted close to
buildings.

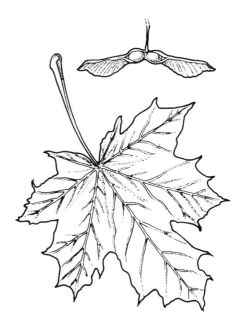

*Norway maple leaves are typically lobed, and the
points on the end of each lobe help to distinguish
this species from the sycamore.*

Hybrid Black Poplar (P. × euramericana*)*
This tree is very demanding in terms of site
fertility and intensity of cultivation.

Balsam Poplar (P. tacamahaca × trichocarpa*)*
Balsam poplars are similar to the hybrid
black poplars.

White Poplar (P. alba*)*
At one time considered native, the white
poplar is now thought to have been introduced into England during the mid-16th
century, probably from central Europe. It is
particularly useful as a windbreak in coastal
regions.

Robinia, False Acacia or Locust Tree
(*Robinia pseudoacacia*)

One of the first trees introduced to this
country from North America, the robinia is
named after the nurseryman to Henry IV of
France. It is capable of growing quickly to a
large size and, in the past, the timber was

Robinia leaves are a pale yellow when they first flush.

BELOW: *Leaves and unripe fruit of the common walnut. Like the sweet chestnut, the fruit used to ripen in Britain when the climate was milder.*

highly valued, surpassing oak for hardness. It is, however, very susceptible to high winds, with brittle branches and a short lifespan. It is usually grown on good soils in Britain, whereas in its native range it grows more slowly on poorer sandy soils.

Walnut (*Juglans regia* and *J. nigra*)

Both the common (*J. regia*) and black (*J. nigra*) walnut will grow well in many regions of Britain, but they prefer fertile sheltered lowland sites. They may grow up to 30m tall and form broad, impressive trees, particularly when grown in the open. The common walnut is a native of the Caucasus while the black walnut originates from the east coast of North America.

Highly prized for its timber, the tree also produces valuable fruit but our summers are not warm enough for these to ripen. It can grow quickly, and research is currently under way to identify the best provenances for British conditions. Once common, many trees were killed by the heavy frosts experienced during the mini ice age in the 18th century.

CHAPTER 4

The Conifers

Britain is unusual within Europe in having only three native conifers. However, it does have a climate particularly well suited to the conifers that grow in the more oceanic conditions found in the Pacific Northwest of America. Furthermore, centuries of plant collecting have introduced a variety of species from other parts of the world. Most of Britain's commercially important conifers have been introduced from abroad, mainly within the last 200 years. A visit to any arboretum will demonstrate the great legacy left to Britain by the early plant hunters and explorers, while our urban parks and great landed estates would be much poorer without the mature conifers introduced mainly during the 19th century.

The conifers are Gymnosperms, meaning 'naked seeds', and the leaves are either needles or scale-like. They are particularly well adapted to extreme environments, and are found growing throughout the boreal zone, extending across Siberia, northern Canada and much of Scandinavia. In the most northerly regions, very slow-growing conifers merge into the Arctic tundra. The great Siberian forests of larch and pine provided one of the first examples of forest conservation when Tsar Peter the Great of Russia established a reserve for the sable in the early 1700s.

Although most conifers are 'evergreen' some are deciduous and lose their leaves over winter, the best known of these in Britain being the larches.

Table 8 summarizes some of the important features of our more common conifers.

The most notable feature of the list, compared with Table 7 for the broadleaves, is that all bar one have been introduced comparatively recently. In many cases, some of the original plantings are still growing strongly and show no signs of reaching maturity yet. Most of these species are now naturalized and will regenerate naturally under woodland conditions.

The Native Conifers

Juniper (*Juniperus communis*)

The common juniper is scattered widely throughout Britain, but is found only occasionally as extensive woodland. Tolerant of a wide range of soil types, it suffers from poor regeneration and its range is contracting. Traditionally used to flavour gin, it is an important component of many natural mixed woodlands. It provides an important source of food for many bird and insect species, as well as nesting cover, particularly in upland areas.

Juniper is difficult to regenerate from seed and is usually planted or grown from cuttings. The tree bears flowers of different sexes on different plants. There is currently a move to plant more juniper woodland, and research is underway to determine the reasons for its decline.

The berries are an important winter food for thrushes, and a number of new plantations have been established in the Scottish Borders with a view to re-establishing gin production.

Table 8: Some features of the common conifers found in British woodland

Common name	Date first introduced to Britain	Height range (metres)	Distinguishing features	Silvicultural characteristics	Preferred soils and sites	Age range and typical timber rotation (years)
Scots pine	Native	20–36	Pointed crown when young becoming flattened with age. Orange bark, fissured in old trees. 2 needles	Light demander. Frost hardy. Pioneer species. Seed source important if planting in native range	Freely drained soils but not calcareous. Prefers easterly sites with warm, dry summers	150–300, 60
Corsican pine	1814	20–40	Compact dark green crown. 2 needles. Old trees have deeply fissured grey bark	Light demanding. Frost hardy. Salt tolerant	Lowland sites. Low rainfall with warm summers	120–200, 55
Sitka spruce	1831	20–50	Pointed crown. Needles bluish-green. Bark flakes	Windfirm and salt tolerant. Light demander	Ideally deep soils but will tolerate shallow soils	100–160, 50 Earliest plantings still growing well.
Norway spruce	Pre-1500	20–45	Mid-green needles	Very frost hardy. Shallow rooted and liable to wind-throw	Fairly fertile. Sensitive to air pollution	100–200, 50
European larch	~1620	20–42	On old trees bark deeply fissured, reddish coloured. Branches droop. Deciduous	Very light demanding. Central European seed source best	Freely draining mineral soils. Dry climate preferred	120–350, 60
Japanese larch	1861	20–35	Branches level and crown wider than European. Deciduous	Light demanding	Similar to European but milder sites. Will grow on heathland	100–200, 50

Common name	Date first introduced to Britain	Height range (metres)	Distinguishing features	Silvicultural characteristics	Preferred soils and sites	Age range and typical timber rotation (years)
Hybrid larch	1897–1904	20–30	Similar to European parent but longer needles	Very light demanding	Well-drained mineral soils	100–200, 50
Douglas fir	1827	Commonly to 50m+	Bark smooth when young with resin blisters, becoming deeply fissured with age	Shade bearing, particularly when young	Well drained mineral soils. Sheltered	120–180, 55 Earliest plantings still growing well
Western red cedar	1853	18–40	Cinnamon-brown bark, peeling in strips. Scale-like leaves smell when crushed	Shade bearing.	Deep fertile soil. Not sandy or acidic	100–150, 60
Western hemlock	1851	20–45	Drooping leading shoot. Needles of different lengths	Shade bearing. Frost sensitive and needs shelter	Moist mineral soils in west	100–150, 60

NOTE: The figures for height and age exclude the largest and oldest trees, many of which exceed these figures considerably. The optimum age for timber production may, for certain species, be higher or lower than that given above. The figures are for guidance only. Trees in urban areas often grow quite differently from those in a woodland.

Juniper woodland growing at an altitude of about 300m above Haweswater, Cumbria. The trees are not regenerating and suffer high levels of grazing from sheep and deer.

Mature Scots pine showing the fissured bark and domed crown typical of older trees. (Photo: Ted Wilson)

Scots Pine (*Pinus sylvestris*)

The archetypal tree of the Highlands of Scotland, Scots pine once grew naturally in England on sandy soils, particularly in the east. As a native, it is now restricted to Scotland, although it has been widely established throughout Britain in plantations.

Scots pine is a valuable timber tree in its own right but, increasingly, its habitat is valued for other reasons. Scots pine woodlands remain one of the last strongholds in Britain of the native red squirrel, and considerable effort is under way to extend the once-great Caledonian forest of the Scottish Highlands. It is often used as a nurse species for broadleaves, and is common in mixed woodlands. It has a high landscape and conservation value, and there are strict rules governing the planting of native races within clearly defined zones of semi-natural woodland in Scotland.

Yew (*Taxus baccata*)

The yew is often asociated with churchyards, but it may also be found growing in woodlands, either as isolated trees or as substantial components of the canopy. On occasions, it may even be found growing in commercial plantations since the timber is highly valued. Most high-quality yew timber is exported to the continent for veneer production.

The yew is very long-lived, tolerant of shade and capable of surviving on a wide range of sites, including chalkland. The foliage of the tree is poisonous, as are the seeds and bark, so care needs to be taken when planting where animals or children may be present. Birds eat the fruit quite safely and the dense foliage provides good nesting habitats.

The Common Introduced Conifers

Pines (*Pinus* spp.)

Corsican Pine (Pinus nigra *var.* maritima)
One of the four black pines found throughout Europe and Asia, this species has been planted widely in the past as a timber tree, particularly on the drier east coast of Britain. It is common in East Anglia and forms a major component of Thetford Forest.

It should not be planted in the uplands and prefers light sandy soils, although it will also grow well on heavy clays. It is quite difficult to establish, needing to be planted either in early autumn or late spring when the roots are able to make new growth. On the right site, it grows much faster than Scots pine.

It has a much more open crown than the closely related Austrian pine and is tolerant of airborne pollution.

Yew plantation in southern England growing on chalk with flints soil. On the right soil yew can grow quite fast. Note how the dense shade results in very poor ground flora.

The needles, mature cone, and outline of a mature Corsican pine.

Mature, high-quality Sitka spruce growing on the west coast of Scotland.

Lodgepole Pine (Pinus contorta)
A native of North America and used by the Native Americans for the central post of their 'lodges', it was introduced to Britain as a timber tree ideally suited to poor upland sites. The hollow roots are capable of growing in the waterlogged conditions, making it one of the few species able to grow on peat soils.

The often extensive plantations, many of which were established in the far north of Scotland, became a cause for concern in the 1980s when the high conservation value of peat bogs was recognized.

Spruces (*Picea* spp.)
Sitka Spruce (Picea sitchensis)
The most widely planted conifer in Britain, Sitka spruce was introduced from the Pacific Northwest of America in 1831.

It is an important commercial species: it grows quickly in Britain's oceanic climate, and its strong white wood is useful for paper and sawn-timber production. On more sheltered sites, it may grow to a great height, and trees introduced in the 1830s are still growing vigorously. It thrives best in areas of high rainfall — ideally over 1,000mm a year.

Although it is thought of primarily as a timber tree of large commercial monocultures, it has the potential to grow well in mixed woodlands and to be managed in more uneven-aged systems. On wind-firm sites it may develop into an attractive tree with high landscape value.

Its natural range extends in a narrow belt from Alaska down to northern California, and the choice of the correct provenance for the site is important. Increasingly, British provenances are preferred as the tree is now naturalized in many regions of the north and west.

Norway Spruce (Picea abies)
Norway spruce is found growing throughout Europe and is one of the most common trees in woodlands from Scandinavia through to northern Asia. Like Sitka spruce, it is a good timber tree, preferring the wetter west coast. It was first introduced into Britain during the 16th century and is now widely planted, but may also be regenerated from seed.

The traditional Christmas tree across much of Europe, it is to some extent being replaced with more exotic species such as the Nordmann and Caucasian firs.

Norway spruce does not like dry sites and is often found on similar sites to Sitka spruce although it does not grow as quickly. In the past, it was sometimes planted to replace broadleaved woodland, and many established plantations are now likely to be converted back to these, particularly on ancient

Closed cone and needles, and open-grown specimen, of Norway spruce.

sites. It is often planted as a nurse species for oak, and the choice of provenance is important if grown for timber.

Larches (*Larix* spp.)
A number of these deciduous conifers are found growing extensively across the northern hemisphere, including the Siberian larch and, in Canada, the western larch.

They are light demanding with fast early growth. Their deciduous nature adds landscape diversity to predominantly evergreen conifer woodlands.

European Larch (L. decidua)
One of the commonest larches in Britain, this tree is capable of growing up to 40m tall on better soils. It was introduced to Britain in the early part of the 17th century and is now naturalized throughout the country. It is an important timber tree and the preferred species for building boats (boatskin larch). In addition, it has a very high amenity value, and is often a prominent feature of plantations, especially on private estates. It is an excellent nurse species but ideally requires deep and well-drained fertile soils. New plantings should use British provenance material. Along with the Scots pine, the seed is a good food source for the red squirrel.

Japanese Larch (L. kaempferi)
Not as demanding as the European larch, this fast-growing species is an important pioneer, suppressing vegetation and acting as a good nurse for broadleaves. It is found throughout the wetter west and north, often in large plantations where it grows faster than either European larch or Scots pine.

It is resistant to larch canker, but suffers from frost and poorly drained sites. The timber is of poorer quality than the European larch, and on fertile sites has a tendency to produce spiral grain which reduces its value still further.

Hybrid Larch (L. × eurolepis)
This hybrid arose in Dunkeld, Perthshire at the turn of the 20th century as offspring of the Japanese and European larch. More

Hybrid larch at Dunkeld, Perthshire. In the background is Dunkeld Cathedral. (Photo: Ted Wilson)

Douglas fir regenerates freely in Britain and may be managed under a selection or shelterwood system. The trees here have been lightly thinned to allow sufficient light to reach the woodland floor and promote seedling growth.

A native of the coastal region of the Pacific Northwest of North America, it thrives in Britain's oceanic climate and in many areas sets seed and regenerates freely. Capable of very fast growth, it is one of the tallest trees in Britain, often exceeding 55m. It grows best on deep, fertile soils and produces a valuable timber sought-after for high-quality flooring and joinery.

It has a deeply fissured bark when older and is increasingly retained as a specimen tree in sheltered valleys. In many areas, the older plantations established over the last one hundred years are looking like 'cathedral groves' with very high public amenity value. In some cases they are designated as long-term retention, and may in time reach the 800-plus years found among the 'old growth' forests in their home range.

Other Introduced Conifers

A number of other conifer species may be found in woodlands, possibly planted as an experiment to take advantage of a particular site, to mimic other natural woodlands, or to add diversity to the structure and ecology. Some, such as the western red cedar, are quite common in certain regions, while others, such as coast redwood plantations, are unusual.

Western Red Cedar (*Thuja plicata*)
Another native of North America, this tree requires a sheltered site with deep, fertile and freely draining soils. It grows best in the wetter west of Britain and is particularly useful when planted in mixtures.

It has a narrow columnar crown with a straight stem. It makes a good hedge, and its dense foliage and shade-bearing character provides good cover in woodlands designed for game. It is commonly used for greenhouses, shingles and cladding; the heartwood is very durable.

Western Hemlock (*Tsuga heterophylla*)
This shade-bearing species is very versatile, growing on a wide range of different soils.

vigorous than either parent on most sites, it does not suffer larch canker or die-back, and is more frost hardy.

In general, its silvicultural characteristics are intermediate between the two species, and it is particularly useful on sites where the European larch struggles. It requires plenty of space to grow well and often requires early thinning to maintain strong growth and good timber quality.

Douglas Fir (*Pseudotsuga menziesii*)
Douglas fir is named after David Douglas, the Scottish explorer, who in 1827 sent seed home, and Archibald Menzies, the Scottish botanist who first discovered the tree in 1791. The Douglas fir is now a common sight in both woodlands and parks.

Mature tree with the elegant fluted trunk typical of open-grown specimens of western red cedar.

Leaves and an open cone of western hemlock.

Although it prefers more westerly areas of Britain, it will grow in quite low rainfall regions. Often planted in mixtures, it is best established with some shelter and is valuable in continuous cover systems. The best seed for British conditions comes from Vancouver Island in Canada.

It should not be planted on sites where previous conifer crops may have been affected by either honey fungus or butt rot (*see* Table 18, Chapter 7).

Cedars (*Cedrus* spp.)

Atlas Cedar (C. atlantica), *Cedar of Lebanon* (C. libani), *Deodar* (C. deodara)
Although rarely found as woodland trees in Britain, they are common in parklands on large estates and often make an impressive landscape feature. Three species are usually grown in Britain and all look quite similar, with very large cones that sit upright on the branches. The needles resemble the larch but are evergreen.

A useful but not always infallible guide to distinguishing between them is:

Ascending twigs = Atlas;
Level twigs = Lebanon;
Drooping twigs = Deodar.

Silver Firs (*Abies* spp.)

A large genus with over fifty species of primarily shade-bearing conifers, many are extremely fast growing and often among the tallest of trees. They are found growing throughout the northern hemisphere and, in Europe, are an important constituent of many mixed forests.

Mature deodar showing the overall shape of the open-grown crown and the drooping tips of the branches. (Photo: Ted Wilson)

Three in particular are found in British woodlands.

Noble Fir (A. procera)
Occasionally found in woodlands, it is planted for amenity as well as timber, and the silver-grey trunk and blue foliage are notable features.

It is capable of withstanding severe exposure and might prove useful in future if the climate becomes more unpredictable. It grows better in the wetter west of Britain. Along with many of the silver firs, it often takes a while to establish and then grows rapidly.

This species is fast becoming a popular Christmas tree, retaining its blue foliage far better than the ubiquitous spruce and commanding a premium from buyers.

Grand Fir (A. grandis)
Introduced to Britain in 1832, in its native range specimens can reach over 100m tall. This very fast-growing species has reached over 60m in Britain and may grow up to 1.5m a year. It grows well on a wide range of sites, including limestone. The best seed for British conditions comes from the more northerly parts of its natural range, such as Washington State and Vancouver Island.

Common (European) Silver Fir (A. alba)
Found throughout Europe, particularly in the Alps and the Balkans, it was introduced to Britain in 1603. It grows best in the north and west of Britain and is quite unusual in the south and east. Many of the earliest specimens planted as a forest tree in the 19th century are now very large, in some cases reaching 50m tall. This species is no longer widely planted on account of its susceptibility to aphid attacks and fungal diseases.

Lawson Cypress (*Chamaecyparis lawsoniana*)
Originating from the west coast of North America, Lawson cypress is commonly planted as a specimen amenity tree, often as one of over 200 cultivars of varying form, colour and height. The dense foliage offers good nesting habitats, and the tree is often used in hedging as the foliage is retained down to the ground.

This shade bearer is useful when planted in mixture with other species, particularly in uneven-aged systems. Although fast-growing, it requires fertile and well-drained soils; frosty sites should be avoided. It has been planted in Weasenham New Wood, the subject of the case study in Chapter 5.

Pines (*Pinus* spp.)
Monterey Pine (Pinus radiata)
The Monterey pine is a native of the coast of California, where it grows on isolated rocky outcrops above the Pacific Ocean. It is an important timber tree in New Zealand, Chile and South Africa, where it is planted commercially.

Mature silver fir planted in 1820 and still growing well on a steep slope above Thirlmere in the English Lake District. At over 43m tall it is one of the largest trees in Cumbria. Note the tree-sized limb growing horizontally about 12m above the ground.

It is particularly useful for coastal plantings, and a fine plantation has been established on sand dunes on Anglesey at Newborough Warren by the Forestry Commission. It is hardy throughout Britain except in the uplands and far north.

When open grown, it can form a magnificent, tall crown and is often seen in resorts along the south coast where it is known as the 'Insignis pine'.

Maritime Pine (Pinus pinaster)
Originating from the coastal zone of western Europe and north Africa, the species was first introduced to Britain possibly in the late 16th century. Visitors to the Atlantic coast of France will have seen extensive plantations established on the sand dunes of the Landes region south of Bordeaux.

It is now quite common in southern Britain where it regenerates freely and has become naturalized. It thrives on the sandy soils in the New Forest in Hampshire. Warmer summers are likely to see its range expanding.

An open-grown Monterey pine, illustrating the broad spreading crown.

Austrian Pine (Pinus nigra *var.* nigra)
Closely related to the Corsican pine, the Austrian pine is commonly seen near towns and in shelterbelts close to the sea. Introduced to Britain in 1835, it is sometimes used as a nurse species for beech as it grows well on dry, shallow, calcareous sites.

A sawn coast-redwood log showing the thick bark, lighter sapwood and heartwood (penknife is 10cm long). The bark is spongy and absorbs moisture, which protects the tree from the forest fires that regularly sweep through its natural range.

Coast Redwood (*Sequoia sempervirens*)
Originating from a narrow coastal strip running from northern California to southern Oregon, the coast redwood is the world's tallest tree, reaching a height of over 112m (368ft). In Britain, it is occasionally planted in groves for both amenity and timber production.

It is one of the few conifers able to coppice, and the regrowth is very shade tolerant. It also has the ability – rare in conifers – to send up root suckers, and small groves may well originate from a single tree. It will grow well on mild and sheltered sites, and is capable of reaching over 40m tall in forty years.

The species has been planted in Weasenham New Wood (*see* Chapter 5), along with other species from a similar range within North America.

CHAPTER 5

A Vision for the Woodland

From the outset, it is important to define the management objectives clearly, and these will be set within the context of an overall aim or vision for the woodland. The case study at the end of this chapter underlines the importance of these objectives for a family that has owned the same woodland for many generations. Once a clear vision has been articulated and a decision on the objectives has been made, it is important that the actions carried out in the woodland contribute directly or indirectly to the achievement of these objectives.

If grant aid is being sought from either the Forestry Commission or another public body, it is of paramount importance that the objectives are clearly set out. Where possible, they should be framed in such a way that they support the aspirations of the relevant grant-aiding organization. In the past, grant aid was given for timber production alone; today, the overriding principle is one of demonstrable 'public benefit' and the achievement of various sustainability criteria. The benchmark standard for woodland management in Britain is the UK Woodland Assurance Standard (UKWAS), explained briefly below.

The structural complexity discussed in Chapter 2 lends woodland the ability to meet many different objectives of management. For example, a pure even-aged conifer plantation managed primarily for timber will still contain a variety of habitats, including ride edges and footpaths, all important for their nature conservation value. Even felled woodland will provide a habitat, albeit a different

one, and, by careful planning, habitat diversity may be maintained in perpetuity.

Although there might be some 'trade-offs', many different objectives may be accommodated in the same woodland. This is quite different from the situation often found in agriculture where annual crops or farm stock may meet only one objective, namely production.

It may be advisable to divide the woodland into different zones based upon the objectives of management. Each zone may still contribute to a number of different objectives, but one objective will take overall precedence. In this way, management may be targeted where it will achieve the best results.

At the outset, the range of objectives chosen for any particular woodland will determine such things as the intensity of operations, the type of management practised, the choice of species for planting or the use of natural regeneration.

Remember that in some cases the location or particular features of the woodland itself may dictate the objectives. For example, if the woodland is designated for nature conservation or is covered by a Tree Preservation Order (TPO), it will not be possible to carry out certain operations without the agreement of the relevant authority, and some objectives may be difficult, if not impossible, to achieve.

Woodland Standards

Over the last few years there have been a number of attempts to define standards for the sustainable management of woodlands all over the world. This need has arisen partly as a result of the signing by Governments of sustainability protocols, and partly through the desire of consumers and retailers for some reliable measure of ensuring good management standards. In some cases, this has led to labelling schemes for timber and timber products; these are described briefly in Chapter 12.

In Britain, the UK Forest Standard has become the benchmark for good management. It is now possible for owners of small woodlands to claim grant aid for the preparation of the appropriate documentation to apply to meet this standard through the UK Woodland Assurance Standard (UKWAS).

Listed below are the key headings that management plans have to address to meet the standards. The aim is at the very least to maintain, or where appropriate enhance, each of these key aspects. These need to be considered when preparing a management plan as discussed in Chapter 6.

1. Soil condition.
2. Water quality, yield and discharge.
3. Carbon sequestration and air pollution.
4. The production of timber and other products.
5. Nature conservation.
6. Workforce competency and safety.
7. Rural development, including access, recreation, quality of life and community involvement.
8. Heritage conservation.
9. Landscape quality.

Objectives

The following are the main objectives likely to apply to woodlands in Britain and elsewhere. The list is not exhaustive but indicates in no particular order those most typically used, with modifications, by private woodland owners. These objectives could be to:

- Grow timber.
- Promote biodiversity (wildlife) conservation.

- Maintain and enhance the landscape value.
- Provide public access.
- Promote and develop informal and formal recreation opportunities.
- Seek greater community involvement.
- Provide shelter for farmland.
- Maintain and enhance, where appropriate, historic and cultural sites within woodland.
- Manage for game and sport.
- Promote traditional forms of management and associated woodland crafts.
- Develop traditional or novel agro-forestry systems.
- Develop and market non-timber forest products.
- Practise non-intervention where appropriate.

Each of these is discussed in a little more detail below.

Timber Production

In the past, most of the woodland in the landscape was managed to some extent for timber production, with the exception of those areas set aside as royal hunting forests. The old adage is worth repeating: 'A wood that pays is a wood that stays'.

There is a close correlation between woodland survival and the production of saleable produce. In the past, woodland that had little value either for timber, shelter or game was invariably cleared for farming or settlement.

Many woodlands are still managed primarily for timber production, and new woodlands are being established for new markets. However, the market for low-grade timber is poor and unlikely to improve in the foreseeable future. In the uplands, poor-quality conifer plantations are now competing with cheap imports from around the world and with recycled materials. Despite its bulk, timber is a globally traded commodity, and British producers have to compete with countries that have lower land costs, cheaper labour and, in many cases, better climates for growing trees quickly.

The decision to manage woodland for timber production is usually based upon one or more of the following:

1. High quality and high value for those timbers likely to remain sought-after in the foreseeable future, particularly where advances in silviculture allow rotation lengths to be reduced.
2. Lower quality but with value added on-site.
3. Lower-value timber where economies of scale and mechanized harvesting allow, and even here the profit margins are very low.
4. Niche timbers and products.
5. As part of an integrated approach to growing energy on-site using short-rotation coppice or firewood.

Biodiversity

Woodlands play an important part in the biological diversity (biodiversity) of Britain. As noted in Chapter 1, one of the reasons for this is the close link many retain to the past. In addition, the relatively low intensity of management supports a rich and varied wildlife. In many woodlands, particularly those classed as ancient semi-natural, nature conservation will be the overriding management objective.

As well as providing important habitats in their own right, many woodlands support nature conservation by providing buffer zones and linking areas of high conservation value, which act as corridors for wildlife. With an increasingly fragmented landscape, newly planted woodlands may be designed specifically to link together existing areas of

ABOVE: A high-quality stand of timber.

RIGHT: Bird-boxes are particularly useful in semi-mature and young woodland where the absence of natural cavities and mature trees inhibits breeding. Other species that benefit from artificial structures include bats, the pine marten and other arboreal species such as the dormouse.

high biodiversity. In many cases, substantial benefits may be obtained by planting relatively small areas of land.

It is also important to remember that seemingly uninteresting monocultures might have special value for nature conservation. In many of the larger upland conifer forests of Britain the relative scale and remoteness is attracting species such as the goshawk, osprey and the pine marten.

Although, in many cases, conservation objectives might focus on certain birds or mammals, woodlands are also very important for invertebrates, fungi, lichens and mycorrizae. In older, especially westerly woodlands, the conservation of bryophytes may be an important motive for woodland conservation and it may be necessary to maintain canopy closure to keep the humidity high (*see* Chapter 7).

Landscape

The contribution that woodland and trees make to the landscape is incalculable, and they are an integral part of the British countryside. The conservation of woodland as a landscape feature is often an important objective and may include the preservation of ancient trees within a woodland mosaic, such as traditional wood pasture.

While landscape objectives are often important on a regional scale, in some areas, where the landscape is more intimate, individual woodlands can have an effect out of all proportion to their size. It is for this reason that incentives may be available to help meet landscape objectives in certain localities.

In areas where it is deemed important to maintain continuity of woodland cover, it might be necessary to consider alternatives to clear felling. This requirement might

The archetypal landscape of lowland England is illustrated here in a view across the Eden valley in Cumbria. The intimate mix of woodland, farmland and hedgerows, so important for wildlife, has now been lost in many regions. New woodland has an important part to play in connecting isolated habitats.

71

arise within a designated area such as a national park or within an area where woodlands make a special contribution to the local landscape character.

Public Access

Historically, the general public has been largely excluded from privately owned woodland in Britain, except on a few private estates where a more enlightened approach has been taken. The rise in car ownership, changing political and social attitudes and a greater awareness of the rural environment over the last few decades have resulted in an expectation of increased access, exemplified in the recent 'right to roam' legislation.

It should, however, be noted that such access brings with it the requirement that the general public behaves responsibly. While in many European countries open access is the norm, this tends to be accompanied by a greater cultural understanding of woodlands and an increased awareness of the sensitivity of such areas to disturbance.

The provision of public access to woodland is now a key requirement for many forms of grant aid. The decision of an individual owner to include access as an objective will depend on many personal factors. However, there may be situations where access will be required as a result of existing legal rights, or as a result of current legislation (*see* Chapter 12).

Public access may be provided in a number of different ways:

- Restricted to permissive footpaths.
- Restricted to public rights of way.
- Restricted to certain parts of the woodland.
- Paid access.
- Open access.

The type of access allowed and the facilities on offer will affect the availability of financial support and will help determine the type of management adopted over some or all of the site. The provision of access might actually help in achieving certain other objectives, particularly if the woodland is close to urban areas, or there is a strong sense of community involvement. Operations that might prove controversial, such as clear felling mature woodland, are often easier if the context in which they are being carried out is explained to local people in advance. In fact, in some cases, you will have to demonstrate that you have actively sought local views as part of approval for a management plan under the UKWAS.

Finally, the provision of public access needs to be seen in the context of the other

Public access is an important objective, and one that may attract grant aid for the provision of footpaths, trails and interpretation facilities.

objectives, and in many cases these will be mutually supportive. Increasing public access should be seen as an opportunity to promote the cause of woodlands and to educate members of the public on approaches to management and conservation.

Recreation

Informal
The provision of informal recreation facilities – such as way-marked trails, interpretation displays, or archaeological and heritage trails – may all attract grant aid and help inform members of the public of the importance of well-managed woodland.

This may also be done as part of a business, as demonstrated in the case study on Low Bridge End Farm in Chapter 11.

Formal
Often part of a business enterprise, formal recreation opportunities include such things as:

- Paint-balling.
- Off-road experiences.
- Wilderness and survival camps.
- Rope-access courses.
- Ranger-led walks.
- Mountain-biking trails.
- Licensed fishing.

An owner intending to provide paid recreational opportunities will need to obtain legal advice with respect to the Occupiers Liability Acts, the Health and Safety implications and any planning controls on development. There are a number of very successful woodland enterprises of this type, but market research is essential and the location of the woodland is of critical importance.

Community Involvement
It is becoming quite common for local communities both to own and manage woodlands for the benefit of local residents. In some situations, grant aid might be available to help residents purchase woodland on

Log cabin under construction in the Scottish Borders, partly financed through grant aid designed to improve public access through a woodland SSSI (Site of Special Scientific Interest). Unusually the cabin, which is being constructed by Alex Hampton and Grant Rowley, uses low-value Sitka spruce and will be roofed with turf.

Shelterbelts linking larger woodlands in this view across the Yorkshire Dales. Grants may be available towards the costs of fencing and extending moribund shelterbelts, and promoting a more sustainable structure.

the open market. Alternatively, residents might become involved in working with a local landowner to achieve certain objectives. This approach is sometimes referred to as 'social forestry', and is quite well developed in a number of countries.

One of the best examples of this approach is to be found in the Laggan Community Forest in Scotland. Following initial soundings by the local community association, a full Partnership Agreement was signed with the Forestry Commission, and this has recently been renewed for a further twenty-five years. Among the achievements of the local partnership are:

- A twenty-year forest design plan with significant changes made to the forest structure and the species mix.
- 150 hectares of new native woodland planted.
- Way-marked trails.
- The employment of local contractors.

Over the coming years, other initiatives planned include mountain-bike trails, business accommodation and the provision of local housing through land exchanges with local estates.

In some situations, the active involvement of local people may be one objective among many for an individual owner. This might be purely altruistic, or might help reduce the potentially damaging effects of local access and recreation.

Shelter

Many smaller woodlands on farms have been established to provide shelter for stock and crops. In addition, they help reduce soil erosion, maintain biodiversity and reduce the effects of high wind speeds. They may be important landscape features in their own right, and are often local landmarks with historic connotations.

There is now a realization that farmed landscapes require a more diverse range of habitats, and changes planned for the Common Agricultural Policy (CAP) are likely to support the maintenance of existing shelterbelts and the planting of new ones. Although many of these will be in upland areas, lowland areas will also benefit along with an integrated approach to hedgerow maintenance and restoration. Woodland, shelterbelts and hedgerows may then provide the essential links for wildlife ('connectivity', in the current jargon), supported by changes to rural grants.

Historic and Cultural Sites

Many woodland owners gain tremendous pleasure and satisfaction from researching the role their woodland has played in the economy of the land. The longevity of woodland, the importance of management to our ancestors and the relative lack of disturbance of the land, mean that many retain important and valuable records of past activities. These might include:

- Place names such as 'dingle', 'clough', 'hurst', 'carr'.
- Boundary markers, including veteran trees and standing stones.
- Earth banks and ditches, the shapes of which are often specific to the locality.
- The site itself, perhaps adjacent to a stream or spring for a specific reason.
- Woodland structure and internal boundaries.
- Old workings, including saw-pits, charcoal hearths and lime kilns.
- Cultural artefacts, such as the cockfighting circle illustrated below.
- Features adjacent to farmland, including embankments.

Many of these features need positive protection, and their conservation may be included in management plans and attract grant aid for restoration or protection. They are also important features for public interpretation and inclusion in trails.

The 'cock pit' in woodland above Thirlmere in the English Lake District. At one time this now-drowned valley was home to a number of scattered farming communities, and they would gather above the valley to enjoy cock fights. This flat area is built up and surrounded by mature beech trees.

Game and Sporting

In many parts of Britain, woodlands provide shelter and cover for field sports, while on many traditional estates the mosaic of woodlands will have been designed specifically to achieve a variety of habitats and cover for different species.

The conservation and management of habitats for game and sporting interests also meet many of the requirements for biodiversity, including the provision of open space, maintaining the woodland edge and the development of the shrub layers. In addition, deer management relies upon maintaining a diversity of habitats and monitoring the impacts of mammals on the woodland structure and regeneration.

The management of game is a specialized occupation, and advice should be sought from professionals before planning such activities. If poorly planned or managed, substantial damage can be done to the woodland itself and to the ecology of the site.

In many cases, informal sporting activities will help reduce the impact from woodland mammals such as the grey squirrel, and may maintain populations of other species at acceptable levels. Chapter 7 considers the main woodland mammals that may need to be managed to ensure the long-term health of the woodland ecosystem.

When buying woodland, the sporting interests, which might include the fishing rights, are often retained by the previous owner, and care should be taken to ensure that the price reflects this (*see* Chapter 12). In many cases, the sporting components contribute substantially to the capital value of woodland.

Traditional Management and Woodland Crafts

The traditions of woodmanship and greenwood techniques have undergone a renaissance in recent years. Many owners of broadleaved woodland now actively manage them using traditional techniques, with the aim of producing handcrafted products for local markets. In some instances, this is a reaction to mass production while, in other

Sweet chestnut coppice with cleft timber used to make chestnut paling.

cases, lifestyle changes have meant a demand for courses teaching traditional techniques.

Grant aid to support biodiversity may require a return to the traditional forms of management that will lead to the creation of particular habitat types and species associations. For example, over-mature coppice woodland is sometimes managed to produce local charcoal. This has a number of benefits, including a reduction in imports from the tropics, a reduction in transport costs, higher quality and local job creation. At the same time, the resumption of a coppice cycle maintains the vernal plant communities and associated wildlife that are part of the fabric of our countryside.

The decision to adopt traditional greenwood techniques does not mean that more advanced labour-saving techniques cannot be used. However, central to the philosophy of green-wood working is the highly skilled labour involved in the production, the use of the low-value underwood and the low 'embedded energy' of the final product.

Agro-forestry

Agro-forestry is the practice of agriculture in combination with trees to provide the benefits of short-term income from annual crops or from stock, with the longer-term input from tree cover. A number of different systems may be adopted to meet different objectives. It is a discipline in its own right and includes traditional techniques, together with systems that make use of advances in both forestry and agriculture.

With changes to farm-support mechanisms, and a move towards more sustainable approaches to land use, it may be that such systems will increase in importance. Of the systems currently being used in Britain, the following are the most common:

Silvo-arable

Trees are planted in rows and arable crops cultivated in alleys between the trees. One such system uses fast-growing poplar on a thirty-year timber rotation, with winter wheat as the annual crop.

Silvo-pastoral

Trees (suitably protected) are planted at wide spacing, with animals grazing in between.

Woodlands are a major source of edible fungi. Inoculation of logs with the spores of commercially valuable species is discussed in Chapter 11. (Photo: Tom Kent, courtesy of Grampus Heritage)

Research has shown that there is no loss of agricultural productivity at a tree spacing of 5 × 5m, 400 trees per hectare or wider.

A decision to adopt an agro-forestry system might be done when planting a new woodland, or it might be an objective that will determine the operations to be carried out within an existing woodland.

Non-timber Forest Products

It has always been a tradition in Britain for woodland to produce a wide range of locally useful materials in addition to timber. However, over the last fifty years or so, many of these products have been replaced with either man-made alternatives or imported goods.

The potential range of non-timber forest products is enormous, and some woodland owners have built up expertise in one or more of these niche products. With the recent decline in timber prices, especially for lower-grade material, a great deal of interest has focused on alternative sources of income. In many cases, woodland owners have had to learn new skills of marketing and adding-value to realise the potential. NTFPs are discussed in a little more detail in Chapter 11.

A decision to manage woodland, either partially or wholly, for non-timber products will entail extensive market research and an assessment of its potential to meet likely demand. There will also need to be consideration of the woodland management techniques best suited to maximizing the product or products.

Non-intervention

To many woodland owners the concept of 'doing nothing' is very appealing! In certain circumstances, this might be the best approach to management. In fact, it is always worth asking the question: 'Why do we need to do anything in this woodland?'

It is a good question and well worth thinking carefully about. We do tend to think that 'management' means having to do something, but in many cases a woodland will carry on quite well without our intervention.

CASE STUDY:
Weasenham New Wood

Weasenham New Wood is a testimony to the value of keeping a woodland in the same family for generations. Originally established on heathland in west Norfolk in the 1880s by the Coke family, it has grown into an outstanding woodland of some 22 hectares, meeting many different objectives. It is a good example of why an owner should have a clear vision and not necessarily believe everything written in forestry books.

During the later part of the 19th century, the heathland, where the rainfall is amongst the lowest in Britain, was planted with a variety of conifers from the Pacific Northwest, including Douglas fir and noble fir, species that thrive in oceanic conditions! Over the following decades, and despite damage by spring frosts, more species were planted until, by 1920, enough shade was cast to be able to underplant with more shade-bearing species. A number of broadleaves were also planted, inclu-

ding oak, ash and sweet chestnut. At the same time, a variety of flowering shrubs such as azaleas and magnolia were planted alongside the rides. The shrubs and under-planting helped maintain a damp micro-climate and contributed to the build-up of soil humus on what were originally quite sandy acidic soils.

Group-selection system with high-pruned conifers and an understorey of azaleas, photographed in early summer. The variation in structure and species, including both broadleaves and conifer, suits many bird species.

The mix of species and ages has allowed the owners to develop a woodland run on continuous-cover principles (*see* Case Study, Chapter 10). It is managed on a group selection system, felling small areas and encouraging natural regeneration within them.

Among the more surprising species to be found growing and thriving here are coast redwood, western hemlock and western red cedar, together with rarer species such as the Macedonian pine (*P. peuce*) and the Chinese handkerchief tree (*Davidia involucrata*).

The owner's objectives are:

• The sustained production of high-uali-ty timber.
• The encouragement of wildlife, especial-ly songbirds.
• The maintenance and improvement of the amenity value.

In pursuit of these objectives, the current owner, Toby Coke, prunes the timber trees to 12m for both timber and amenity value. The main pressures on the woodland now come from deer and the grey squirrel, the latter arriving here in 1973. The costs of squirrel control in this wood amounts to the price of an average family car every year, trapping between 250–350 animals in traps set at a density of one per hectare. Without this level of control, the woodland would be unable to regenerate the mix of species for which it is justly famous.

The continuous cover favours many songbirds, including coaltits, goldcrests, crossbills and many warblers. A one-mile walk through the woodland is open to the public on certain dates in May and June to coincide with the flowering periods, and it is difficult to believe that underfoot is a sandy soil deemed too poor for agriculture. There is also a plan for the construction of an aerial ropeway giving access to the tops of some of the largest trees, over 30m above the ground.

The important lessons from this remarkable wood are that owners should:

• Have a clear vision.
• Ensure continuity of ownership if possible.
• Have a few clear objectives.
• Be willing to experiment and to trust their instincts.
• Look after the soil and microclimate.
• Remember that even poor soils can grow good timber.
• Control pests if they are out of balance with the woodland and affect the achievement of the objectives.
• Think long-term.

It is just that if we wish to have the many benefits that woodland can provide, and given that the structures and species mix are often the result of our intervention in the past, we are often obliged to continue with more active management.

In many woodlands it may be desirable to set aside some areas for non-intervention, particularly for those species that are sensitive to disturbance or are less mobile than others. The possibilities for non-intervention are discussed in Chapter 7.

CHAPTER 6

Getting to Know Your Woodland

A woodland is a complex place and it requires time to get to know it properly. An essential first step is the site survey and assessment of the woodland in the very early stages of ownership. Depending upon the size of the woodland and the range of objectives, this might take some considerable time, particularly if an ecological survey of plants and animals is required. Some of the more unusual plants, such as the orchids, flower infrequently, while fungi are seen best in the autumn. It might also be necessary, or at least advisable, to carry out some historical research.

In addition to the site survey, a detailed map of the woodland is essential for many reasons. Management plans are increasingly map based and large-scale plans can be annotated and included in grant applications. It is often far easier to express your ideas and plans in visual form and, in the case of landscape design, sequential plans can detail the stages over many decades. The interpretation of the woodland for members of the public is often best achieved with maps, possibly linked to photographs of ongoing operations.

Together, these two techniques help build up a picture of the woodland past and present, and act as a baseline against which future changes can be measured. While the traditional methods of site survey are tried and tested, more modern approaches using PC-based programmes and digital mapping techniques also have their place.

Professional foresters have long extolled the virtues of management plans founded upon site survey and detailed maps. In fact, in many European countries management plans dating back over 400 years are still in use today. One of the legacies of the British presence in India – less well known than the railways – is the existence of long-term forest plans written in colonial times and still in use by the Indian Forest Service today.

A recent development in Britain is the provision of grant aid for the preparation of a management plan using standard forms, or a template produced by the Forestry Commission in England. This is a welcome step for woodland owners as it helps clarify and simplify some of the more technical aspects of management.

Site Survey

The amount of time devoted to the site survey will inevitably depend upon the management objectives and the time available. Furthermore, the results of any survey might well alter some or even all of the objectives or, at the very least, the priorities given to each. However, the survey should include most, if not all of the following headings, albeit in varying degrees of detail:

- Ownership and boundaries.
- Surroundings.
- Historical and archaeological evidence.

- External constraints.
- Habitats.
- Woodland age and structure.
- Soils and climatic influences.
- Biodiversity.
- Statutory designations.

Ownership and Boundaries

The woodland may have clearly identifiable boundaries and these may be delineated by fences, walls, hedges or even by earth banks and ditches. The type of ditch and bank might be a pointer to the age and history of the site. There are distinct regional differences in the patterns of banks and ditches, and these might also be found within the woodland, indicating patterns of past ownership.

The boundaries themselves may well be important habitats in their own right. Hedgerows and boundary trees are often older than the trees within the woodland, and may have been managed continuously for a considerable period of time. Many boundary trees have a strong local resonance and may be historically important as markers for the 'perambulations' that once defined the extent of human settlements. They may also be important wildlife corridors and should be considered in any future planning for new woodland establishment near by. In many neglected woodlands, boundary trees and hedges often require active management if their value is to be maintained.

It is important to identify the boundaries clearly, as the location of these may have legal consequences in the case of disputes arising from overhanging branches or damage to a neighbouring property from fallen trees.

Surroundings

Any site survey should pay attention to the surrounding land uses and, in particular, to any changes that may have an impact on the woodland itself. Such changes might include agricultural drainage or fertilizer application, clearance of shelter or other woodland, changes in farming practices or even buildings and encroachment by residential developments. Local Authority structure plans should be consulted to determine potential changes that might affect the future of the woodland.

Historical and Archaeological Evidence

The permanence of and lack of disturbance to many woodlands mean that they often provide a rich source of information on the history of the locality. In the case of ancient woodlands, links may be found to earlier human settlements and to the impacts of past management on the species found in the woodland.

Woodland soils are often undisturbed when compared with other land uses and may provide rich historical and archaeological information. Seemingly innocuous features such as earthworks and clearings may well be signs of past use. These might include charcoal hearths, saw-pits, lime kilns and other local features. If in doubt, it is always worth seeking specialist advice prior to undertaking any management activities.

External Constraints

These may include:

- Utility wayleaves (access for services) across or close to the woodland.
- Rights of access, both public and private.
- Nearby structures, including reservoirs.

Such constraints may have a bearing on either current or future management, particularly if the woodland is small.

Habitats

It is very important to identify these at the earliest opportunity. In many cases, some of the most important habitats are those found within or adjacent to the woodland itself. In fact, one of the reasons for the generally high conservation value of woodland is this diversity of habitat within the woodland itself.

The more obvious habitats include grassland, hedgerows, streams and lakes, springs, the woodland edge, riparian and bog land. Those less often considered include the woodland canopy supporting communities

Charcoal 'landing' built by levelling the ground, often on quite steep slopes. Charcoal burners would usually site their pits close to a stream and would live out in the woodland all through the season. Large 'burns' would have to be watched continuously to prevent any danger of ignition, which would reduce the quality of the charcoal. Modern methods make use of steel kilns.

of lichens and bryophytes (mosses and liverworts), and wood pasture systems with pollards and veteran trees.

The woodland itself might also be composed of a number of quite different habitats, such as coppice, conifer plantation or ancient semi-natural woodland.

Consideration should be given to Habitat Action Plans (HAPs) as funding may be available for specific habitat conservation or restoration. In some cases, there may be locally rare habitats or species of particular interest that in other regions may be quite common. The most important woodland habitats are:

- Native pinewoods.
- Lowland beech and yew woodland.
- Lowland wood pasture and parkland.
- Upland mixed ashwoods.
- Upland oakwoods.
- Wet woodlands.

Woodland Age and Structure

The age of the woodland, or of the trees within it, may be known from legal or historical documents, or from management plans. If grants have been given, records will show details of planting and felling years.

If no records exist and the ages of individual trees need to be assessed, then a number of different methods may be used:

1. The tree(s) can be felled and the annual rings counted. This destructive method is really only useful for low-grade trees, or for assessing stands that may be ready for thinning or felling.
2. A device called a Pressler borer can be used to take a core from the tree, and the rings counted. In some species, it is quite difficult to distinguish the growth rings using this method. The entry hole may also allow disease or decay into the trunk so this method should never be used for

high-quality timber trees, where the greatest value is in the lower part of the trunk.

3. Conifers grow by producing a 'whorl' of branches radially around the trunk every year. These can be counted to give an estimate of age.

4. Trees in woodland grow more slowly than in the open. As a very rough rule of thumb, the circumference (girth) of a healthy tree, measured at 130cm above ground level, will increase by 1.2cm a year. Thus, a tree with a girth of 120cm will be about one hundred years old.

Because trees grow at very different rates early and late in their lives, this rule is not reliable for young or very old trees.

The current structure is usually a good guide to past management and may be read like a history of the site. The site survey might simply identify the structure at a rather basic level or might involve more detailed assessment of the layers, tree sizes and crown shape. Note should be made of such things as species mix, canopy structure, presence of natural regeneration, grazing pressure and past methods of management.

Cut log indicating the growth rings. The rings may be difficult to distinguish in slow-growing species, or where site factors slow down the growth rate. This log is 'tagged' to identify the purchaser.

BELOW: *A profile, drawn to scale, through a mature Scots pine plantation established in 1895. The crowns of the trees have broadened out with age and the woodland is developing a number of strata with holly and birch as an understorey. (Redrawn from a detailed field survey undertaken in 2003 by students at the National School of Forestry.)*

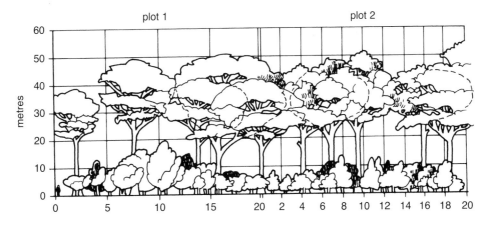

Soils and Climatic Influences

Woodland soils may be quite complex, and even small woodlands may contain a number of different types. The lack of cultivation in even intensively managed woodlands maintains soil structure, so many features not common in agricultural soils will be found. Most woodland soils are capable of growing a wide range of species,

and nutrient availability is not usually a limiting factor. Soil depth may vary considerably across the woodland and should be considered, along with the climatic influences on the site.

Simple soil pits dug across the woodland, perhaps at the same time as an assessment of the canopy structure is being made, will help to identify the changing profiles. A photo-

Table 9: Common woodland soils and their important features

Type	Where found	Features	Limitations
Brown earths	Throughout Britain	Well drained, brown and loamy. Usually deep with good rooting potential. Rich flora	Slightly acidic to neutral
Podsols	North and sandy heaths in south	Freely draining, sandy soils with bleached upper horizon and orange beneath	Ironpans may be present
Ironpans	Throughout Britain, in regions of higher rainfall and freely draining soil	An ironpan is a thin, impermeable layer of minerals that restricts root development and water flow	Needs to be broken to improve drainage and tree growth
Calcareous	Mainly in southern England and the Pennines	Derived from limestone or chalk. Often freely draining	Many trees, particularly conifers, dislike alkaline soils. Often shallow soils
Gley	Both lowland and upland gley soils are found where the water-table fluctuates	Mineral soils where ground water rises from below. Peat may form on top of a gley soil	Rising water-table in winter may kill the roots that develop over summer
Peat	Generally in the higher rainfall uplands to west and Wales, although may occur throughout Britain	Often cover large areas in undulating terrain and previously used for commercial conifer plantations. May be formed in any areas where drainage impeded	Now often protected for nature conservation, and increasingly as carbon sinks

graphic record many also be kept to act as a baseline from which to judge the effects of future management.

A number of microclimatic variables should be noted and recorded. Some of these might change across quite small woodlands if the topography is very variable. Such factors include the presence of frost hollows, altitude and the degree of exposure.

Table 9 summarizes, in a very simple classification, the range of important soil types that may be found in British woodland. In practice, there will be gradations between the types, and variations within each type will occur.

Many woodlands will have been drained in the past, and neglect causes these drains to silt up or to become blocked by trees and vegetation. The initial survey of a woodland should identify these, and consider ways in which they may be restored. Many woodland soils respond well to drainage, and growing conditions can be improved considerably. Trees are especially prone to being waterlogged, and poor rooting often leads to wind-blow. Care should be taken, however, not to drain important wildlife habitats (*see* below).

Biodiversity

Certain woodlands have a very high ecological value, and many others can make a substantial contribution to the biodiversity of the region. One of the motivations for the purchase of small woodlands is often the enjoyment of wildlife and the restoration of habitats within the woodland itself.

Over the last few years, there has been a shift in thinking away from the conservation of particular species towards the conservation of habitats themselves. If the habitats are cared for and protected, then the species within them will also be conserved.

Although mammals, birds and plants are often the most obvious indicators of biodiversity, woodlands are important habitats for other groups, notably the fungi, lichens, bryophytes and invertebrates.

An assessment of biodiversity is required under the UKWAS, and when applying for grant aid. The management of woodland for biodiversity is discussed in more detail in Chapter 7.

Ecological Site Classification (ESC)

The classification provides a sound ecological basis for the sustainable management of forests for timber production, wildlife conservation and other benefits. It is applicable to all kinds of woodlands, from plantations of a single species through to semi-natural woodlands of many species.

The ESC has been designed by the Forestry Commission to enable an assessment to be made of the ecological potential of the site, following a field survey during which the vegetation and soils are classified. A standard field-survey pack with detailed instructions on identifying the soil types and the important plant indicator species is available to download from the website (*see* Table 11).

Statutory Designations

A number of these might apply either to the woodland or to the surrounding land. Since they are legally binding, an owner should have received detailed information from the relevant agencies. Those most likely to apply to woodland are noted in Table 10.

If you are buying woodland, you should check in advance for any restrictions that may be placed upon management. For example, if a woodland is designated, or includes within it an SSSI, then permission may be required to carry out a number of operations, including felling and thinning. A list of these Potentially Damaging Operations (PDOs) will be included in the SSSI notification.

Mapping

Good-quality maps are an essential component of management plans and a prerequisite for grant-aid applications. Although many woodlands have historical maps associated with them, it is important to use current Ordnance Survey (OS) maps whenever applications are made to government bodies.

Table 10: Some Statutory Designations that may affect woodland in Britain

Designation	Purpose	Responsible authority
Site of Special Scientific Interest (SSSI)	Protection of important sites for plants, animals, geological or physiographical features	English Nature (EN), Scottish Natural Heritage (SNH), Countryside Council for Wales (CCW)
Special Protection Area (SPA) (will be an SSSI)	Protects habitats of rare or vulnerable birds	EN, SNH, CCW
Special Area for Conservation (SAC)	Protects wildlife habitats other than birds	EN, SNH, CCW
Ramsar site (will be an SSSI or NNR)	Wetlands of international importance	EN, SNH, CCW
National Nature Reserve (NNR)	The most important sites for nature conservation	EN, SNH, CCW
National Park (NP)	Conserve and enhance the natural beauty, wildlife and cultural heritage	Countryside Agency, SNH, CCW
Environmentally Sensitive Area (ESA)	Farmland with national environmental importance	Defra, Scottish Executive, Welsh Assembly Government
Area of Outstanding Natural Beauty (AONB)	Landscape	Countryside Agency, SNH, CCW
National Scenic Area (NSA)	Landscape	SNH
Scheduled Ancient Monument (SAM)	Nationally important archaeological sites	English Heritage, Historic Scotland, CADW (Welsh Historic Monuments)
Conservation Area.	Protection of all trees within important built-up areas	Local Planning Authority
Tree Preservation Order (TPO)	Trees or woodland of high amenity value	Local Planning Authority

Care should be taken to use originals rather than photocopies for detailed measurements. You should make sure you have permission to use OS maps for the purposes intended.

In the case of small woodlands, simple well-annotated maps may be the only documents needed. It is usually preferable to have a number of different maps, each containing more specialist information.

In addition to the physical boundaries and geographic features, maps for use in a woodland plan should indicate the following:

• Grid reference.
• Scale.
• North (arrow).
• The types of woodland marked out, usually in compartments.

- Rights of way.
- Access routes and point(s) of entry to the woodland.
- Archaeological features.
- Designated areas.
- Safety hazards.
- Areas of high ecological value.
- Recreational areas.

The Ordnance Survey produces maps at a range of different scales. The most commonly used scales for woodlands in Britain are:

- 1:2,500 for detailed mapping and for use with small woodlands.
- 1:10,000 for larger woodlands and where detail is less important.

OS maps are available as sheets; many are also available in digital format (accessible via the OS website – *see* Useful Addresses). It is also now possible to order OS 'Superplan' maps centred on the woodland itself, which is useful as this is likely to reduce the number of sheets that must be purchased.

GPS Techniques in Woodland

Techniques and equipment that were once the preserve of specialists are now readily available to woodland owners. One of these techniques is the use of a Global Positioning System (GPS) for measuring and marking out woodland boundaries, for locating sites and perhaps individual trees of historic importance, and for estimating such things as the length of a fence line or the position of drains.

In addition, GPS data can be integrated with off-the-shelf, PC-based management and mapping software. This is especially valuable for larger woodlands, where a number of properties are being managed, or where there is a lot of information to be stored.

Sources of Historical Information

In many cases, there will be quite extensive historical information available, particularly where a woodland has been actively managed over, say, the last few hundred years. In addition to estate records, maps might be available together with records kept by government agencies. It is possible that local naturalist trusts could have survey records of flora and fauna, and other groups with an interest in the local landscape might have access to useful information.

Aerial surveys, often done at regular intervals, may prove very useful in tracing past activities and in monitoring changes in both species and woodland area. These records may be held by planning authorities, government departments, academic institutions or by private aerial survey companies.

In some cases, university departments might have carried out applied experimental work in the woodland, or some of the land-based government agencies or their predecessors might provide access to useful material.

Sources of Current Information

Often the first point of contact is with the local Forestry Commission Woodland Officer. He or she will be able to provide some initial advice and guidance, and provide information on the current range of both FC and other grants that may be available. In most situations, they will also be able to advise a woodland owner on other sources of information and help.

Increasingly, rural advice is being streamlined and integrated and, in many cases, the first point of contact for those with agricultural holdings will be the local farm adviser. A list of the key agencies is included at the end of the book (*see* Useful Addresses).

Table 11 details the main sources of information together with their websites. Increasingly, information is most easily accessed from the relevant websites, which are often the source for the most up-to-date documents. Often, grant forms and guidance notes can be downloaded, and sometimes applications can be made electronically.

Table 11: Sources of information useful for preparing site surveys and management plans

Organization/Source	Website
Multi-Agency Geographic Information for the Countryside:	www.magic,gov.uk
UK Biodiversity Action Plan:	www.ukbap.org.uk
Red Data Book for Endangered Species:	www.jncc.gov.uk
Countryside Agency:	www.countryside.org.uk
Forestry Commission – Ecological Site Classification:	www.forestry.gov.uk/esc
Forestry Commission – Management Plan Template:	www.forestry.gov.uk
Ordnance Survey:	www.ordnancesurvey.co.uk
Scottish Natural Heritage:	www.snh.org.uk
Countryside Council for Wales:	www.ccw.giv.uk
English Nature (includes NVC classification):	www.english-nature.co.uk

Part of a 1:10,000 aerial photograph of mixed woodland and farmland taken in June 1999. The compartments and woodland boundaries are clearly visible, and the image was used to produce the map on the opposite page. (Photo: Unit for Landscape Modelling, Cambridge University, reproduced with permission, Copyright reserved Cambridge University Collection of Air Photographs)

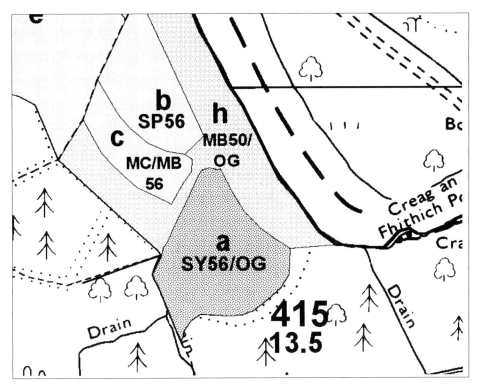

Woodland map drawn from the aerial image opposite and indicating compartments, sub-compartments and other management information. Sub-compartment 'a' is a plantation of sycamore established in 1956 together with open ground. The crowns of the mature trees are visible in the aerial image. (Base map copyright: reproduced by permission of Ordnance Survey on behalf of HMSO © Crown Copyright 2005, All rights reserved. Ordnance Survey Licence Number 100043982; woodland map courtesy of Robin Surveys, www.robinsurveys.co.uk)

The Management Plan

This document sets out your vision for the woodland in the long term, and details the operations to be carried out in the woodland in both the short and medium term. The plan is important as it is both a working document and a baseline from which to measure the longer-term success of your vision and objectives for the woodland.

The Forestry Commission in England and Wales has produced a management plan template that is available on-line in electronic format (Table 11). In Scotland, detailed information on the preparation of a Forest Plan is available either from their website or by post.

Although in some countries a management plan has to be drawn up by a professional forester, this is not the case in Britain. However, a woodland owner might be well advised to seek professional help, at least in the early stages of its preparation.

The Forestry Commission now expects that a management plan will broadly address the following headings within their preferred framework. You may use other approaches and headings, but the information noted below will need to be included somewhere in the plan.

• Background information.
• Woodland information.

89

- Long-term vision, management objectives and strategy.
- Management prescriptions and operations.
- Consultation.
- Monitoring-plan summary.
- Work programmes.
- Maps.

Although some information collected through a site survey will be included, other information will need to be gathered to enable any application for grant aid to be assessed adequately.

Background Information
The location of the woodland should be shown on a map at a scale of either 1:25,000, or 1:50,000, and should include a six-figure grid reference and the nearest town or village. You should include any historical information to hand, for example on past management, and a description of the woodland in the landscape. This may be done by using annotated maps together with brief notes. This section 'sets the scene' and should not include detailed woodland survey information.

A six-figure grid reference is accurate to 100m and usually marks the access point to the woodland. When identifying the grid reference, a useful rule may help in deciding which edge of the map to start with: 'along the hall and up the stairs'. In other words, start from the bottom left of the map and move along until you are level with the access point before reading the first three numbers. Then, from the bottom right, move up the map and read the next three numbers.

Woodland Information
The detailed site survey information is brought together in this section. It does not have to be too long, but it should provide the relevant authorities with sufficient information to judge whether or not you have taken into account the range of habitats, other features and designations. It also provides information that is required under the UKWAS.

It is usual for all but the smallest woodland to be divided up for ease of management. This is done by dividing it into compartments and, if necessary, subcompartments. These are management units in which part of the woodland, or stand, is either similar in species and structure or has similar management objectives.

Long-term Vision
- Vision. 'The big picture', the longer-term view over the next twenty to thirty years.
- Management objectives. What you will do, and monitor, to achieve your vision.
- Strategy. How you will actually carry out the work needed to achieve your objectives. This might, for example, include the allocation of resources, some explanation of how constraints will be dealt with, and the use of zones within the woodland with different objectives.

Management Prescriptions and Operations
This section details the methods you will use to achieve your objectives. It is also sometimes called a plan of operations. It will include the range of practical operations you intend to carry out, as described in Chapters 7–11.

Consultation
It is now expected that woodland owners will actively consult with all interested parties before carrying out any operations that might affect them. This will certainly include the statutory bodies where a designated area is concerned, but it might equally well apply to a neighbour who may be affected by tree felling or thinning.

The aim of a consultation exercise is to give local people a chance to voice their concerns, and then to show that you have taken these into account in your planning.

Monitoring-plan Summary
In most small woodlands this will be quite a simple task and might only require a note to confirm that certain actions have been undertaken. Part of the joy of owning woodland is the monitoring of the effects of various oper-

ations on the trees themselves, the wildlife or the habitat diversity.

This might also include records of collaborations with other organizations and progress towards specific targets, such as increasing aquatic diversity or reducing damage by squirrels.

Work Programmes

The proposed work needs to be set out, often in map form with annotations, in two subsections:

1. Long-term work over the next twenty years, listed as 6–10, 11–15 and 16–20.
2. Short-term work for each of the next five years.

Detailed plans are required for the first year, with rather less detail for years two to five. The use of maps is highly recommended and they can be clearly marked and copied, with changes made in successive years. In many cases, maps alone will suffice, perhaps supplemented with small amounts of supporting text.

Maps

These are becoming increasingly important in identifying clearly the operations that are planned. The usual approach is to prepare a base map showing key information such as the boundaries, internal rides and compartments, and other distinguishing features. This is then used to build up more detailed maps showing specific features and/or proposals.

For example, there might be a habitat map showing in quite a bit of detail the types and areas of each different habitat, with notes on particular species. The use of PC-based mapping programmes will enable the owner to print them, and they may then be used for information boards, school visits or public consultations.

Table 12: Types of map appropriate for different planning purposes

Type of Map	Information
Base	Boundaries, compartments, subcompartments and species, open spaces, roads and rides, access point(s)
Thinning and Felling	Areas to be thinned and/or felled. Include extraction routes, stacking or loading areas, storage of machinery and fuelling areas
Planting and Restocking	Information on species mix, any new compartments or changes to existing ones, if using planting, natural regeneration or a mixture of both
Habitats	Different habitats, including areas of non-intervention or long-term retention
Archaeological Sites	Any Scheduled Ancient Monuments and other features, including earthworks, tumuli, etc
Special Interest	Statutory designations

CHAPTER 7

Biodiversity Matters

Woodland is one of the most diverse of all our natural habitats, and one on which the passing centuries have had perhaps the most profound effect. The interactions between plants, animals and human use have in many cases resulted in greater diversity than would be found in purely 'natural' woodland.

This chapter is concerned with the maintenance and enhancement of biological diversity, usually shortened to 'biodiversity'. In this extremely complex system, the biological activity takes place as much below ground as it does above. If a woodland is left

to itself, it will, over time, reach its own equilibrium in which the various living organisms all play a part. However, this approach may not provide all the things we wish for in terms of, for example, landscape, timber, certain animals and plants, freedom to wander, views, and tall trees. Only by actively managing the woodland can we hope to meet the objectives we have set for it. The key to this is 'getting the balance right'.

Many books on woodland management include a chapter about 'protection', but the issues involved in protecting woodland are

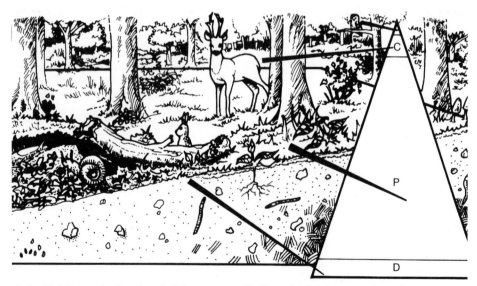

A simplified diagram showing where the living component (the biomass) is found in a typical British mixed woodland on deep, well-drained, brown-earth soil. In relation to the decomposers (D) and the producers (P), the herbivores and carnivores – together known as the consumers (C) – represent a tiny proportion of the total biomass.

really ones of wildlife management and ecology. To some extent, the acceptable balance is a personal matter and depends upon the objectives of the owner. For example, deer may cause extensive damage to young trees, but some owners may be happy to accept this if the reward is watching them in their 'natural' habitat. However, over time, an owner may come to realize that if the habitat itself is to remain healthy, deer numbers may need to be kept under control after all.

The diagram opposite illustrates the importance, and the large biomass, of the decomposers and producers in relation to the herbivores and carnivores. It also indicates where the range of biodiversity is distributed and why such elements as deadwood and the associated invertebrates are so important in a woodland ecosystem. When one component is out of balance – for example if the herbivore population becomes too great – many other parts of the system suffer and overall biodiversity declines. This is now the situation in Britain where the top predators, the carnivores, have been largely lost from woodland.

The difficulties we face in managing woodland for biodiversity in Britain are:

- The loss of all the large predators on woodland mammals.
- Large numbers of introduced plants and animals.
- Farming systems reliant on grazing animals, particularly in the uplands.
- High human population density, predominantly urban based.
- An almost non-existent woodland culture.

The remainder of this chapter is divided into two main sections: wildlife conservation and habitat management, and protecting the woodland.

Wildlife Conservation and Habitat Management

In general, diversity of habitat is the key to successful conservation in woodlands. By maintaining or creating a range of habitats suitable for all the key wildlife groups, the woodland owner will attract the wide diversity required. Many woodland species are mobile and will, particularly if other woods are close by, rapidly take up residence in newly created habitats. There are exceptions to this, notably some of the flowering plants and bryophytes, but it is surprising how quickly sites are colonized if the conditions are right.

In woodland there are on the whole four major options that should be considered if an increase in habitat diversity is required:

1. Adoption of alternative forms of management, including group felling, possibly with a change in species (Chapter 2).
2. Reinstatement of traditional forms of woodland management, including coppicing, pollarding and coppice-with-standards (Chapter 6).
3. Provision of more open space and better managed rides and roads (Chapter 9).
4. Setting aside areas for non-intervention or minimal intervention (*see* below).

Here is a check-list of things to do to improve habitat diversity:

- Leave deadwood and, if safe, dying trees.
- Avoid operations in nesting and breeding seasons.
- Maintain edges and let light into the woodland.
- Where possible, ensure rides are not straight, but sinuous.
- Do not carry out work throughout the woodland in any one year.
- Leave some tree and shrub species for long-term retention.
- Avoid damage to rides and compaction of soil when harvesting.
- Use low-impact harvesting systems, including horse extraction.
- Maintain thick ground cover and coppice hazel for small mammals.
- Erect bat boxes.
- Allow climbing plants to grow, perhaps in non-intervention areas.

- Thin the trees to increase light levels.
- Resist the urge to 'tidy up' as you work through the wood.
- Protect areas such as rock outcrops, water-logged sites and damp hollows.

Non-intervention

In Chapter 2, one of the possible management objectives discussed was 'to do nothing' in the woodland. This approach, sometimes called minimum or non-intervention, may be appropriate when conserving certain species or groups, but there are a number of potential pitfalls to be aware of. These include:

- The composition of the tree species may alter over time.
- Certain plants and animals may disappear from the woodland because its structure may change.
- The woodland could be smothered by invasive species such as rhododendron.
- Natural regeneration may be affected by high levels of grazing or browsing.
- The historic links with past management practices may be lost.

Wildlife Groups

The aim of this section is simply to highlight a few of the factors or species of interest in each group. Specialist societies and publications will provide further information with respect to the particular needs of each group.

Birds

Woodland is an important habitat for many different types of bird. The range of species is to some extent dependent upon the size and shape of the woodland and on the number of other habitats within and adjacent to it. As with mammals, birds are not so much dependant on the species of trees or plants as on the structure of the woodland. This is why diversity in tree age and height is so important and, of course, why coppice plays such an important role in providing some of this diversity. An increasing number of larger woodlands are home to raptors such as buzzards and sparrowhawks.

Deadwood and old trees are extremely important, with over 30 per cent of woodland birds nesting in the holes of more mature trees. In predominantly broadleaved wood-

---

Table 13: Relative importance of different woodland habitats for the main animal and plant groups and species

Woodland habitat	Important for
Minimum intervention	Birds of prey nesting sites, bats, pine marten, fungi, invertebrates, climbing plants and the taller shrubs
Mature high forest	Woodland birds (prefer uneven-aged), larger mammals, fungi, lichens and mosses
Veteran trees and deadwood	Woodland birds including woodpeckers and owls, bats, invertebrates, fungi and lichens
Coppice (active)	Songbirds, smaller mammals including hazel dormouse, vernal flowering plants
Open spaces, woodland edges and rides	Birds, smaller mammals, larger mammals, reptiles, invertebrates especially butterflies, grasses
Ponds	Birds, aquatic mammals, invertebrates (and, in turn, aquatic diversity), amphibians
Wetland	Invertebrates, especially dragon and damsel flies, carnivorous plants

land, conifers play an important role in providing winter shelter and nesting sites, particularly the softer-leaved species such as western red cedar.

The main breeding season for birds is from April to May, with a number starting as early February while others may extend into September. Try to carry out woodland maintenance work at other times, or at least concentrate activities in a different area each year. Felling and thinning work should always be carried out over winter. Some species, notably the larger birds of prey, always return to the same sites and these should be left undisturbed, possibly by including them within areas zoned for non-intervention or long-term retention.

Recent research has shown an alarming decline in the numbers of certain woodland species, including the spotted flycatcher, the tree pipit and the lesser redpoll. It is too early to identify the cause or causes for this decline but possible reasons include:

- Climate change, affecting insect emergence or the drying-out of woodland.
- Loss of invertebrate habitats, including deadwood.
- A reduction in the active management of lowland woodland.
- High levels of deer, affecting regeneration and modifying habitats.
- Greater predation on nests by grey squirrels and crows.
- Changing land uses adjacent to woodland and the effect on edge habitats.

Interestingly, many of these possible causes underline the importance of an active rather than non-interventionist approach to woodland management.

Small Woodland Mammals
Like many mobile species, small mammals are in general less dependant upon individual species than on the woodland structure and such things as ground cover and ease of movement. There are notable exceptions, with the hazel dormouse requiring, as its name suggests, the presence of hazel to

flourish. However, it also thrives in conifer woodland and its serious decline is probably due to a number of factors, the decline in actively managed coppice being only one.

Table 14 summarizes the habitats and breeding seasons for the small woodland mammals seen in Britain. The timing of the breeding seasons supports the practice of delaying many management operations until autumn and winter.

Bats
The importance of woodland for bats has tended to be overlooked in recent years. However, it is now becoming apparent, especially with the advent of radio-tracking, that broadleaved woodland is extremely important for many British bat species. This is because bats use woodland for both foraging and, in some cases, roosting. While some are true woodland mammals, others use broadleaved woodland as their primary foraging habitat.

Bechstein's bat is one example of a species that roosts in hollow branches, dead trees and decay sites in veteran trees. This species prefers closed-canopy woodland with a well-developed understorey; in fact, exactly the type of habitat that might be zoned as minimum intervention.

Bat studies also underline the importance of deadwood habitats in broadleaved woodland. All bats species in Britain are protected by law.

Large Woodland Mammals
These include both the common and rarer species, but all are more influenced by the woodland structure than by any particular plant species. This group has been most affected by the extermination of the large predators, leaving human beings as the only means of population control. As a result, many cause serious problems for woodland regeneration and, in some cases, it is impossible to put a reliable estimate on population numbers. This is particularly the case with roe deer, which lie up in dense conifer plantations and whose numbers have increased dramatically over the last thirty years.

Table 14: Small woodland mammals: their habitats and breeding seasons

Common name	Scientific name	Breeding season	Distribution and habitats
Bank vole	*Clethrionomys glareolus*	April–October	Broadleaved woodland and scrub. Dense cover
Brown hare	*Lepus capensis*	May–July	May be locally abundant in the lowlands. Usually broadleaved woodland
Common shrew	*Sorex araneus*	April–September	Open woodland with dense herbaceous layer
Hazel dormouse	*Muscardinus avellanarius*	June–September	Woodland, particularly mid-age coppice with dense shrubs, including hazel; scrub
Edible dormouse	*Glis glis*	June–August	Mature broadleaved woodland in the Chilterns. Introduced and now abundant in some conifer plantations
Field vole	*Microtus agrestis*	March–September	Widespread. Open woods, young plantations, dense grass
Grey squirrel	*Sciurus carolinensis*	February–April and July–September	Widespread and throughout Britain
Hedgehog	*Erinaceus europaeus*	May–October	Open woodland and scrub
Mole	*Talpa europaea*	March–May	Not usually in pure conifers
Mountain or Blue hare	*Lepus timidus*	February–May	Uplands. Open woodland, usually in winter
Pygmy shrew	*Sorex minutus*	April–September	Open woods with dense herb layer
Rabbit	*Oryctolagus cuniculus*	January–August or later	Widespread
Red squirrel	*Sciurus vulgaris*	March–May and July–September	Amongst conifers and wind-pollinated broad-leaves only (small seeds). Protected: population in decline
Water shrew	*Neomys fodiens*	April–September	Close to streams
Wood mouse	*Apodemus sylvaticus*	April–September	Widespread. Open field layer and scrub

Table 15: Large woodland mammals: their habitats and breeding seasons

Common name	Scientific name	Breeding season	Distribution and habitats
Badger	*Meles meles*	January–June	Mainly in broadleaved woodland. Protected species
Fallow deer	*Dama dama*	May–June	S. England, Midlands and Wales with isolated populations throughout Britain. Open woodland with dense undergrowth
Fox	*Vulpes vulpes*	March–July	Widespread
Muntjac	*Muntiacus reevesi*	All year	S. England but spreading into the Midlands and west. Woodland with dense shrubs and herbs
Otter	*Lutra lutra*	Young born at anytime	Near water. Range extending. Use woodland more than at first thought. Protected species
Pine marten	*Martes martes*	March–June	Larger woodlands of all types. Mainly Scotland but range extending, albeit slowly. Protected species
Polecat	*Mustela putorius*	April–September	Woodland and scrub, mainly in Wales. Protected species
Red deer	*Cervus elaphus*	May–June	Mainly Scotland. Some English populations. All types of woodland and moorland
Roe deer	*Capreolus capreolus*	May–June	Widespread. Open woodland and dense thickets. Young conifer plantations
Sika deer	*Cervus nippon*	May–June	Mainly Scotland, but in pockets throughout England. All types of woodland
Stoat	*Mustela erminea*	April–May	Widespread

(continued overleaf)

Table 15: Larger woodland mammals, their habitats and breeding seasons *(continued)*

Common name	Scientific name	Breeding season	Distribution and habitats
Weasel	*Mustela nivalis*	April–August	Widespread, with access to water
Wild boar	*Sus scrofa*	February–August. Peak in April	Small naturalized populations in S. England. No natural predators
Wild cat	*Felis sylvestris*	May–September	Scottish Highlands and possibly the Scottish Borders and Northumberland. Protected species

NOTE: Chinese water deer (*Hydropotes inermis*) are also found in woodland, mainly in the south and east of England. They are increasing in extent and population and pose a potential threat to broadleaved woodland establishment in the lowlands.

Red deer bucks in the Scottish Highlands in late spring. The vegetation on the hill behind is birch and juniper scrub; regeneration is being prevented by the high numbers of deer. (Photo: Malcolm Riding)

Lyme's disease affects humans and is carried by deer ticks, although small mammals are thought to be the main reservoirs of these parasites. Although still rare, with increasing numbers of deer in woodland and greater public access, owners should be aware of the problem.

Invertebrates

Invertebrates are possibly the most neglected animal group yet, perversely, probably the most important in terms of the ecology of woodland. Invertebrates range from bark beetles through woodlice and spiders to springtails and mites.

They are usually found in the litter layer where they help recycle rotting vegetation and aerate the soil. They are also an important food source for many mammals including voles, dormice and shrews.

The conservation and management of deadwood is partly justified by the close association of invertebrates with this habitat. The use of 'Waterhouse' piles (log piles) is one way of building up the invertebrate ecology quite quickly.

Non-flowering Plants

This very large group of plants includes some that are known to have existed over 250 million years ago. Rather than relying on seeds, they reproduce by spores, which are single cells and may be carried considerable distances from the plant. The main groups found in woodland are: ferns; mosses and liverworts; fungi; algae; and lichens.

Many are important in helping to identify the age and history of woodland, as they are very sensitive to environmental disturbance, including pollution, light levels and bark chemistry. Their identification and biology are very specialized, and readers interested in finding out more should contact the relevant society.

Fungi are intimately associated with woodland ecosystems, and many thousands of species occur within them. The biology of fungi is extremely complex, and the fruiting bodies we see above ground are a visible indicator of much greater activity under the surface. Fungi are nature's waste recyclers, releasing nutrients locked away in dead tissues and making them available to living plants.

The largest living organism on earth is believed to be a fungus discovered in a forest in Oregon a few years ago. Estimated to cover nearly 1,000 hectares, the honey mushroom (*Armillaria ostoyae*) lives about 1m under the soil surface. It is 5.6km across and estimated at between 2,400 and 7,000 years old. Genetic analysis has shown it to be a single organism.

Old-growth temperate forest in North America showing the conservation of deadwood habitats. In Britain many woodlands have been cleared of deadwood in the past. This type of habitat is now a major priority for nature conservation.

Hart's tongue fern growing under ash woodland on a limestone pavement. The woodland includes yew, holly and hazel.

A number of different types of fungi and associations are recognized:

1. Mycorrhizae are associations of fungi and tree roots. The fungi live in intimate association with the roots, providing them with nutrients and water. In return, the fungi obtain sugars from the tree roots.
2. Toadstools and bracket fungi are the large fruiting bodies designed to spread the spores of the fungus. Below ground are the mycelia (roots) of the fungus.
3. Lichens are associations of a fungus and a blue-green algae.

Many fungi are strongly associated with other species or groups. For example, over 200 species of beetles, moths and flies breed in the large fruiting bodies, and some nowhere else! Some animals, notably the ambrosia beetles, 'farm' certain fungi. There is the possibility of harvesting fungi in woodland (*see* Chapter 11).

The beech tuft fungus growing in the crown of beech in late summer. Not all fungi grow on the ground, and a number may be found quite high up in the tree crown.

Flowering Plants

The use of flowering plants is central to the NVC discussed in relation to woodland structure (*see* Chapter 2). They are closely associated with certain types of woodland, and for many owners and members of the general public flowering plants remain a particular interest and source of enjoyment.

Table 16: Conservation value of the common native woodland shrubs and climbers

Common name	Scientific name	Where found and conservation value
Alder buckthorn	*Frangula alnus*	Damp and peaty sites, berries for birds
Bilberry (blaeberry)	*Vaccinium myrtillus*	Acid soils, berries in autumn
Blackthorn	*Prunus spinosa*	Dense thickets, nesting sites, butterflies
Broom	*Sarothamnus scoparius*	Heathland and sandy soils, insects
Bramble	*Rubus fruticosus*	Common, nesting cover, autumn fruit
Buckthorn, purging	*Rhamnus catharticus*	Similar to alder buckthorn but drier
Butcher's broom	*Ruscus aculeatus*	Dry soils in south, nesting
Clematis	*Clematis vitalba*	Climber. Calcareous soils in south and Wales, insects
Cowberry	*Vaccinium vitis-idea*	Evergreen shrub on acid soils, butterflies, fruit
Dogwood	*Thelycrania sanguinea*	Calcareous soils
Elder	*Sambucus nigra*	Common, flowers for insects, berries for birds, nesting sites. Resistant to rabbits
Gorse (furze, whin)	*Ulex europaeus*	Common in open woodland, insects, nesting sites
Guelder rose	*Viburnum opulus*	Widespread on damp soils, fruits for birds and small mammals (esp. wood mouse)
Honeysuckle	*Lonicera periclymenum*	Widespread climber and in field layer, flowers, fruits, invertebrates
Ivy	*Hedera helix*	Evergreen climber and in field layer, nesting, cover, winter deer browse
Ling, Heather	*Calluna vulgaris*	Widespread in open woodlands. In old pinewoods, important for black grouse and capercaillie
Privet	*Ligustrum vulgare*	Common on calcareous soils, nesting, invertebrates
Roses	*Rosa* spp.	Several species, nesting and fruit
Spindle tree	*Euonymous europaeus*	Calcareous soils, mainly southern, insects and fruit
Spurge laurel	*Daphne laureola*	Evergreen shrub, calcareous, butterflies, moths, bees on flowers. (Rare: Mezereon, *D. mezereum*)
Wayfaring tree	*Viburnum lantana*	Calcareous soils in south, insects and birds

Protecting the Woodland

A number of protection issues are very complex, in particular pests and predator control, and tree diseases. The Forestry Commission prepares a wide range of up-to-date publications, and also offers telephone advice through the Tree Advice Trust. Membership of various societies allows owners to share common problems and to discuss solutions; a list of relevant organizations is included in the list of useful addresses.

It is important to remember that trees and woodlands are generally well adapted to many forms of damage, and that death and decay are a natural part of the woodland ecosystem. Indeed, in some woodlands, time might be spent in promoting deadwood and decaying habitats in order to achieve certain ecological objectives.

Some damage may be cyclical in nature, making it necessary to assess the extent to which control is achievable or cost-effective in practice. For example, many pest populations build up rapidly if conditions are right

Spindle, a native shrub, flowering in southern England. The wood was once used to make spindles for use in the knitting industry.

for them, and by the time a problem is seen it may be too late to effect any real control. However, new pests and diseases are entering the country and vigilance is required in order to spot these.

Recent moves towards less intensive forms of silviculture, together with greater restrictions on chemical applications, have resulted in a more holistic approach being adopted by many woodland owners. In some cases, the use of natural regeneration may reduce damage in the early stages of woodland regeneration. In addition, some of the smaller mammals are opportunistic and their populations will increase dramatically if the site is disturbed, for example when clear-felling.

If, on reading this section, it appears that woodlands are subject to a multitude of protection problems, it is worth remembering that they are some of the most advanced, stable and longest lived of all ecosystems.

Some of the pests and diseases mentioned in this chapter are notifiable, meaning that there is a legal duty on a woodland owner to inform the relevant authorities if any are found in the woodland.

Mammals

There is a wide range of mammals, both large and small, which may cause damage in both newly planted and established woodland. Some tree species are more susceptible than others and consideration needs to be given to this when planning new woodland.

While damage is most common in the early stages of a woodland's development, greater financial or amenity loss may occur much later on when individual trees have a greater value.

Mammal populations are subject to quite rapid changes, caused by such variables as climate, food sources, predator populations and human intervention. There are also large regional differences in both distribution and population density. Changing countryside management, including the use of set-aside land, is altering the distribution of many mammal species.

In and adjacent to urban areas it may be more difficult to control certain mammals, such as the grey squirrel, due to cultural attitudes and the close proximity of the general public. While government policies target woodland expansion in these areas, urgent efforts will have to be made in finding acceptable methods of control if the new woodlands are to survive and meet the objectives set for them.

Types of Mammal Damage

All the larger mammals listed in Table 17 might, in addition to their specific actions, cause general browsing damage. The use of terms such as browsing and grazing are often used interchangeably, but they have quite different meanings, which are important when applied in a woodland situation.

Browsing is the removal of leaves, buds and shoots from the tree. It rarely kills a tree but the leading shoot may be damaged. In some cases, this may require formative pruning if quality timber is being aimed for (*see* Chapter 10).

Grazing is the habit of feeding on grasses and other vegetation close to the ground. This actively promotes competition with newly planted trees, although in some situations grazing animals may be used in agroforestry systems to provide early financial returns.

Fraying is caused by male deer marking territory or cleaning the antlers of velvet. Bark hangs down in strips from the main stem and branches. Fraying is often found on the edges of woods.

Bark stripping is the removal of bark and the underlying tissues from the main stem and branches.

Pith removal takes place when the tree is in full leaf, usually in older trees, and is carried out by grey squirrels. Ash, sweet chestnut and walnut are most affected but damage is generally minimal.

As mentioned briefly in Chapter 1, browsing is integral to the ecology of many woodlands and, as a result, trees are adapted to it. In many species, for example holly, the lower leaves are spiky to protect the tree, and the form of many trees in the landscape is partly attributed to the effects of grazing.

Where grazing is inevitable, it may be appropriate to leave some woody vegetation on-site as protection for the trees.

Depending upon the objectives for the woodland, browsing may be acceptable but it will stunt young trees, result in a loss of vigour and cause multiple leaders to form. For this reason, trees grown for timber should be protected from the effects of browsing until they are of sufficient height. In agro-forestry systems involving stock, widely spaced trees will usually be individually protected.

Table 17 summarizes the damage that may be caused by the more important mammals found in Britain. The list is not exhaustive, and the severity of any damage is very dependant upon local conditions, the presence of other woodland, the species and age mix and factors as varied as soil type and public access. The optimum densities quoted are for guidance only and will depend to a large extent on the habitats in which the deer are found. The changing nature of farming practices, rural employment and subsidies are all likely to have a major impact on mammal distribution over the coming decades. Close seasons operate for deer control.

Control Methods

If the risk of damage is low, it may be sufficient to respond as and when it occurs, making sure that regular inspections take place at times when damage is most likely. If damage is expected to be serious, or if it will affect the achievement of the management objectives, a number of approaches may be adopted, as follows:

1. Individual protection of trees or the fencing of larger areas (*see* Chapter 8).
2. Control of the mammal population by measures such as trapping, shooting or the use of poison. There are strict controls on these methods, including close seasons, and further advice should be obtained from the relevant authorities.
3. Increasing habitat diversity, either to provide alternative food sources or to make

Table 17: Summary of the more important woodland mammals that may cause damage to trees

Common name	Type of damage caused	Comments, tree species and habitats most affected	Protection measures
Red deer	Fraying of bark March–May. Stripping at any time	Optimum density around 4 per 100ha. Oak and beech	Fencing (2m), tree shelters (1.8m). Sitka spruce very tolerant
Roe deer	Fraying March–July	Optimum density 8 per 100ha	As for red deer, but fencing (1.8m) and shelters (1.2m)
Fallow deer	Fraying March–May.	Optimum density 6 per 100ha. Coppice	As for red deer
Sika deer	Fraying March–May. Stripping at any time	Optimum density as for red deer. Very secretive deer	Fencing as for red deer
Muntjac deer	Fraying March–May	A major problem in lowland broadleaved woodland	As for red deer, but fencing 1.5m
Grey squirrel	Stripping May–July. Ring barking. Eats seeds, cones and buds. Particularly affects oak, ash, beech and sycamore	If numbers are high may severely affect species choice. Major threat to the viability of many broadleaved woodlands	Choose less susceptible tree species. Remove trees with large seed if within red squirrel zones
Rabbit	Stripping in winter	Populations on increase with changing farming practices. Ash and sycamore very susceptible to 20 years	Fencing (90cm), tree shelters
Brown hare	Clipping of leading shoots in winter and spring	Trees survive but often with multiple leaders	Fencing
Blue hare	As brown hare	As brown hare	As brown hare
Field vole	Stripping and girdling young trees at any time	Populations may increase dramatically over short period	Tree or vole guards (inserted into ground). Weed control

control easier by providing more open spaces (glades).

4. The use of alternative silvicultural systems that are less susceptible to damage.

5. Small mammal populations may be partially controlled by providing improved habitats for predators such as owls and hawks. However, predator numbers will not increase fast enough to control adequately sudden increases in small-mammal numbers.

6. In some situations, small areas of regeneration may be protected from deer by fencing with circular enclosures, or by allowing trees to regenerate through dense woody growth such as holly or thorn.

7. Deer management groups have been set up in some regions to co-ordinate efforts.

Insects

There are many insects associated with trees and woodlands, and some of these are quite specific to certain stages in the life of the tree. They are usually kept in check by natural enemies, ranging from birds to viruses.

Insects attack trees in a number of quite different ways depending upon their life cycles and methods of feeding.

Defoliators

This group of insects eats the leaves of the trees, often causing complete loss of the foliage. This results in a loss of growth, reduction in flower and fruit production, and an increased possibility of secondary attacks by other pests and diseases. Conifers are more susceptible to defoliation than broadleaves, and may even be killed if attacks continue for a second year. Many broadleaves are adapted to such attacks: oaks, for example, produce new 'lammas' growth in summer if defoliated.

In conifers, these insects include the pine beauty moth (*Panolis flammea*) and the pine looper moth (*Bupalus piniaria*). In broadleaves, one of the more common defoliators is seen in oak woodland in early summer. The oak-leaf roller moth (*Tortrix viridana*) may defoliate entire woods. Pedunculate oak is more susceptible as it comes into leaf earlier than the sessile oak. However, damage is restricted to the current year's growth.

Bark Beetles

This group can do immense damage and is usually specific to one tree species. Probably the best known in Britain is the large elm

Roe deer buck fraying a young tree. The bark is stripped from the main stem and the tree suffers deformed growth and decay. (Illustration: Colin Blanchard)

Defoliation of oak by the oak-leaf roller moth in early summer. New 'lammas' growth will appear later in the season, and tree growth will be slightly reduced.

bark beetle (*Scolytus scolytus*), responsible for carrying the spores of the fungus that causes Dutch elm disease. Bark beetles produce characteristic tunnels under the bark in which they lay their eggs, and in many cases the trees die through an inability to conduct nutrients from the roots to the shoots.

The great spruce bark beetle (*Dendroctonus micans*) is an important pest of conifers in Wales and the Marches, and is a notifiable disease. The European eight-toothed spruce bark beetle (*Ips typographus*) is another species that should be reported if found.

Bark Gnawers and Root Feeders

A specialized group of beetles, the adult stage is adapted to feed on young saplings, either in the nursery or on the natural regeneration of both conifers and broadleaves.

The pine weevil (*Hylobius abietis*) is probably the best known of this group, and populations can soar after clear-felling. Biological control is available to keep this in check.

Shoot Borers

These are insects that live mainly on the young twigs and terminal buds of trees. The boring tends to weaken shoots and twigs, which blow off in the wind.

The pine-shoot borer (beetle) (*Tomicus piniperda*) is quite common in Scots pine woodland, where the ground may be littered with twigs whose pith has been bored out.

Sap Suckers

Better known as aphids, they reduce tree growth by feeding on the sugars in the sap. In large numbers, they can produce a 'rain' of sap secretions recognizable to those who park their cars under lime or sycamore trees in summer.

The green spruce aphid (*Elatobium abietinum*) is often found in Sitka spruce, and outbreaks may follow mild winters. Damage is usually restricted to reduced growth, and control is usually undertaken only in Christmas-tree plantations.

The felted beech coccus (*Cryptococcus fagisuga*) produces a waxy wool on the stems and branches of the tree. It is often associated with the fungus, *Nectria coccinea* (beech bark disease), causing canker and die-back.

Types of Insect Damage

Usually any damage caused by insects will be minimal and should be accepted as part of the woodland cycle. However, in some situations, insect populations may increase dramatically and have a major impact on the woodland.

Conifers tend to be more prone than broadleaves to insect attacks, both in the establishment phase and even more so when replacing conifers with the same species. This is because the previous woodland often played host to the insects which will emerge to damage the new plants.

Large plantations of single-species conifers planted in the uplands sometimes succumb to serious attacks by a number of different insect pests. This is especially the case when they are planted on more marginal sites where a combination of stress and a large food source allow populations to grow unchecked. Most of the commercial conifers are introduced species and have not yet had time to develop protection strategies. In woodland where there is a greater diversity of conifer species and ages, these conditions are less likely to occur. This is partly why there is a shift towards continuous cover management. However, vigilance is still required and new pests occasionally find their way here from abroad.

In general, broadleaves are managed less intensively than conifers, and pest populations do not tend to reach such high levels. In addition, many of the broadleaved species are native and are planted on better soils at lower elevations. As a result, they tend to suffer less stress than many of the conifer species.

Detailed guidance on the identification and control of these insects will be found in the current Forestry Commission publications. The FC website carries updates on recent outbreaks and control measures.

Control Methods

The use of biological control has had some success in Britain. This involves the application of naturally occurring controls such as parasites or the active protection and habitat enhancement of natural predators. Such an approach, sometimes referred to as Integrated Pest Management (IPM), has a number of potential advantages including:

- Reducing the reliance on pesticides and herbicides.
- Reducing costs.
- Increased biodiversity.

The protection of seed and seedlings in the nursery is complex and outside the scope of this book, as are the particular insect pests of amenity trees in urban areas.

Bacterial and Fungal Diseases

In general, bacteria and fungi are very beneficial in woodland, and play key roles in breaking down plant nutrients and in recycling the products of decomposition and decay. In addition, many fungi live in intimate contact with tree roots as mycorrhizae, helping to ensure the uptake of nutrients directly from the soil.

Many of the diseases that attack woodland trees are fungal in origin. As a result, they tend to be difficult to identify until the fruiting bodies appear, by which time it is often too late to do anything. If in any doubt, it is always advisable to seek specialist help and advice.

Diseases of nurseries are specialist and complex in nature, and will not be dealt with here.

Two diseases found in Britain recently are causing concern and woodland owners should report any suspected infections. They are:

1. Sudden oak death (*Phytophthora ramorum*), with a more virulent strain *P. kernovii* now identified in south-west England. This is a notifiable disease, with potentially very serious consequences for oak trees across Britain.

Table 18: Tree diseases sometimes found in woodland

Scientific name Common name	Indications and symptoms	Control measures	Resistant species
Heterobasidion annosum. Fomes root and butt rot of conifers	Serious cause of loss in British conifer woodlands. Fruiting bodies at base of stump. Crown die-back. Wind-throw due to root rot	Stump inoculation. In pine, a suspension of *Peniophora gigantea* to stumps	Douglas fir and silver fir
Armillaria spp. Honey fungus	A number of species, causing damage at different stages. More common on stumps of broadleaves. Fungus has black shoelace-like strands and honey-coloured fruiting bodies	If serious, change to more resistant species	Douglas fir and broadleaves
Phaeolus schweinitzii	Stem rot of conifers	Common on Sitka spruce, Douglas fir and the larches. On old woodland sites. Fruiting body bracket at base of tree. Decayed wood cubical and dry. Linked with Honey fungus. Avoid susceptible species on likely sites	Other conifers and broad-leaves
Rhizina undulata. Group dying of conifers, or 'Fire Fungus'	Initiated by fire as spores germinate above 35–40°C. Attacks conifers only. Fruiting bodies are cushion-like brown on floor, spreading in ever-widening circles	Do not set fires in forest or burn debris on site	Douglas fir
Brunchorstia pinea. Brunchorstia shoot killing of pine	On Corsican and Scots pine. Die-back in crowns of young trees	Mainly in uplands of north and west Britain	Other conifers

Scientific name Common name	Indications and symptoms	Control measures	Resistant species
Peridermium pini. Resin top disease of Scots pine	Found only in E. of Britain where rainfall low. A parasitic fungus (rust) which enters young shoots but may girdle main stem	Remove infected trees at thinning stage	Corsican pine rarely infected
Lachnellula willkommii. Larch canker	Disease of the European larch, especially Alpine provenances. Severe damage to branches and even death	Plant-resistant provenances of European larch. Most hybrid larch resistant	Japanese larch rarely infected
Nectria coccinea. Beech bark disease	Linked to initial infection by the felted beech coccus. Rarely affects the final crop but causes loss mid-rotation	Remove infected trees at thinning stage, or earlier if timber valuable	Drought may predispose beech to attack
Xanthomonas populi. Bacterial canker of poplar	Cankers form on branches and trunks. Bacteria ooze from infected bark and spread	Remove infected trees. Plant resistant varieties of poplar	Use approved varieties only
Ophiostoma novo-ulmi. Dutch elm disease	Pathogenic fungus spread by the elm bark beetles (*Scolytus* spp.); causes death by blocking xylem vessels in growth rings	Sanitation felling of limited success. In N. Britain climate moderates spread	Root suckers likely to maintain 'pockets' of the species
Phytophthora spp. Ink disease of sweet chestnut	No visible signs of fungus seen. Die-back of trees followed by inky-black exudations on roots and stumps. On wetter soils	Improve drainage. Both beech and Lawson cypress very susceptible	If severe, change species
Pseudomonas syringae. Bacterial canker of cherry	Lesions on twigs and branches. Gum oozes from cankers. Stem may be girdled. 'Shot'-like holes in leaves	Plant in mixtures. May be more common on shallow soils. Site selection important	Correct choice of planting material

A house built around a tree in New York State. Although this has been done with the best of intentions, and is no doubt a talking point around the dinner table, the tree will in time outgrow the house and the roots may be starved of moisture, causing dieback.

2. Red band needle blight. This is a fungal disease currently affecting Corsican pine in East Anglia.

People

The old adage, 'You hurt the things you love', is often true when it comes to trees. Time and again, important trees are 'protected' by building walls around them, paving over the roots,

taking samples or just by the sheer weight of numbers. Trees need air and water just as much as we do, and the unseen roots are sensitive to disturbance, compaction and pollution. Insensitive developments, careless access to underground services and inappropriate activities are just a few of the 'people pressures' that can cause damage to woodland.

Climate Change

Perhaps the greatest threat to woodland will come from the climatic changes predicted as a result of the rising level of CO_2 in the atmosphere. While it is too early to predict with any certainty the detailed changes that might occur, enough is now known of the broad-scale effects to suggest the adoption of some 'guiding principles' with respect to the management of trees and woodlands:

- Plant a number of species to spread the risk.
- Consider planting species from south of their current range.
- Consider using plants with a more southerly provenance.
- Maintain conditions that favour soil protection and water conservation.

More specific, but still tentative ideas from work being carried out by Forest Research suggest that:

- The planting range of Douglas fir may extend eastwards.
- Beech may extend northwards and may become marginal in the south-east.
- Sitka spruce may extend its range northwards but may become marginal in the south-west.
- Corsican pine may flourish in the warmer south and extend northwards into the eastern side of Scotland.

CHAPTER 8

Regenerating and Creating Woodland

This chapter considers the regeneration of trees within an existing woodland, and with the creation of new woodland on bare land. The following topics are included:

- The choice of tree species.
- The importance of provenance.
- Site factors to consider.
- Planting.
- Natural regeneration.
- Plant spacing.
- Fencing and individual tree protection.
- Creating new woodlands in Britain.
- Shelterbelts.

There is also a case study on creating a new woodland.

Regeneration is a term used here to include both the planting of young trees and the natural regeneration obtained from the existing trees in the woodland. The planting of young trees, or the promotion of natural regeneration, is one of the more important tasks to be undertaken in woodland management. It may need to be done for a variety of reasons, including:

- The replacement of trees previously felled for protection or safety.
- The restocking of woodland after either clear-felling or selection-felling.
- After group-felling to promote an uneven-aged woodland.
- After disturbance such as disease or pest damage.

- To add diversity to a woodland.
- After a natural occurrence such as storm damage.
- To supplement either existing natural regeneration or previous planting.
- To strengthen woodland edges and hedgerows.

Natural Regeneration or Planting?

In most cases, the decision on whether to use young plants or to use natural regeneration will be based on a number of factors. Table 19 lists some of the more important factors to consider when making a decision. If the decision is taken to plant, then the choice of species becomes all important.

Choosing Species to Plant

Chapters 3 and 4 list and describe most of the woodland trees likely to be planted in Britain. They comprise a rich and varied selection of trees appropriate to many different sites and regions. Some are more demanding than others, and some will grow faster, taller and for longer than others. Many have particular features such as good autumn colour or high conservation value.

The selection of the correct species for the site is the key to successful establishment. The choice should not be taken lightly and, if in

---

Table 19: Natural regeneration or planting?

Natural regeneration	Planting
Ensures species are matched to local microhabitats.	With care this can be done, but time-consuming.
Relies upon good seed years, which may be infrequent.	Ease of planning and of costing before work commences.
Local genotypes are maintained.	May use local stock grown in nursery.
Difficult to predict success due to the range of variables.	Fewer variables and greater control over plants and planting.
More intensive management, particularly where many species regenerate.	Generally easier to control and manage.
Only those species present will regenerate.	Gives the opportunity to change or add species if appropriate.
Can be used to supplement planting and aid diversity of structure and species.	Enrichment of natural regeneration by planting may be used.
Requires greater skill and flexibility, and might take a number of years to achieve adequate stocking density.	More predictable and greater level of knowledge among contractors.
More likely to lead to uneven-aged woodland.	Will tend towards even-aged but, with planning, this can be addressed.
A more natural process.	Well-considered planting designs can mimic natural patterns to some degree.
If carried out correctly, it can be more cost-effective than planting.	Costs clearly known in advance.

---

any doubt, a professional forester should be consulted. However, there is also a very personal element involved and, as long as the chosen species will survive and grow reasonably well, there is no reason why personal preference should not be taken into account.

Local woodlands will give an indication of what grows well, and semi-natural woods will feature locally native species. Disused quarries and similar sites may well indicate a range of tree and shrub species that regenerate naturally. Younger woodlands will demonstrate the prevailing trends as well as past mistakes! There is also the possibility of planting more unusual species for clearly defined objectives, such as hybrid walnut for furniture-quality timber.

Table 20 gives an indication of the more common species planted in the soils listed. It is a guide only and should be read in conjunction with local knowledge and the detailed site survey (*see* Chapter 6).

Mixtures and Nurse Species

In general, it is better to plant a number of different species than to limit planting to just one species, unless group sizes are small or where a decision has been made to grow for a single specialist market. A species-diverse woodland will tend to be more stable, healthier and may meet more objectives than one planted with a single species.

Because trees root at different levels, and their crowns sometimes occupy different

Table 20: Tree species commonly planted in woodland

Soils and site	Broadleaves	Conifers
Brown earths, sheltered and well-drained in lowlands	Wide range, including ash, beech, cherry, lime, oaks, sweet chestnut, sycamore, walnut, poplars, hornbeam, hazel, holly	Larches, Douglas fir, western red cedar, western hemlock, spruces
Upland brown earths, acidic, well drained	Beech, birch, cherry, sessile oak, sycamore	Larches, spruces, western hemlock, Douglas fir, Scots pine
Chalk and limestones (calcareous)	Ash, beech, sycamore, lime, wild service, box	Western red cedar, Japanese larch, Corsican pine, Norway spruce
Lowland gley soils, poor drainage, heavy	Ash, oaks, sycamore, poplars, willows, hornbeam	Norway spruce, western hemlock, western red cedar
Upland gley soils, acid	Sessile oak, rowan, aspen, downy birch	Spruces, western hemlock
Upland peaty gley soils	Downy birch, rowan, willow	Sitka spruce
Podsols, sandy soils, ironpans	Birches, rowan	Scots and Corsican pines, western hemlock, hybrid larch

spaces, planting in mixtures may actually increase the growth of the trees and contribute to the stability of the woodland.

On some sites, it may be better to plant a pioneer species to act as a nurse for those species that will eventually form the woodland proper. Nurse species may often be cut out of the woodland once they have done their job, or left to form an understorey. Typical pioneer species that may be used as a nurse include alder, birch or pine. Another approach is to use a nurse species to improve the nutrient status of the soil.

Hybrid walnut (NG23 – Juglans nigra × J. regia*) two years after planting in Sussex. It was planted as a 60cm bare-root transplant in a nurse mixture of* Alnus cordata *and* Elaeagnus umbellata. *(Photo: The Walnut Tree Company, www.WalnutTrees.co.uk)*

Provenance, Origin and Seed Sources

In Chapter 1, we briefly considered the ways in which trees migrated from Continental Europe after the last ice age and the use of introduced species to complement a fairly impoverished native tree flora. Unlike agriculture, where there have been many thousands of years of breeding and stock improvement, woodland trees still remain essentially wild populations. The small amount of selection and improvement that has occurred over the last few hundred years has affected only a small number of generations, owing to the longevity of trees in comparison with annual plants. While breeding programmes for crops and animals can take place quite quickly, there may be a wait of over thirty years before a tree even sets its first seed.

Recent advances in tree selection, propagation and genetics are now paying practical dividends, with improved planting material for a number of species coming on to the market. A good example of this is the introduction of improved clonal native wild cherry under the trademark 'Wildstar'. These ten clones have been selected for improved growth, disease-resistance and better form.

Although this is a highly complex subject, it is important to understand the rudiments, since there are legal obligations on a woodland owner or manager to use the correct material for certain timber-producing species. Details of the legal requirements for forty-six tree species and for the genus *Populus* (the controlled species), under the Forest Reproductive Regulations (FRM), may be obtained from the local Forestry Commission office or via their website.

The FRM Regulations divide Britain into four 'Regions of Provenance' and, for native species, the regions are further subdivided into twenty-four 'Native Seed Zones'. The common terms used are:

- *Origin* This is the place where the species originally came from.
- *Provenance* The particular region within the natural range of a species, or the region in which introduced trees have naturalized and set seed. Different provenances will display variations in characteristics, such as frost hardiness, that reflect the local climate. For example, if you buy Douglas fir seedlings, they may be from seed collected in Washington State, USA, or from a collection made in Devon but, in both cases, the origin is from within the natural range in North America.
- *Native* Tree species that arrived in Britain naturally following the retreat of the ice sheet after the last ice age and before the formation of the English Channel.
- *Locally native* This refers to native trees from a local region. Some species, such as beech, are only native in particular regions. Adaptations and characteristics alter in response to local conditions. In some situations, you will be required to plant trees from within your own local zone.

Site Factors to Consider

Plants need protection from a number of site factors. Trees are at their most susceptible to damage when young and towards the end of their natural life-span.

Although the past history of a site will give some indication of likely damage, the possibility of climate change means that extra care needs to be taken on sites that are either more exposed than average or more marginal for tree growth. In upland areas wind is a major factor in determining the height to which a woodland will grow and hence its stability.

Drainage
One of the first signs of neglected woodland is often a rise in the water-table owing to blocked and poorly maintained drains. This results in waterlogging of the soil and consequent lack of oxygen, leading to root death and eventually to tree death and wind damage. This is particularly a problem on heavy soils where rooting may be impaired in any case. Drains, ditches and watercourses should all be maintained to ensure a free flow of water from the woodland.

Salt Damage

Woodlands near the coast may suffer the combined effects of high wind and salt. The wind may cause severe restriction in annual growth together with deformation of the crown. The resulting trees will be most valuable as a wind-firm edge to the woodland and should be felled only as a last resort. The salt will also cause damage to the trees, primarily by 'burning' the leaves and thus reducing the growth rate (*see* the photograph on page 8). Certain species, including ash, hawthorn, sycamore and a number of conifers, are more resistant to the effects of salt and wind, and should always be planted along the leading edges of any coastal woodland.

Drought

During a prolonged period of drought, such as might happen in many parts of Britain in unusually warm summers, trees may die or be severely affected. In older trees, the symptoms may be delayed for many years.

Beech leaves are retained on the lower leaves of the tree over winter as protection against ground frost.

Trees within woodland are less susceptible than those on the edges, or those growing on their own. Soil depth and structure is also a major factor in determining the likelihood of long-term damage.

Trees with predominantly surface roots, including birch, beech and larch, are all very susceptible to drought. The effects of severe drought can be very long lasting, and older woodland trees may take a number of years to show the full effects, and even longer to recover.

Frost

Spring frosts, or 'late' frosts, may damage or even kill leaves and shoots, particularly with sensitive species. The resistance to frost varies within species as well so, on frosty sites, choosing the correct provenance may be important. Beech, ash, oak, Douglas fir and larch are all frost-sensitive, as is Sitka spruce. Frost-hardy species include Scots pine, sycamore, hornbeam, cherry and birch. The habit of beech to retain its dead leaves into winter is an adaptation to spring frosts, acting as a blanket for each bud.

Autumn frosts, or 'early' frosts, may also damage younger shoots. This is quite common on a number of conifers where the tender needles near the terminal bud may become brown.

Winter Cold

Damage by winter cold may be caused in a number of ways. Cold winds may desiccate foliage, particularly if they occur before the tree is fully hardened for winter. If warmer spells alternate with cold this may also cause damage. A number of introduced species are also susceptible to very low temperatures, notably many of the eucalypts, *Nothofagus* species and the Monterey pine. The latter is often seen in coastal regions where the climate tends to be milder.

Planting

The choice of species will be largely dictated by what is growing well already and by

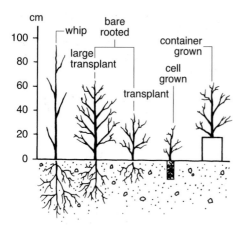

The range of tree sizes and types typically planted in a woodland situation.

the objectives for the woodland. In the case of semi-natural woodland, the species present will generally be well adapted to the site, whereas in a plantation a change of species, or the addition of some new species, may be required. Planting is an opportunity to add diversity to the woodland and possibly to experiment with new species, or to consider mixtures of species.

In general, it is better to plant as small and sturdy a tree as possible, subject to constraints such as protection and microclimate. Small trees tend to establish faster, do not go into a period of shock (check), and grow with better form and vigour. However, there are situations where larger plants may need to be used, particularly if weed growth and control is a problem.

Buying Plants

It is possible to grow your own plants from seed and, if planting locally native species, this may be viable. However, in general, it is far better to buy plants from a reputable nursery specializing in woodland trees. Some even specialize in growing trees of native origin. When bought in bulk from wholesale nurseries, young trees are a surprisingly cost-effective method of establishment. Many nurseries

have excellent websites with useful planting information and stocklists.

The amount of grant aid payable for planting is linked to the cost of bulk plants and not to larger specimens bought in from domestic suppliers. Do not buy plants from a local garden centre: they will be prohibitively expensive and may not meet the requirements of the regulations for the supply of certain species. In addition, a specialist supplier will be able to give more informed advice and assistance in the selection of the appropriate species and sizes. Do, however, try to buy from nurseries in a similar climatic region and ideally one where the plants are grown on-site and not imported.

Young trees may be bought in a number of different size categories, and the choice will depend upon such factors as price, species and potential site factors. A good tree-nursery catalogue will give the buyer most, if not all, of the following information:

- Species name – both common and botanical, to avoid any confusion.
- Provenance and/or origin, to help in site matching and, in the case of forest trees, to meet the FRM regulations.
- The registered seed-source number for those species covered by the FRM regulations.
- The size of the plants indicated by the treatment in the nursery, such as 1 + 1, 2 + 1 (*see* below).
- The stem diameter range.
- The height range.
- Minimum root-collar diameter (for cell-grown plants).
- Whether container-grown or bare-rooted.
- Additional information where necessary.

The indication of treatment in the nursery is as follows. The first number indicates the time in the seed-bed in years, followed by an indication of whether the plant was then moved to another transplant bed (+) or undercut *in situ* (u) and then grown on again for a number of years. The process of undercutting or transplanting promotes the growth of more fibrous roots at the expense of height growth, which increases the likely success of establishment in the woodland.

A procedure called side air-pruning has been adopted by some nurseries. Deep channels are cut in the soil on either side of the transplants in the nursery. The roots emerge into the air, and this encourages the formation of compact, fibrous roots. This is believed to combine the sturdiness of transplants with the flexibility and ease of use of container- or cell-grown material.

Transplanting also allows the nursery to cull poor-quality plants, and to grade them in relation to the needs of the market and the use to which they are being put. (A transplant sold for timber production will need to be of better quality than one sold for hedging.)

A typical example from a nursery catalogue for a bare-rooted transplant is shown below:

Common ash, *Fraxinus excelsior*, Zone 204, 1 + 1, 40–60cm (16–24in).

'Zone 204' indicates that the tree is of British provenance: from north-east Britain (20) and the native seed zone (4), including the area around Durham. The 1 + 1 transplant has had one year in a nursery bed, followed by one year in a transplant bed. 40–60cm refers to the height range of the plants supplied.

Woodland transplants are usually sold in multiples of fifteen or twenty-five and, in some years, certain species may be in short supply. Some broadleaved trees set seed infrequently, and good mast years for oak and beech may only occur every five years or so. Order plants as early as possible, ideally by July at the latest, for the planting season in the following autumn or spring.

Take care of plants prior to planting, as follows:

- Ensure roots do not dry out and keep plants sheltered and out of the wind.
- Maintain as many short, fibrous roots as possible.
- Handle gently – even dropping them affects tree survival.

- Do not leave in the sun, either in transit or on site.
- Avoid damaging the roots, stems or bark.
- Plant when dormant with no new growing roots.

The main reason for failure following planting is moisture stress. The roots need to be healthy and viable. In some nurseries, the root-growth potential (RGP) is measured to give an indication of health and vigour.

Planting Methods
While there are many different techniques in use, they divide into two basic types depending on the plant material used.

Features of a good-quality plant, in this case cell-grown but applying equally to bare-rooted stock. Important features include fibrous roots, a balanced root/shoot ratio, and shoots free from damage.

Table 21: Common methods for planting woodland trees

Method	Advantages	Disadvantages	Comments
Notch (Slit)	Fast: for use with bare-root transplants and cell-grown trees only	Not suitable for larger trees or on wet sites	Commonly used for larger-scale woodland establishment. Reliable on good sites with competent contractors and high-quality plants
Turf	Use on wetter soils	Time-consuming	Can give good weed suppression, possibly without the need for chemicals
Ridge	On ploughed/drained sites gives good planting position	Ridges dry out in exposed situations and may also suffer from erosion	Plant either on top or to leeward side of ridge
Mound	On wet soils good planting position	Time-consuming on a small scale. Stability issues on windy sites	May use mechanical mounders on larger sites
Pit	Good soil cultivation and space for root growth	Expensive on all but the smallest sites	Usually used for specimen plantings with larger trees and for container stock
Mechanical	Speed and consistency	Only for single species at standard spacings	Usually only on large uniform sites, or for SRC on farmland

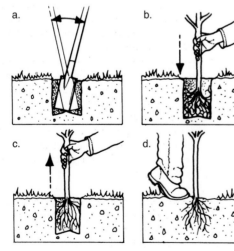

a. Make a notch or slit in the ground with a small garden spade or lightweight planting spade, moving it to and fro to open up the soil.
b. Place the transplant gently in the notch, making sure the roots are all pointing downwards and that the collar of the tree is slightly below ground level.
c. Pull the transplant upwards so that the root collar is level with the soil surface. Take care not to damage any of the fine roots.
d. Remove the spade carefully and firm the soil around the roots, ensuring that the tree is upright.

Transplants and cell-grown stock are usually planted with a slit or notch method.

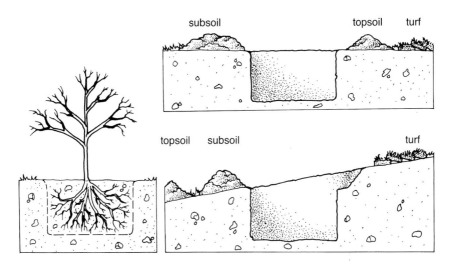

Larger bare-rooted plants, container-grown stock or valuable specimens are usually pit planted.

These are bare-rooted transplants and cell-grown stock.

Direct Sowing or Seeding

Although used in other countries, direct sowing or seeding is rarely used in Britain. The method offers the advantages of both planting and natural regeneration but with more control over species choice and plant spacing.

Direct sowing is ideally suited to the larger-seeded trees such as oak and beech, and follows the pattern laid down in many natural woodlands where small mammals bury seeds over winter. Where mammal predation is high, for example if there are large numbers of squirrels or woodmice present, this might be a viable option only if adequate control or protection can be put in place.

It may also be used with smaller-seeded species where the seed is broadcast either mechanically or by hand over ground previously prepared by cultivation of some sort. Seed mixtures, possibly of native trees and shrubs, may be used to create a more 'natural' woodland with random open spaces and areas of denser growth.

The following points should be borne in mind if attempting this method on a small scale:

- Many tree seeds go into dormancy (sometimes for over a year) if allowed to dry out after collection; they should be sown 'green'.
- Many native species, including the willows, birch and alder, have very small seeds that are difficult to collect (but *see* below).
- The young seedlings will have to compete with other vegetation unless this is controlled in some way.
- If using large seeds such as oak or walnut, consider planting individually and deeply, possibly with some sort of 'quill' or narrow tube inserted into the ground to deter small mammals.
- Small-scale experimentation, where the labour is 'free', is what marks out a passion for woodland management and faith in the future!

A 250-hectare native woodland is currently being created in Wales using a novel approach. Rather than planting the seed in the ground, or broadcasting it at high density on prepared ground, branches heavily laden with seed are being placed upright into the ground in the hope that the wind will do the rest.

The Forestry Commission's *Practice Guide* is excellent on this subject (*see* Further Reading).

Natural Regeneration

In certain types of woodland, the use of natural regeneration is often preferred, or at least desirable. However, it is important to try to assess well in advance whether it is likely to be successful in any particular woodland. While grant aid may be available at the same rate as it is for planting, payments may be delayed until successful regeneration occurs and, in some cases, planting may have to be undertaken anyway if the regeneration fails or is sporadic.

Advance Regeneration

In some situations, particularly with shade-bearing species where the mature woodland is quite open, advance regeneration might occur under the mature stand. This is used in a number of silvicultural systems, notably the shelterwood system.

Scarification

The obvious reasons for lack of regeneration are poor seed years or animal damage.

However, the effect of the ground vegetation, and competition for light and water, particularly where there is a thick mat of organic matter, should not be overlooked. In these situations, it is best to break up the vegetation by scarifying it. This usually entails mechanical methods but may also be done by animals including pigs, or by the action of harvesting and extraction machinery in the woodland.

In many parts of Britain, the climate is not ideal for natural regeneration, although the prospect of increasingly warm summers might change this to some extent. In Continental Europe, the use of natural regeneration is more common, and this is largely due to the positive effect of cold winters and warmer summers, resulting in better seedling germination and early summer growth.

Natural regeneration may fail owing to:

- A poor seed year.
- Planning that does not coincide with a mast year.
- Heavy predation by mammals or birds.
- Insufficient light on the woodland floor.
- Competition with other vegetation.
- Inclement weather – a damp spring and cool summer.

Mast Years

Most of our native, large-seed trees exhibit what is called masting. This is the production

Dense spruce regeneration, which will need to be respaced to maintain good growth and form. (Photo: Ted Wilson)

Table 22: Mast years for the major woodland species

Species	Age in years of first good seed mast	Frequency of mast years	Timing
Ash	20–30	3–5	September–March
Beech	50–60	5–15	September–November
Sessile oak	40–50	3–5	November
Pedunculate oak	40–50	2–4	November
Hornbeam	20–30	2–4	November–April
Small-leaved lime	20–30	2–3	September–November
Sweet chestnut	30–40	1–4	October–November
Sycamore	25–30	1–3	September–October
Wild cherry	15–25	1–3	July–August

The Harvard Forest Dioramas showing colonization of farmland in New England in the 19th century. The top picture shows a farmstead in 1830 following large-scale clearance of woodland by the early European settlers. The bottom picture shows the same (winter) scene in 1915 after colonization by pine followed by broadleaves. By 1930 over 80 per cent of the land had reverted back to broadleaved temperate woodland. (Photo: John Green, reproduced by courtesy of Harvard Forest Dioramas, Fisher Museum, Harvard Forest, Petersham, Massachusetts)

of seed on an irregular cycle, in response to both environmental and physiological processes. When planning for natural regeneration, it is important to determine when a particular species is likely to mast, and to open up the canopy accordingly. Invariably, seed germinates best when light conditions are good, when the soil is well drained and the ground vegetation sparse. In some cases, the site may need to be scarified prior to seed production.

Creating New Woodlands by Natural Regeneration

The creation of new woodland using natural regeneration has a number of advantages over planting. The resulting woodland will be composed of species already growing in the locality and, since they have produced seed, they will be well established. The costs of establishment may be reduced and protection problems less severe.

However, to be successful the new woodland needs to be close to an existing woodland and timed to coincide with good seed production. Planning needs to take place well in advance and ground preparation carried out prior to seed dispersal.

In the case of trees bearing lighter seeds dispersed by the wind, regeneration may be more predictable if the ground conditions are good for germination, perhaps assisted by scarification in advance.

In some areas of Britain, land is being deliberately fenced to exclude browsing and grazing animals, and then left in the hope that colonization by trees will occur. This approach is under way in a number of national parks in England and is also the preferred method of regenerating the Caledonian pinewoods in the Highlands of Scotland.

Plant Spacing

It is necessary to plant trees at a density that will allow for natural losses and the effect of interventions such as cleaning and thinning over the life of the woodland. When applying for grant aid, you will have to have a sufficient

density of young trees to ensure that, should the site become neglected, it would still form woodland. If one of the objectives is high-quality timber, it will be necessary to plant at a higher density to allow for the selection of the best trees over the life of the timber crop.

The planting density for an evenly spaced area is given by the formula:

$$N = A/d2$$

N is the number of trees, A is the area in square metres/feet, and d is the planting distance between each tree. The minimum planting density for grant aid varies depending upon the species and the objectives. In some cases, where productive woodland is an objective, there is a requirement for a minimum density at the end of the first five years after planting.

Increasingly, and particularly where quality timber is not a priority, planting might be clustered or grouped randomly. Sometimes the advantages of closer spacing can be obtained by this method if a more open structure is required.

Natural regeneration is more difficult to manage, as it will usually germinate at much higher densities than those noted above, and will then have to be thinned out (cleaned). On good soils and with good seed years there may be as many as 300,000 trees per hectare!

To Fence or Not to Fence?

One of the first decisions to take when regenerating an area of woodland will be the methods of protection best suited to the site. In the early stages of growth, trees are susceptible to many types of damage. Protection is particularly important when trees are planted at quite low densities because losses will be more noticeable. While it is impossible to protect against every eventuality, some thought in the early stages will pay dividends later. The decision that has to be made is basically whether to fence the area to be planted or to use some form of individual tree protection.

122

Table 23: Indicative tree spacings in common use

Spacing (metres)	Number of trees/cuttings per hectare	Comments
0.8 x 0.8	15,000	For SRC biomass plantations on 1–4 year rotations, using willow or poplar cuttings
1 x 1	10,000	Traditionally used for broadleaved timber. Now rarely used, but recommended by some if serious about quality timber and long rotations. Spacing used for growing Christmas trees
1.5 x 1.5	4,000	Use where high-quality timber is an objective, and take care over the choice of provenance
2.1 x 1.5	3,200	A compromise between cost and choice. Allows for ease of access for maintenance. May be planted with conifer/broadleaf mix in rows
2 x 2	2,500	Usual minimum spacing for grant aid for conifers with timber as an objective
2.1 x 2.1	2,250	Common spacing for multi-purpose woodlands
3 x 3	1,100	Usual minimum spacing for amenity woodland. Cherry and poplar for timber if high-pruned
4 x 4	625	May be used with some faster-growing broadleaves if selected for vigour and form prior to planting, and managed under a more intensive regime involving regular pruning. Examples include cherry and possibly walnut
5 x 5	400	Suitable for agro-forestry systems where other crops or stock are also part of the management system. Species such as sycamore, oak and other light demanders may be suitable
8 x 8	156	Used for poplar plantations established under high-maintenance regime with pruning and no thinning. Wider spacings have also been used in agro-forestry systems

There is still much debate amongst foresters as to the wisdom of planting at wide spacing. In essence, the argument is that over a long rotation, with the inherent loss of trees from damage, disease and poor genetics, wide spacing will not leave enough good trees to ensure a final crop of any financial value. This is not an issue if the objectives are purely for wildlife or amenity, but it does raise concerns about the viability of some of these woodlands in the longer term.

While grant aid may be available today for certain operations, it might not always be there. It may be that at some time in the future, owners will need to earn money from more saleable goods, and timber might be one of these. The following points need to be considered:

- *Objectives* What are they and how might they guide the choice of protection? If high-quality timber is the aim, a relatively high degree of protection will be required to ensure that sufficient quality trees reach maturity. If, however, the woodland is to be managed primarily for biodiversity, then some losses will be acceptable.
- *Establishment method* Planting tends to be more susceptible to damage than natural regeneration. The trees tend to be more visible, they might be more prone to vandalism, and there is some evidence that mammals are more attracted to planted trees on account of the higher sugar levels found in transplanted trees.
- *Mammals and insects* These can have a major impact on young trees. In new woodland, the common mammals, farm stock and, possibly, people are the most likely to cause problems. If large mammals are present, deer fencing may be required.
- *Size and shape* In general, small and irregular areas of planting are best suited to the use of individual tree protection. As the area increases, there comes a point at which fencing tends to be a better option. Although this varies considerably, woodlands over about 2 hectares are more likely to be fenced.
- *Surrounding land* This will have a direct influence on the protection of both the boundaries and the trees themselves.
- *Current use* The existing vegetation on the site may have a direct effect upon the survival of the young trees, and any existing pests might have to be dealt with before any trees are established. On larger sites, there might be resident populations of rabbits or hares which will need to be cleared before fencing takes place. In some cases, badgers might be present and may dictate the boundary shape and possibly the use of individual tree protection. Where the site has been abandoned, woody vegetation might need to be controlled, while in some areas bracken or rhododendron may need dealing with prior to planting.
- *Cost* In general, and assuming all other things are equal, it is cheaper – per unit

area – to establish a larger woodland than a smaller one. Economies of scale are evident with materials, labour, fencing and plant purchase. In addition, a larger woodland will tend to provide its own microclimate that will help tree survival and growth.
- *Grants* Many grants are tiered by size to reflect the increased costs of smaller woodlands. However, the longer-term benefits of larger woodlands should not be underestimated and the ongoing management costs associated with individual tree protection are often forgotten.

Fencing

There are a number of different types of permanent fencing that may be used, the choice depending on the sort of damage that may be encountered. Detailed specifications on fencing may be found in Forestry Commission publications and in the BTCV's, *Woodlands: A Practical Handbook* (*see* Further Reading).

The permanent fence types are summarized in Table 24. In addition, there are both old and new approaches that aim to provide protection for a limited period, sometimes at greatly reduced cost. These include:

- Plastic mesh up to 1.8m.
- Dead hedging, using cut coppice material and stakes, to protect coppice regrowth (this will not control muntjac deer).
- Temporary electric fencing (roe deer are the least susceptible).

The FC in Scotland produces an excellent guide to standard costs and specifications for a wide range of operations in woodland. Although the costs will be higher in certain regions of Britain, the indicative costs should prove useful throughout the country. It is available on their website under Grants.

Individual Tree Protection

The development of tree shelters in the 1980s revolutionized the planting of small areas of woodland and copses. In effect, each one is a mini-greenhouse providing an improved microclimate and protection from mammal damage. A number of designs are on the market, with adaptations for different species and site conditions.

Although they have many advantages over other methods of establishment, they do need regular care and attention, and they are unsightly. Some of the practical problems associated with them include:

- Damage to the trees when they emerge from the shelter.

- Height growth at the expense of sturdiness.
- They are susceptible to wind damage.
- They make an ideal nest for mammals if not correctly erected.
- Their use may lead to planting at too wide a spacing.
- They may not break down as quickly as planned.
- They are energy intensive in manufacture and maintenance.

However, in many small woodlands their advantages outweigh the problems, and they

Low-cost plastic deer fencing used to protect recently cut coppice. This type of fencing needs to last only until the coppice shoots reach above browsing level. (Photo: Edward Mills)

Table 24: Specifications for the main types of woodland fencing used in Britain

Protection from	Specification (metres)	Relative costs
Sheep	Standard stock fence	**
Rabbits	90cm netting, 15cm turn out	**
Hares	1m and as for rabbits plus additional wire 10cm above	**
Roe and muntjac deer	1.8m, with hex mesh for rabbits and centre-line wire for sheep	****
Red, fallow and sika deer	2m, as for roe but heavier-duty	*****

NOTE: All the above use spring-steel wire with pressure-treated posts and rails. Exceptions are if hardwood posts, cleft or sawn, are used.

Badger gate constructed in stock and rabbit fencing. Badgers and their setts are protected in Britain under the Wildlife and Countryside Act (1981).

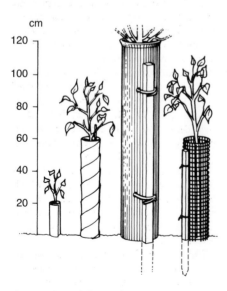

A range of tree shelters and guards are available for use in small woodlands or new plantings.

provide a cost-effective solution to the problem of establishing trees on certain sites.

Creating New Woodlands in Britain

In comparison with most European countries, Britain is sparsely wooded. Even though the average woodland cover across Britain has increased from 4 per cent to 11 per cent over the last hundred years – itself a remarkable achievement – there is still an aspirational target of 30 per cent within the next fifty years or so.

Large differences in woodland cover exist both between and within the counties and regions of Britain. Although the large-scale afforestation of the uplands, carried out primarily with conifers, has now declined, there is an urgent need to plant new woodlands that reflect the changing needs of society and that meet a wider range of objectives.

Financial incentives are now targeted specifically at smaller woodlands, often located closer to urban areas or with clearly defined social or ecological aims. High-quality timber rather than bulk cellulose is also preferred, and species choice is driven by a wider range of objectives.

There are many different reasons why new woodland may be created. These include the obvious ones such as landscape and shelter, and the perhaps less obvious ones such as improving biodiversity or creating something 'for posterity'. Well before embarking on a project that, if successful, will certainly outlive those who initiated it, it is important to decide clear aims and objectives. It is also important to consider the surrounding landscape and the types of woodland within it.

Depending upon the size, complexity, species, method of establishment and location, it may take anything from one season to many years to achieve the desired outcome. Before embarking on any woodland establishment, you should ensure that the proposed site is fully surveyed and that any statutory designations are identified and the relevant authorities notified.

Until quite recently, most woodland establishment in Britain was carried out by the Forestry Commission, by large privately owned estates, or by management companies on behalf of private investors. While this still continues, others – including charities, individuals, community groups, local authorities and farmers – have taken a much more active role. The work of the National Forest in the Midlands is an excellent example of farmers becoming foresters. Over 65 per cent of woodland in Britain is owned by individuals or organizations other than the Forestry Commission.

Woodlands come in all shapes and sizes, and the latest census of woodlands in Britain shows that there are more than 59,000 individual woodlands of under 10 hectares, and nearly all of these are in private or charitable ownership.

The most common broadleaved species in these woodlands are oak, ash, birch, beech and sycamore; among the conifers, Scots pine, the spruces and the larches predominate.

Objectives

Chapter 5 considered how the management objectives for woodland help inform the decisions that need to be taken in the future. When creating new woodland, the objectives are likely to be the same or very similar, but may also include:

- The creation of new native woodlands.
- Habitat restoration.
- Land reclamation.
- Planting farmland surplus to requirements.
- Connecting fragmented habitats, including other woodland.

Location

Although creating new woodland is nearly always a 'good thing to do', it is worth giving some thought to where it is to be located, assuming there is some choice in the matter. Increasingly, grant aid is targeted at achieving national or regional priorities and, in some cases, additional payments are made if the location fits in with these. For example, a region might have a lower than average woodland cover, or, through planting, the landscape may become less fragmented.

There are no clear rules, but it is worth remembering that, where possible, it is generally better to create new woodland:

- Adjacent or near to an existing woodland.
- Where there is already woodland in the locality.
- By enlarging an existing woodland.
- By linking to other woodlands, thereby providing corridors for wildlife.
- Adjacent to other semi-natural habitats.
- That is as large as possible.

The Type of Woodland

At the outset, it is important to decide on the type of woodland you wish to create. This will be directly influenced by the objectives you have set for the woodland, and possibly by such constraints as the location, any designations or perhaps the presence of indicators of historic woodland management (for example, scattered pollards or earth banks).

- *High forest: even-aged* Most easily established by planting in a formal arrangement, either with native or introduced species.
- *High forest: continuous cover* Woodland established with the intention of creating diverse ages and species.
- *New native* The creation of new native woodland is currently strongly supported by grant aid. As noted above, this should ideally be adjacent to existing native woodland, and established either by natural regeneration or by planting with trees from seed collected locally.
- *Semi-natural* This implies the use of natural regeneration using locally available seed trees. The natural succession that occurs results in a woodland reflecting local conditions and tending towards an uneven-age structure.
- *Wood pasture* This will invariably be established with native species capable of responding to the traditional forms of management, including pollarding. Such species commonly include ash, beech and

Small woodland established adjacent to a larger one, planted in tree shelters with oak and mixed broadleaves at 3m spacing. Access routes have been left adjacent to the hedgerow and the river.

oak together with hornbeam in the southern parts of Britain.

- *Coppice* It is quite unusual to establish new coppice, since so many older woodlands are neglected. An exception might be willow coppice for basket weaving or osier production. However, it may be desirable to extend an existing area of coppice, or to establish a new one with more unusual species. Almost any broadleaved species will coppice, although it is important to assess the market demands before establishment as the value of this form of management relies upon regular cutting and the alternation of light and shade produced.
- *SRC* Depending upon the species, this is usually planted with cuttings or transplants of selected, often 'clonal', material. Established in a formal layout to allow for machine harvesting, the growing of this crop has more in common with agriculture than with woodland management. The crop may be planted mechanically and initial management is intensive.

- *Mixed amenity* This is often planted close to urban areas where visual amenity is paramount, perhaps on 'brownfield' sites.

What Size is Best?

This is not an easy question to answer since it depends upon so many different factors. In financial terms, grant aid will be given only for areas over 0.25 hectares. In practical terms, such a small area will have a large boundary and edge effect. In general, the larger area the better, with 2 hectares being the minimum needed to sustain a woodland community and to provide a range of different habitats.

In small woodlands the trees will eventually become very large in relation to the site, and the crowns and roots may spread some considerable distance across a boundary. They might affect the use of the adjacent land – for farming, market gardening or other uses – or become a liability for the current or future owners. If in doubt, plant smaller trees and shrubs along the edges and keep the larger woodland trees well back from the boundary.

What Shape is Best?

While a long, narrow woodland may be quite large in area, the edge effect means that true woodland conditions of shade and shelter might not occur at all. Conversely, a large square woodland might follow the existing field boundaries but will look out of place in many landscapes. In general, it is advisable to follow the character and scale of the local landscape.

When planning the woodland, remember that boundaries are often expensive to maintain, and that complex shapes are more difficult to manage than simpler ones. Where possible, make use of existing boundaries such as roads, footpaths, stone walls, rivers, streams and ditches. The edge of any woodland is an important habitat in its own right and, where possible, edges should join up with semi-natural habitats rather than with intensively managed farmland or industrial landscapes.

Shelterbelts

The detailed site assessment and design of shelterbelts is a complex matter, taking into account such variables as topography, wind direction, soils, crops and species choice. The following points need to be considered:

1. The use of a mix of tree species, including some conifers to provide winter shelter, with the faster-growing and more wind-firm species planted on the windward edge. The planting density should allow wind to filter through the shelterbelt. It is better to plant at too high a density and thin out later than to have to plant again.

2. Plant shrubs and smaller-growing trees around the edges to provide the best conditions for shelter. A multi-layered woodland is far better able to withstand the force of the wind.

3. Consider the use of screens to help establish trees, using small plants in preference to larger ones.

4. The mechanics of wind hitting shelterbelts is very complex. If wind hits a wall of trees it will tend to rise up and cause eddies on the downwind side. Ensure wind is able to move through the trees, and if necessary plant in a staggered formation.

5. Neglected shelterbelts, particularly where stock have grazed intensively beneath the canopy, may need fencing for some time to allow the understorey to develop. Grants may be available to support this.

6. In some cases, it may be necessary to plant a new shelterbelt adjacent to the old one, or to consider some thinning and replanting in a structured way over a number of years. This should be done with care as many species have quite shallow roots and are likely to blow down in high winds.

7. Trees situated on the edges of established shelterbelts will tend to be the most wind-firm, and these should be retained where possible. Make use of the silvicultural characteristics of shade-bearing species such as beech, and underplant following thinning.

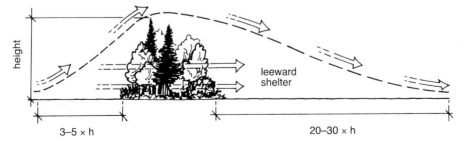

A well-designed shelterbelt may offer protection for up to thirty times its height downwind. The effect of eddies is reduced if air flows through the trees rather than hitting a dense wall of vegetation.

CASE STUDY:
Barfil Farm, Kirkcudbrightshire, Scotland

Barfil Farm is situated near Dumfries in the south-west of Scotland. It was bought by Maggie Gordon and Bob Lee in 1990. It occupies 146 hectares of upland previously let for grazing but it did have some improved ground. The farm contains a number of important habitats for wildlife and includes part of the Milton Loch SSSI.

One of the attractions of Barfil was the potential to develop an integrated farm and woodland enterprise developed along organic principles, retaining the important habitats and improving the poor upland grazing by diversification and woodland planting.

The land is at an elevation of between 120m and 155m, and the site has a mild but quite exposed climate. The soil is generally acidic, and in the distant past would have supported oceanic-type, temperate, deciduous forest. The land is generally fertile for woodland trees, but the soil is quite shallow in places and has become eroded owing to the lack of vegetation. The farm contained both improved and unimproved grassland.

In 1992, the owners, advised by the author, planted some 65 hectares of mixed woodland under the Forestry Commission woodland grant scheme (WGS), with additional support from the Farm Woodland Premium Scheme (FWPS). The grants provided capital payments for the planting, and the premium scheme annual payments offset (some of the) loss of farm income. The final planting was approximately 60 per cent broadleaved, 20 per cent conifer and 20 per cent open space, including rare-orchid and wetland habitats. The compartments were planted in mixtures, with woodland shrubs along the edges of the rides and the main access route to the farm.

At the outset, the vision for the woodland was to create a sustainable resource available to local craftspeople and to use horses for extraction to the ride side.

The objectives for the woodland, which was designed to shelter the central part of the farm holding, were as follows:

• To produce a mixed but predominantly broadleaved woodland capable of growing timber.
• To create wildlife habitats.
• To provide shelter for the farm enterprise.
• To act as an educational resource in conjunction with farm building developments.
• To improve the site's microclimate.

The trees were planted using both cell-grown and bare-rooted transplants at a spacing of 2.1 × 2.1m, and the site was ring-fenced against roe deer, apart from some small, outlying areas and roadside edges where tree shelters were used.

The main tree species planted, some in mixtures, were:

Sessile oak
Ash
Beech
Sycamore
Cherry
Japanese larch
Scots pine

Ten Years On

Maggie and Bob's stamp is now firmly on the farm. The woodland is developing well, with canopy closure in many areas. The farm has a well-known herd of Galloway cattle. The organic produce is sold locally, and the farm buildings house a small conference centre and interpretive facility. A wind generator supplies power for the farm, and some of the willow has been cut for basket-making.

A recent bird survey of the woodland, conducted towards the end of February

Mixture of Scots pine and beech planted as cell-grown trees at 2.1 × 2.1m spacing, with elder and spindle along the ride edge. The Scots pine has acted as a nurse for the beech.

2005, identified thirty species, many of which are new to the farm. Most of the shrubs, including spindle, dog rose and hazel, are flowering and fruiting consistently, and both the larch and Scots pine are setting seed, providing an abundant food source for many tit communities. The ground-feeding birds such as fieldfares make use of the woodland edges, and the woodland areas are all connected to allow movement of mammals and birds. The woodland supports a number of birds of prey including buzzard, kestrel and both barn and tawny owls.

CHAPTER 9

The Seasonal Cycle and Woodland Maintenance

The seasonal nature of the woodland cycle dictates many of the practical tasks required to meet the objectives of management and to carry out the annual operations noted in the woodland plan. The timing of some of these tasks is very important, while others are more flexible from month to month or even year to year.

Although Britain is quite a small island, there are recognizable differences across the regions in the start of the seasons. An appreciation of this variability is important, as it may dictate the timing of operations and the availability of plants, labour or even of machinery. Contractors tend to be quite mobile, and those specializing in planting, for example, may move with the seasons.

Because woodland is layered, the plants below the canopy are very dependent upon the time when the leaves flush. Many woodland plants are adapted to flower just before the leaves of the trees. Two good examples of these vernal plants are the bluebell and wood anemone, both species that thrive in coppice woodland. One very interesting use of this is evident in the application of phenology to the monitoring of the onset of spring in different parts of the country. Monitoring these shifts might provide valuable information on climate change.

Phenology is the study of the times of recurring natural phenomena, especially in relation to climate. It is recording when you heard the first cuckoo, saw the first frogspawn or noticed the first bluebells appear in the wood. Robert Marsham was Britain's first phenologist and started recording his 'Indications of Spring' as early as 1736. If you are interested in the subject, visit www.phenology.org.uk.

Autumn

Traditionally the season when many woodland operations begin, autumn is characterized by leaf fall and the die-back of the field and shrub layer. This is also when the various layers of the canopy become more obvious, and decisions may be taken about felling and thinning. As the soil and air temperature falls, growth slows down and tree sap stops moving through the trunk and branches. It is also a time when the soil might still be very heavy, rainfall high and the ground difficult to work.

This is often the season of the highest winds, and in upland areas in the north and west especially, severe damage may occur in woodland. In areas particularly prone to wind damage, there may be little opportunity for thinning, and early felling may be the only option.

While tree planting can start at any time after growth has finished, the owners of small woodlands have far more flexibility than the larger commercial forestry enterprises in the timing. In general, broadleaved trees are planted before the conifers, and wet sites are usually left until spring. In practice, it is best to plant when conditions allow, when time is available to do a good job and when good-quality plants can be delivered and planted quickly.

Autumn is also the time to collect and possibly sell fungi, and to keep a watch out for the fruiting bodies of the various fungal tree diseases noted in Chapter 7.

Winter

Once the trees are dormant, vegetation has died back and wildlife is hibernating, many woodland operations take place over the relatively short period from about November to early March, depending on location. When the ground is frozen over, timber harvesting and the extraction of produce may be carried out, particularly on sites where damage to the soil needs to be minimized. This is the time when many of the traditional woodland practices of pollarding, coppicing and pruning are also done.

Broadleaved timber is generally felled over winter and before the sap starts to rise in spring, while conifers may be felled at any time. Some species, notably ash, beech, cherry and sycamore, should not be left on-site for long but taken to a sawmill promptly before degrade sets in.

Tree planting may also continue over winter, but is often delayed if the ground is frozen or if snow is lying, as damage may occur to the roots of the young plants.

Spring

In Britain the early woodland plants are highly adapted to making the optimum use of the rising temperatures and light levels associated with the start of spring. As early as late January in the most southerly parts of Britain, soil conditions improve and the early vernal plants, such as the snowdrop, emerge and make use of the higher light levels found on the woodland floor.

This is often a busy time for tree planting, but care must be taken to ensure that the plants have not started growing as the young roots are especially vulnerable to damage.

Summer

This is the season to enjoy your woodland and to assess the site, to survey and record the plants and animals, and to plan thinning or harvesting operations. Newly planted areas should be inspected regularly for damage by mammals, and fences checked to ensure they are sound. In some cases, the application of herbicide may be required depending on the site, and on farm woodlands a watch should be kept out for weeds such as thistle that might affect nearby arable farm crops.

Practical Tasks

The rest of this chapter is devoted to the day-to-day tasks that may be required to meet the objectives set for the woodland. Some of these tasks may need to be done regularly, while others may only need doing very infrequently.

One of the joys of owning woodland is the pleasure to be gained from doing the practical tasks, and the rapid response of the woodland to many of these operations. To many people, such activity is a welcome change from their normal routine and often a prime motivation for buying woodland.

Equipment
It is very tempting to go out and spend a lot of money on what Hans Morsbach calls 'yuppie tools'. Most woodland tasks require a few simple tools and, when the occasion demands, more expensive equipment can be hired or borrowed. In some areas, informal woodland co-operatives may hold equipment. Probably the most useful motorized piece of equipment in all but the smallest woodland is the all-terrain vehicle/cycle (ATV/C), which can be used to transport materials and people in most conditions.

Some woodland tools, notably the chainsaw, are potentially very dangerous and it is

Table 25: Seasonal strengths and weaknesses

Factor	Autumn	Winter	Spring	Summer
Soil	Becoming colder. Often wet. Poor drainage apparent	May be frozen	Warming	On dry sites newly planted trees may suffer drought
Ground flora	Late-season plants die-back	Vernal plants emerge before canopy leaves		Shade-bearing plants emerge
Tree physiology	Senescence and leaf fall. Production of late wood	Dormancy	Sap rises. Flushing and root growth initiated. Production of early wood	Late flushing of shade bearing species
Fungi	Fruiting bodies appear			
Seed germination			Once soil temperature exceeds 5.6°C	
Wind	Often highest speeds experienced		Late spring winds when trees have flushed can cause major damage	

now a legal requirement to have approved training before using one (*see* Chapter 12). After a training course many years ago, a management consultant who had recently bought a woodland told me how his walk changed to a swagger when he carried his chainsaw, and how using it competently gave him immense pleasure and a sense of achievement.

A list of essential items might include:

- Planting spade.
- Mattock.
- Billhook.
- Herbicide applicator.
- Weeding 'hook'.
- Safety gloves and clothing.
- Pruning saw (pole saw).

- Small hand axe.
- Helmet with visor and ear protectors.
- Chainsaw and breaking bar.
- Clearing saw (petrol-driven).
- Coloured tape.
- Tree-marking paint.
- Height stick.
- Hypsometer and diameter tapes (*see* Chapter 10).

Maintaining Newly Planted Trees
Once planted, the trees will require regular inspections in the first few years. These inspections should include:

- Assessing losses and the numbers of plants required for beating-up.

Tree-felling with a professional chainsaw and full personal protective equipment (PPE). Once felled the Scots pine will be 'snedded' (trimmed of the side branches), and then cross-cut into different lengths to meet certain product requirements.

- Checking for the firmness of planted trees.
- Checking the stability of any tree shelters, spiral guards and protection against voles.
- Assessing weeding requirements.
- Checking for signs of damage.

Beating-up

This is the procedure carried out to replace any losses that might occur during the first few years after planting. This is usually only done where between 10 and 20 per cent or more of the planted trees fail. Losses may be caused by mammal or insect attack, by natural losses or by extreme drought. In addition, poor-quality plants, careless handling or inappropriately trained planting contractors or volunteers may all lead to substantial losses. It may be necessary to beat-up with larger plants to avoid them being suppressed, or even with faster-growing species.

Beating-up does not normally occur after the first few years, unless losses are high or unless structural diversity is an objective. To claim grant aid, a high standard of planting and survival is required; this will usually be assessed on-site by the local woodland officer.

Weed Control

There are four main reasons why weeding may be necessary:

- Transplants may be smothered by tall plants and woody vegetation;
- Access rides and paths may need to be kept clear.
- Some invasive species, including rhododendron, may need to be controlled.
- Tree roots compete with weeds for moisture and nitrogen.

135

However, a weed is simply a plant that is not wanted and, in many situations, weeds are important components of the woodland ecosystem. In addition, clearing the weeds is costly and may involve herbicides that have some environmental drawbacks, or are restricted in their application. For these and other reasons, weed only when absolutely necessary, bearing in mind the following:

• Woody and other vegetation is an important habitat in its own right, and clearance should be restricted to an area adjacent to the planted trees.
• Ground vegetation helps to maintain soil moisture and to moderate the effects of drying winds.
• Excessive weeding, particularly of woody growth, may actually encourage grasses which compete even more vigorously with young trees.
• Some woody plants, including holly, thorns and brambles, may help protect young trees from browsing by mammals, including deer.
• Some light sandy soils, particularly in exposed situations, need ground cover to prevent erosion occurring.

Competition with the surrounding vegetation for light and nutrients is one of the commonest reasons for the poor survival of planted trees. Natural regeneration is less prone to this owing to the higher initial seedling density. An open woodland site encourages weed species, and any ground preparation will prove an ideal seed-bed for weed growth. The aim is to suppress the vegetation until such time as the trees are tall enough to form a canopy and reduce the amount of light reaching the woodland floor. The higher the initial planting density, the faster this will occur.

In addition, weeds compete with tree roots for moisture as well as nutrients and have a severe effect on both height growth and general vigour. This competition is often at its highest during summer when the young trees need moisture the most. This is even more important on well-drained soils, especially in the south and east of Britain.

Another factor to consider is the shelter that weed growth provides for small mammals, notably voles, which can decimate new planting if weed control is poor. While small mammals are partly kept under control by birds of prey, the birds need to be able to see them in the first place.

In many cases, the most cost-effective approach is to ensure a weed-free zone around the tree about 1m in diameter. Manual cutting of the vegetation, often practised in the past, may actually increase competition by stimulating the root growth of weed species.

Must I Use Chemicals?
The short answer is 'no!'. There is now increasing pressure to reduce the use of chemicals in woodland, and the UKWAS specifically requires foresters and owners to 'seek alternative means of controlling unwanted vegetation'. The use of herbicides is still the most commonly used means of weed control in Britain, but considerable effort is under way to find alternatives. Research on a number of natural herbicides, including citronella oil, is still at an early stage.

In small woodlands, where the number of newly planted trees is likely to be low, alternative methods should work well. However, where larger areas are concerned, or where new woodland is being created on bare land, the decision will be more difficult and an owner may decide to accept higher costs for environmental or ethical reasons. Bear in mind that the 'ecological footprint' of many woodland operations is extremely low, and that directed application of herbicides involves very low doses of chemical.

How to Weed
The following options are available to control or to reduce the effects of weeds:

1. Hand weeding.
2. Mechanical systems.
3. Herbicide application.
4. Mulching and other non-herbicide applications.

5. Planting at a higher initial density.
6. Planting larger, sturdier trees.
7. Under-planting prior to felling the over-storey trees.
8. Use of advance natural regeneration.

The first four are practical solutions while the others are silvicultural in nature and need to be planned for well in advance (these are discussed further in Chapters 8 and 10).

The equipment required for weeding divides into four main categories:

1. Hand tools for cutting weeds and woody vegetation.
2. Tools for mechanical weeding.
3. Hand applicators of herbicides.
4. Mechanical herbicide application, usually adapted for use on tractors or ATV/Cs.

Hand Tools
Before the advent of herbicides, weeding was invariably carried out with hand tools, usually a weeding hook designed for the purpose. In small woodlands, or where there is little new planting, hand weeding may still be preferable as it has certain advantages over the use of chemicals:

• No specialized training or certificates of competence are required.
• The tools are cheap to buy and often have other uses.
• A greater degree of selection can be used.
• There is cause for concern over the long-term effects of herbicide use on both human health and on biodiversity.
• In some woodlands of high ecological value, herbicide use will either be restricted or banned altogether.
• They are in keeping with the UK Woodland Standard's commitment to reduce the use of chemicals;
• The main cost is time and energy – and in your own woodland this may be counted as free!

The following are some practical tips for hand weeding:

• Make sure the tools are sharp
• Wear gloves.
• In the first year, start weeding in June.
• Two or even three weedings may be needed in the first year.
• Weed along the row of trees, about 1m wide.
• In later years, just weed around the trees.
• If there is tall weed growth between the rows, cut this down.
• Use a stick to protect young trees from the weeding hook.
• If deer are present, weed between the rows so the trees are less visible.
• As you progress, check the trees are firm and upright.
• Some vegetation, notably bracken, is better crushed as cutting may cause some plants to regrow even faster.
• Take care! It is too easy to end up with a lot of damaged trees.

Mechanical Tools
These are either purpose-built machines or adaptations of farm machinery. Apart from the clearing saw noted below, most of these are really suitable only for large commercial plantings, or for new woodlands established on farmland or other relatively flat sites.

The petrol-driven clearing saw is a hand-held device in which a motor turns a shaft with a blade or other cutting device attached to the end. They are balanced to hang on a harness, and can be used for long periods without undue strain. While not especially cheap to buy, they do have many uses. When fitted with a circular saw blade, they can even be used to clear woody vegetation and to fell small trees and coppice.

Herbicides
The commonest method of weeding is to apply a 1m diameter 'spot' of herbicide around the tree. This should be carried out until such time as the tree is well established and capable of growing above the competing vegetation, usually within two to four years.

The application of forest chemicals is controlled, and users have to possess the appropriate certification provided by the NPTC.

Approval to use a herbicide for agricultural or horticultural use does not mean that it will necessarily be approved for use in woodlands, or vice-versa. There is a legal requirement for the potential users of pesticides and herbicides to read and follow the product label.

It is usually preferable to employ contractors for chemical weeding than to do it yourself as they will have the appropriate certificates and understand the importance of application rates, timing and species susceptibility to the chemicals.

There are two main types of herbicide in general use:

1. *Pre-emergent* These act on the soil and are then absorbed by the growing roots. They are usually applied either prior to planting or immediately afterwards. They are also called residual herbicides as they remain active in the soil for some time.
2. *Emergent* These are applied while the weeds are growing and are taken up directly by the foliage. Timing is critical here, as the weeds need to be sprayed before they cause damage to the young trees.

Detailed recommendations on the herbicides currently approved for forestry use, and on the timing and application rates, may be found in the relevant Forestry Commission publications.

By far the most common means of applying herbicide is with a hand-held applicator. The major advantages lie in the speed of application and the low cost per treated tree. In many cases, better control over weed growth is obtained and it may not need to be done as often as hand weeding. The most commonly used hand applicators include:

- Forestry spot gun, adapted from an agricultural drench-gun.
- Knapsack sprayer.
- Weed wiper.
- Pepper pot.

Table 26 summarizes the advantages and disadvantages of each type of hand applicator.

Table 26: A comparison of the commonly used hand-held applicators

Equipment	Operation	Advantages	Disadvantages	Relative cost
Spot gun	Sprays a 'cone' of herbicide, 1m in diameter	Easy to use and calibrate. Light – 5-litre capacity	Can be tiring if there are many . trees to treat. Spot application only	***
Knapsack sprayer	A pressurized reservoir with coloured nozzles for different application rates	Very versatile. Can spray in bands, spot, overall, etc. 15-litre reservoir	Skill needed to calibrate. Heavy when full	*****
Weed wiper	Pole with rope wick at one end, for direct application to weeds only	Easy to use. Can apply the herbicide directly on to weeds	Little control over application rate. Wick can dry out and needs regular replacement.	*
Pepper pot	For granular herbicides only	Easy to use. Lightweight	Application can be a little hit and miss	Free with granules

Herbicide application using a forestry spot-gun.

If planting large areas on mainly flat ground, perhaps as part of a farm holding, then a mechanical applicator may be preferable to a hand applicator. Adaptations of mechanical applicators are available for agricultural tractors or even ATVs. Tractor-mounted boom sprayers may be used if applying a broad-spectrum herbicide before planting takes place. Alternatively, a well-designed planting scheme with 3m-wide access routes will allow boom sprayers to be used with selective herbicides even after planting has taken place.

Alternatives to Using Herbicides

There is an increasing interest in alternative approaches to weed control. Some of these rely on traditional methods while others make use of advances in materials and the use of forest residues. As noted previously, the cost associated with training and certification for herbicide use is increasing, and for owners of small woodlands these costs may not be justified. There are also valid

concerns being raised as to the safety of some of the chemicals in current use, and it seems wise to be cautious if there are good alternatives on the market.

Mulches

These may be made from either organic matter or some form of artificial material such as plastic sheeting in the form of a mat. The mulch or mulch mat should cover about 1 sq. m around the tree and, in the case of mats, be firmly fixed to prevent them blowing away. Other mulch materials include old carpet, underlay and roofing felt. One disadvantage is the tendency for small mammals, such as voles, to build their nests under some of these sheet mulches. Organic mulches include bark chippings, farm waste and even treated sewage sludge.

The following are some of the other possible alternatives that are currently being assessed by the Forestry Commission for use primarily on new planting sites.

Soil Inversion

This method uses a soil-inversion plough that has two tines. It is connected to a tractor by a three-point linkage mechanism. As the plough is pulled through the soil, all the ground vegetation is inverted, creating a bare planting medium. This method is suitable only for use on large sites prior to planting.

Thermal Weed Control

The use of propane gas as a weed-control method is still in the early stages of development. It is based on tractor-mounted equipment and is best suited to pre-planting weed control on fairly flat arable sites.

Waipuna (Hot Foam)

This is a hot-water-based technology and is designed to control weed growth by applying an organic foam solution of coconut oils and hot water directly on to the weeds. The application boils the contents of the cells and breaks down the cellular structure of the weeds; within a few days the treated weeds wilt and die. The technology is currently in the very early stages of development for woodland use.

Cleaning

After successful establishment, it is sometimes necessary to clean the trees of woody growth. This is particularly true when using natural regeneration, where the higher initial plant density will need reducing, and where unwanted species may need removing.

If a decision has been made to aim for high-quality timber, cleaning may be required to maintain the correct spacing (respacing), and to remove invading species. In the case of natural regeneration, a number of cleaning operations may be required before the first thinning. It is often the cost of cleaning that makes the use of natural regeneration as expensive as planting, since the labour costs may be quite high when dealing with dense woody material.

Cleaning is often carried out with brush-cutters, although it can also be done by hand using billhooks. The high cost of cleaning, together with the recent decline in the value of small-diameter conifer timber, means that this operation is often neglected.

Rhododendron Control

Originally planted as pheasant cover, rhododendron has become a nuisance in many woodlands, smothering the ground, preventing regeneration of young trees and acidifying the soil. It suckers and seeds freely, and is a particular problem in westerly regions, especially in ancient semi-natural woodland. Prevention is far easier than control – eradication requires a lot of time and expense. In some areas, its removal may be grant-aided.

The preferred method of control depends on the extent of the problem and the size of the plants:

- They may be cut to ground level and the new re-growth sprayed with herbicide.
- They can be winched out.
- Lime solution may be applied to the leaves.
- Their stems can be injected with herbicide. This has been very successful, killing trees within six months.

Brashing

This is the removal of the lower branches to a height of about 2m. It is sometimes carried out to improve access, often for sporting reasons. In high-fire-risk areas, it may help reduce the amount of inflammable material on-site and, where public access is important, it may help improve safety.

With the high costs of labour it is no longer a financially viable operation, the only possible exception being in high-value stands where the improved access allows thinning and pruning to be carried out more effectively. It is usually carried out using a pole saw to reduce the possibility of damage to the stems, and the edge trees are often left unbrashed to maintain shelter in the stand.

Pollarding

Traditionally, this was always done when the trees were young, and was then repeated at regular intervals of between fifteen and twenty years. Today, many pollards have been neglected and, as a result, often have very large and heavy limbs in need of felling. In addition, the ability of a tree to regrow and maintain its vigour declines with age and with the increasing diameter of the limbs felled.

There is now a renewed interest in pollards, and grants are available to maintain existing trees and plant new ones. This interest is due to a number of factors:

- Many pollards are very old and have an association with a rich variety of invertebrates and lichens.
- They provide historical continuity with past landscapes.
- They represent a traditional form of land management.
- Interest in agro-forestry systems is increasing, and they are one form of this.
- Wood pastures include natural pollards and this link is important in understanding the role of large grazing animals in woodland ecology.

Coppicing

In small woodlands, or where coppice occupies a small area within the woodland, it

ABOVE: *Many pollards in the English Lake District, some of which are over 700 years old, are now being actively restored, both to maintain their vigour and to provide habitats for rare lichens.*

RIGHT: *Rebecca Oaks cutting seven-year-old hazel coppice on limestone in Silverdale, Lancashire. The material lying on the ground to the left is for fishing nets used to catch flounder in Morecambe Bay, and on the right for the production of the woven hurdles shown in the background.*

may not be necessary to cut an area or 'cant' every year. For small-diameter material, such as hazel, a billhook may be all that is required. Larger-diameter material will usually be cut with a chainsaw, although some coppice workers still use axes or bow-saws.

The coppice shoots should be cut as low as possible, and the individual cuts should slope away from the centre to reduce the likelihood of decay. In the early stages, the amount of regrowth depends on the way in which the stool is cut, although any differences in the number of shoots averages out over time.

Table 27: Coppice species, rotation and some typical products

Species	Rotation (years)	Products
Hazel	6–12	Hurdles, thatching spars, baskets, charcoal, walking-sticks, hedging stakes, peasticks
Ash	12–30	Tool handles, turnery, firewood, tent pegs. May be steam bent
Oak	20–30	Cleft fencing and stakes, tan bark, charcoal, shingles, firewood
Sweet chestnut	15–25	Fencing, split and round stakes, shingles, trugs, charcoal, firewood
Hornbeam	12–30	Charcoal, firewood, wooden cogs

Boundary Maintenance

The woodland boundary is both an important habitat in its own right and a structure defining the extent of responsibility and ownership. If it is clearly in the same ownership as the woodland itself, the owner has a legal 'duty of care' to maintain it as far as is reasonably practicable, and in a safe condition with respect to the neighbouring properties. This will usually entail regular inspections of the boundary and of the trees along it. These inspections need to be carried out by someone knowledgeable and to be recorded and kept on file.

The woodland edge is a very different habitat from that within the woodland and requires careful maintenance. Large boundary trees will have to be inspected for disease or decay on a regular basis, and any work entrusted to a competent arboricultural or forestry contractor.

Fence Maintenance and Upkeep

The decision on the type of fence to use has been dealt with in Chapter 8. Permanent, well-constructed fences will last well into the life of the woodland. However, regular inspections of the fences must be carried out to ensure that they are 'fit for purpose'. This is particularly important after storm damage when trees may fall across fence lines, or during heavy snowfalls when large mammals, such as deer, may be able to get over fences.

Habitat Management

Within and adjacent to the woodland there may be a number of important habitats that require some form of maintenance or, in the case of deadwood, are actually improved by not tidying up fallen trees and removing logs. Detailed guidance is outside the scope of this book but specialist agencies should be consulted, or perhaps volunteers from a naturalists' trust or conservation organizations may be able to help with specific jobs. Many schools, particularly primary schools, are keen to get involved and the 'Forest Schools' movement, and Forest Education Initiative (FEI) might be able to help.

The following is a brief check-list of some of the things to consider while carrying out the regular woodland management tasks:

- Leave sufficient deadwood, both standing and on the ground. Aim for a minimum of three fallen and three standing pieces of deadwood per hectare, spread throughout the woodland. In practice, more should be left, particularly in ancient and semi-natural woodlands.
- Maintain rides, edges and margins to provide alternative habitats to the woodland itself.

1. Long term retention

2. High forest and shade-
   bearing species

3. Light-demanding smaller
   tree species

4. Shrubs and coppice

5. Herbs and smaller shrubs
   or managed hedgerow

1   2   3   4   5

Habitat edges, and the diversity of shade and shelter they offer, are an important wildlife resource and often neglected.

- Maintain hedges and wood-banks, perhaps by pollarding or by other traditional means.
- Allow natural glades to develop where trees are blown down or where planting might have failed due to waterlogging.
- Keep ponds open and cut back trees and other vegetation regularly, but allow shade and overhanging branches to develop in some areas.
- Leave some woody climbers as protection for wildlife.
- Finally, resist the urge to tidy up wherever you go.

Watercourses

This generic term includes rivers, streams, springs and seasonal water as well as lakes and ponds. There are strict controls on management laid out in the *Water Guidelines* published by the Forestry Commission and available on their website.

The maintenance of watercourses should aim to keep the water flowing and to minimize pollution and siltation. However, even here, research suggests that deadwood within watercourses has a vital role to play in maintaining water quality and reducing sediment loads. In addition, migratory fish and aquatic invertebrates benefit from 'debris dams', while deadwood is also a feature of bog woodlands and lake margins.

Drainage

In the past, many woodlands survived because the land was too poor or inaccessible for con-

Watercourse maintained in accordance with the 'Water Guidelines'.

version to farmland. The soils were often poorly drained. In some situations, particularly where they have been converted to plantations, attempts might have been made to improve soil drainage.

The maintenance of boundary ditches and internal drains is important because the position of the water-table has a direct influence on site stability and the rooting depth of trees. A fluctuating water-table will cause root damage and render the woodland more liable to wind-throw.

Rides

These are internal routes within the woodland, often ditched and drained and, in some cases, compacted or topped with hardcore. They should be kept as open as possible to maintain the grassland flora. This is often quite different from the surrounding woodland edge, particularly when material has been brought in for road construction. On sensitive sites, every effort should be made to use local stone when constructing all-weather rides and turning bays.

Thought should be given to alternating the mowing or coppicing of the edges, which should be done over autumn or winter to allow a full life cycle of the plants and associated insects to be completed.

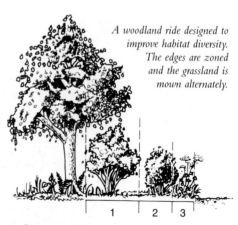

A woodland ride designed to improve habitat diversity. The edges are zoned and the grassland is mown alternately.

1. Cut every 5–10 years
2. Cut every 2–3 years
3. Cut annually

CHAPTER 10

Silviculture and Stewardship

Whatever other management objectives are being followed, the production of timber remains of prime concern to many woodland owners. Many of the woodlands most admired by the public in Britain were originally planted for timber production. The sight of tall, majestic trees with straight trunks still inspires wonder and a sense of awe.

Many woodlands owners practise silviculture with the aim of growing the best-quality timber possible. The quest for quality timber can actually enhance other values such as biodiversity, landscape and amenity while ensuring that, over time, income is earned to support woodland management.

The following quotation by the late Peter Garthwaite, an eminent forester writing in 1995, sums up his view of the importance of growing timber within the wider context of sustainability and conservation.

My forestry philosophy has not changed in the sixty-five years that I have been in practice: it is that wood is a renewable resource, and woodlands and forests should be managed to produce the highest-quality timber of which the site is capable; and that, as a general rule, when trees have reached their prime maturity, they should be felled to live on for many years in such form as their quality dictates: as oak beams supporting the roof of a cathedral; as fine craftsman-made furniture; as a framework for a house.

This chapter describes the silvicultural techniques required to grow trees, and the options for the sale of the timber. The techniques will need to be tailored to the type of woodland and to the silvicultural systems in use.

An innovative building housing a café (Inn the Park) in St James Park, London, developed using low-energy building techniques. The larch timber used on the exterior comes from a certified source, is untreated, and will weather with age. A turf roof helps to insulate the building and links visually with the surrounding parkland and mature London plane trees.

Thinning

The key silvicultural tool available to the woodland owner once establishment is successful is the procedure known as thinning. This involves the removal of predetermined volumes of timber over the life of the woodland, and a reduction in the number of trees from around 2,000 to 4,000 per hectare (or even more if naturally regenerated), to 200 per hectare, or even fewer, by the time the trees are mature.

Thinning mimics the natural selection process that occurs in woodland where species compete and die out. In natural woodland, much of the self-thinned timber is left to rot, whereas in woodland managed for timber much of it is harvested. This is, of course, why it is now so important to leave some deadwood on the woodland floor: it mirrors the natural processes and helps to maintain a better ecological balance within managed areas.

Thinning aims to concentrate the growth on those trees most likely to produce high-quality timber by giving the selected trees more light and reducing the competition for water and nutrients. It may also give an early financial return, but when the trees are still young this will be minimal.

The depressed prices of small-diameter timber have resulted in many woodlands being left unthinned. This is understandable but short-sighted and has led to calls for subsidies to help offset the early costs of growing quality timber. In large commercial forests, many plantations are now no longer thinned at all, but clear-felled at around thirty years old for low-value pulpwood.

The overall aim of thinning is to remove just enough timber from the crop so that the overall productivity is maintained while improving the quality of the remaining trees. If too many trees are thinned out overall production suffers, while if too few are removed, the better trees do not have room to grow.

Thinning is as much an art as a science. Although volumes, ages and heights can all be measured and productivity assessed, the actual choice of trees to retain for eventual high-quality timber, in possibly sixty or more years hence, is made in a four-dimensional world of space and time. Perhaps Einstein should have been a timber grower?

When to Thin?

This will depend on many different factors but as a rough guide, on better soils with faster-growing species it may start as early as twelve to fifteen years old. At the other extreme, slower-growing species on poorer land might not have a first thinning until they are at least thirty years old. The initial spacing is also relevant here, with more widely spaced trees being thinned later than those planted closer together.

How Often?

Younger stands need thinning more often than older stands and conifers more often than broadleaves (with a few exceptions). In the case of faster-growing conifers, thinning might take place every three to five years, extending to five to ten years as the trees get closer to final felling. Broadleaves, however, have a longer cycle, but also a longer rotation. Thinning here might be every five to ten years to start with, extending to ten to fifteen years as the trees mature.

What to Thin?

The aim at the outset is to try to ensure that the trees with the best potential to produce good timber are retained to maturity. At the same time, poor-quality trees with poor form or damage should be 'culled'. In some cases, it is advisable to leave the smallest (suppressed) trees as they help to shade the stems of the better trees and reduce the likelihood of them producing epicormic shoots. These are shoots that appear on the trunk of some trees, particularly oak, in response to high light levels following thinning. They can seriously reduce the value of the timber.

In practice, this means trying to identify, at perhaps twenty years of age, those trees with the potential to produce a final-crop sixty or even a hundred years hence. This is done by selecting, and possibly marking with paint, far more than will actually be needed by the end of the rotation.

When selecting the trees to retain, the following should be looked for:

- A straight, ideally cylindrical, stem with no forking below 6m.
- A stem without other defects, such as cracks or harvesting damage near the base.
- Vigorous, probably dominant or co-dominant within the stand.
- A healthy, well-balanced crown with dense foliage.
- Absence of crown damage (e.g. squirrel damage).

Oak tree showing freedom from heavy branching and epicormics. The bole is straight, without any visible defects, and clean for at least the first 6m. (Photo: Ted Wilson)

- Branching 'light' and branch angles acute.
- Absence of epicormic shoots (especially important in oak).

How Much to Thin

The amount of timber removed at each thinning depends on such variables as the species, site fertility, growth rate and, to some extent, the state of the market for a particular species or size of timber.

It is very important to maintain a healthy, live crown. In general the crown should make up around 40 per cent of the total height of the tree. For some species, notably larch, this should be closer to 50 per cent. This is why it is important not to delay thinning, even if it has to be carried out at a financial loss. Once the live crown is reduced, it is difficult, if not impossible, for the tree to recover.

As a very rough guide, about 30 per cent of the trees may be removed at the first thinning, reducing to as few as 10 per cent towards the end of the rotation. If large areas are to be thinned, or if the woodland has been thinned by previous owners and records have been kept, it may be advisable to consider making use of the Yield Class system for assessing the thinning needs of the stands (*see* page 157).

In some, primarily broadleaved, woodland high pruning might also take place at the same time (this procedure is discussed later). Different species respond differently to thinning and, as a result, care should be taken to treat each wood or stand sympathetically. If in doubt thin 'little and often', or at least until more confidence is gained and a better understanding is developed of how species respond.

Thinning a Mixture of Species

Thinning mixed woodland is more complex – even more so if it is uneven-aged. The same principles apply, with the main timber species being identified and thinned for quality. The decisions as to what to thin and what to leave are more difficult, and more notice should be taken of the silvicultural characteristics of the different species.

Broadleaves: A Special Case

In general, broadleaves show greater diversity in stem form, branching habit and vigour than conifers do. In addition, they are often planted specifically for the production of high-quality timber, and selection needs to focus on this rather than on volume production. Recently, there has been renewed interest in a number of species, and trials are currently under way by the British and Irish Hardwood Improvement Programme (BIHIP) to select trees of better form and vigour for eventual sale as improved planting material.

The trials will take many years to reach seed-bearing age, but the early results look promising. Table 28 indicates the species currently being investigated. They show varying degrees of promise, and have been chosen as they are the species most likely to produce quality timber that will hopefully remain in demand well into the foreseeable future.

Pruning Broadleaved Trees

As noted above, broadleaved trees are very variable and, if quality timber is an objective, it is likely that some pruning will need to be undertaken. This is time-consuming but many owners find it engaging and rewarding. Some species such as ash have high apical dominance. This means that the tree has a single leading shoot likely to lead to a single, straight stem. Other species such as beech tend to have low apical dominance and, as a result, tend to have multiple leaders.

Table 28: Broadleaved species currently on trial for improved planting material

Species	Comments
Ash	Approximately 500 superior trees are to be included in progeny trialing. Ash is a 'dioecious' species – a complete sexual mix-up. Individuals may be male, female, hermaphrodite, or anything in between!
Birch	A collection of forty-five populations was made in 1995, throughout the distribution of silver birch in Scotland and northern England. To date, five provenance trials have been established
Wild cherry	Ten wild cherry clones, selected for good form, vigour and resistance to bacterial canker. Released on the market under the name WildstarTM
Oak	A number of oak trees have been selected for the following characteristics: straight trunks, lighter branching, superior vigour and timber quality. Seed orchards have been established which should begin to produce acorns in twenty years' time
Sweet chestnut	The aim is to establish two clonal seed orchards in Forestry Commission seed zones covering south-east and south-west Britain. In addition, sites will be sought to establish four national clonal trials, representing 100–150 plus trees selected from a wide geographical range
Walnut	Assessment of a range of provenances from across Europe is currently taking place. Potentially of high value and quite fast growth
Sycamore	Over 66,000 hectares in Britain and Ireland. Shows great promise for producing valuable timber on relatively short rotations. The basis for selection will concentrate on factors that most affect the timber value

Table 29: Pruning of broadleaves

Species	Formative	Comments
Ash	Frost sensitive so may lose leader	
Beech	Likely to be required	
Cherry	Likely if planted at wide spacing	Prune July and August only
Oak	Likely to be required	
Sweet chestnut	Likely to be required	
Sycamore	Frost sensitive, treat as ash	Not in spring
Walnut	Prone to frost damage	Prune July and August in full leaf only

There are two types of pruning that may need to be carried out:

1. Formative pruning. This is carried out on young trees up to about 3m tall, and the aim is to promote a single, straight stem. Many young trees have either multiple stems or damaged leading shoots, or they at some stage suffer from wind or frost. The formative pruning operation is best carried out in late spring, just before the trees flush. (One of the reasons to plant at close spacing when establishing the woodland is to reduce the need for such pruning.)
2. High pruning. This is done later in the life of a tree and the aim is to ensure a clean knot-free stem of at least 6m in height. This is the most valuable part of the tree for high-quality timber. High pruning may need to be carried out a number of times during the life of the stand.

Site Factors to Consider

When thinning and felling, it is important to appreciate the impact that site factors might have on the remaining trees. This is particularly important in woodland that may have been neglected for some considerable time, and where thinning or felling might not have taken place for many years.

These site factors include:

High pruning to 6m in Knapp Coppice. (Photo: Jim Ralph)

149

- Wind and wind-throw.
- Frost (*see* Chapter 8).
- Winter cold (*see* Chapter 8).
- Sun scorch.

Wind and Wind-throw

Britain is one of the windiest countries in the world, both in the intensity and the frequency of storms. Even as I am writing this, the damage caused by the gales that hit the north-west of England over the weekend of 7 and 8 January, 2005, is becoming more apparent. Some of the largest and most sheltered woodland trees have been snapped by what appear to be localized winds of considerable force.

A large Douglas fir snapped near the base by gale-force winds. This tree was in a sheltered valley protected from the force of normal winds. The timber is now worthless and may be left on the ground to build up the deadwood component of the woodland.

Foresters use the term wind-throw to distinguish the effect of the wind on woodland from its effect on single trees. There are two types of wind damage:

1. Endemic. This describes progressive wind-throw caused by the gales that are expected to occur naturally every year. In the uplands of Britain, it is almost inevitable that once trees attain a height of between 20 and 25m, they will succumb to wind-throw. At these heights, the leverage of the wind on the stem will uproot a tree, no matter how healthy it is. Once this starts, a domino effect will result in the whole stand being blown down.
2. Catastrophic. This describes the effect of severe but infrequent storms, often devastating whole woodlands. One of the best recent examples was the storm in October 1987, which flattened large swathes of woodland across the south-east of England. Such events are by their very nature unpredictable, but it is worth remembering that in the lowlands of Britain the average return frequency for this type of damage is in the order of once every 200 to 300 years or so, while in the uplands such storms are far more frequent.

In the uplands of Britain, where large commercial plantations have been established, quite sophisticated methods and computer simulations are used to enable forest managers to predict the onset of endemic wind-throw. They can then reduce the risk or fell the crop before serious damage occurs. It is unlikely that smaller woodlands will require such methods (although advice can be obtained from the local Forestry Commission offices). However, a number of practical options are available to help reduce the effects of wind.

Protection Many woodlands are protected by virtue of their location, perhaps in a sheltered valley, or by other local woodlands and shelterbelts in the surrounding landscape. This is why any felling or thinning should take into account the potential effects on the adjacent land. Good long-term planning and replanting will help ensure continuity and reduce the effects of sudden changes in the landscape.

Wind-firm edges The trees on the edge of woodland tend to have a more extensive rooting pattern and a more wind-resistant crown. Furthermore, the woodland edge often has a more complex mix of trees and shrubs of varying height and depth. As a result, the edges are much more wind-firm and offer protection to the trees within the wood. Wherever possible, these edges should be left intact, particularly when thinning or felling trees within the woodland.

Sun Scorch
Although not usually a serious problem in Britain, the sun can scorch the bark of some species, causing damage and allowing disease or decay to enter the trunk. Sun scorch is a particular problem for beech and other species with smooth, thin bark, and is often associated with heavy thinning. It can usually be identified as dead patches of bark on the south-facing side of the tree.

The Market for Timber

Global Trade
The market for timber is complex and affected to a large extent by global supply and demand. As a major importer of timber, Britain is in no position to dictate prices, and with a global over-supply of conifer timber, prices are low and competition intense. In addition to this, there is an increasing reliance on recycled material at the lower end of the market. Points to bear in mind include:

- Britain imports about 85 per cent of its timber needs.
- There is currently no sign of any timber shortage and, over the next twenty years, large plantations, mainly established in the southern hemisphere, will mature.

- Economies of scale and low labour costs in many emerging economies means that British growers find it hard to compete in the global marketplace.
- Most consumers, and thus retailers, are driven by price alone, and few will pay a premium for home-grown timber.
- High-quality broadleaved timber, much of it from North America, is plentiful and available in a range of sizes and species.
- The enlarged EU includes countries with large reserves of both conifers and broadleaves, together with a long history of sound silviculture.

Local Markets
Despite the above, there are still local markets, especially for higher-quality material. Some British growers compete successfully for a share of the market, even exporting timber in some cases. Local sawmills often require smaller volumes of timber, and the growth of bespoke manufacturers augurs well for the top end of the market. There are also a number of other positive points to consider in relation to locally sourced timber:

- It has less embedded energy and will therefore prove more cost-effective in a low-carbon economy.
- Technical developments such as laminating and gluing are allowing lower-value and smaller-diameter timber to be engineered into higher-value products.
- The supply from local woods is more flexible and can respond to peaks in demand more quickly.
- Some consumers of high-value products will pay a premium for locally sourced timber.
- A number of species grown in Britain produce timber that is sought-after for its special decorative qualities.
- Many countries exporting to Britain have their own environmental, social or political problems that mean supply cannot be guaranteed.
- The global trade in bulk, low-value products such as timber depends partly upon the price of oil remaining low.

CASE STUDY:
Knapp Coppice, nr. Kington, Herefordshire

Knapp Coppice is a mixed even-aged woodland of some 8 hectares, planted about forty-five years ago with a mixture of species including Douglas fir, Scots pine, Norway spruce and beech, with a small amount of oak and other broadleaves. About 1 hectare is classified as ancient woodland. The soils are brown earth on a level, south-west facing site. This woodland is quite typical of many that come on the open market, both in terms of the size and the mix of tree species. It has been thinned at least twice, and some of the conifers three times.

The intention of the owners is to create a diverse woodland in which the silviculture follows the principles of Continuous Cover Forestry (CCF). There is a long-term agreement never to clear-fell and a commitment to long-term ownership.

They hope to gradually transform it into an 'irregular' woodland with mixed ages, sizes and species, and to increase the amount of Douglas fir which will respond in small group fellings. Thinning will

A log cabin built in the wood and used to store equipment and provide shelter. The materials for the cabin came from the recent thinnings. (Photo: Jim Ralph)

remove poor trees, but not so as to create gaps that may blow along their edges. There is an attempt to provide shelter along the woodland boundaries due to the surrounding open farmland.

The guiding principles of CCF are to:

- Manage the forest ecosystem rather than just the trees.
- Use natural processes as the basis for stand management.
- Work within the limitations of the site.
- Create a diverse stand structure with a range of species.

The owners' objectives are:

- To experience and learn about the woodland by practice and observation.
- To apply the CCF principles and to learn from them.
- To add value by high pruning, planting and maintaining site vigour.
- To manage the woodland 'holistically' and to take pleasure in watching it develop.
5. Produce the highest-quality timber possible on the site.
6. To take a pride in, and develop the passion for, ownership and management.

Current concerns and woodland operations include:

- Rabbit and grey squirrel damage is a continuing problem.
- Extensive capital investment in rides and lorry access has been completed.
- A further 200m of tracks to be levelled in the coming year.
- The trees will be enumerated (*see* note below) in another two years' time.
- The next selective felling will be done in three years' time.

- Good Norway spruce cone production seen in 2004 and hoping to see more regeneration in the coming years.
- Underplanting of gaps with Norway spruce was carried out in 2002.
- Some signs of ash and Douglas fir regeneration, but seed liable to predation by mice.
- Grants have been received for public access and ride management.

NOTE: Enumeration is the procedure used in uneven-aged systems when the diameter of all the trees is measured. The results are plotted on a graph to ensure that the range of tree size is sufficient to enable the stand to reach maturity and to maintain canopy cover. The procedure allows the owner to thin and fell certain size classes to maintain the correct proportions for the silvicultural system being used.

Sustainable Timber Production

At a time when the word 'sustainable' seems to be on the lips of every chief executive, minister and government official, it is worth remembering that the concept and term was first coined by a forester in the early 19th century. Managed sensitively, woodlands are capable of producing timber indefinitely, while at the same time providing a wealth of other benefits.

One of the concerns about many of the extensive and fast-growing plantations in the tropics is the concentration on produc-tion of timber alone, to the detriment of the ecological and social values that underpin good woodland management.

What Timbers do Merchants Want?

Hardwoods
Table 30 gives the specifications for the better-quality British hardwoods that are currently in demand. In many cases, the merchants buying these timbers will export them, perhaps to Italy or Germany, for

High-value walnut logs with roots dug out to enable the mill to slice the timber and obtain the best figure. Jaguar cars have been involved with the National Forest in planting walnut for eventual veneer production and use in car interiors.

153

Table 30: Merchants' specification for British hardwoods

Species	Minimum length. (feet)	Minimum mid-quarter girth (inches)	Minimum mid-diameter (cm)	Comments
Ash	8	8	25	Preferably white and winter felled
Beech	7	12	33	Clean timber in demand
Cherry	8	9	33	Large-diameter timber hard to find
Sweet chestnut	6	8	25	Quite rare, as much British timber suffers from 'shake'
Elm	6½	12	38	In great demand following losses from Dutch elm disease
Oak planking	6½	14	45	Fresh, winter felled. Clean, straight logs only
Oak veneer	9	18	54	In great demand. British oak severely depleted following centuries of harvesting
Lime	7	13	33	White and freshly felled
Sycamore	7	10	33	Winter felled (October–March) as both planking and veneer. Figured (ripple) is very valuable
Walnut	7	16	54	If possible, keep root on
Yew	6	8	29	A conifer but seen as an 'honorary' broadleaf!

NOTE: Many hardwood timber merchants still use the old 'imperial' measure of Hoppus feet when assessing timber volume. This system converts a round log into the equivalent 'squared' log, enabling the merchant to assess the sawn volume. The system uses special Hoppus girth (diameter) tapes, marked to read directly in 'squared measure'. The mid-quarter girth refers to the diameter of the log at its mid-point, measured using a Hoppus tape. The equivalent mid-diameter in metric measure is also given above.

high-quality veneers. There is no longer any capacity in Britain for high-quality hardwood veneering.

Interestingly, the species listed in Table 30 have hardly changed at all over the last fifty years. The main differences are that smaller lengths and diameters are now acceptable, and that elm is in great demand following the loss of trees to Dutch elm disease. The acceptability of smaller sizes reflects the difficulty merchants have in finding good-quality British hardwoods.

Softwoods

Conifer timber is divided into a number of different categories or 'assortments'. These are based upon the intended product categories, and defined by the length and top diameter of the log. They are sold either by cubic volume, usually under bark (ub), or by weight. It is usual to give an average tree volume when selling conifer timber. The trees should be straight, free from major defects and stain, and clean.

Prices for smaller and lower-grade material are very depressed at the moment and show little sign of recovery. As a major importer, Britain is sensitive to the strength of sterling and the vagaries of global supply and demand.

Unlike the hardwood merchants, softwood sawmills prefer smaller-diameter material, with even the best-quality sawlogs peaking in value at around a volume of 1 cubic metre.

The main categories are:

- Green (higher-grade) sawlogs: 1.8m × 16cm minimum top diameter.
- Red (lower-grade) sawlogs: as for green but fewer restrictions on knots and straightness.
- Short sawlogs: 14cm minimum top diameter.
- Bars: 1.8m × 14cm top diameter.
- Pulp: this is sold by weight, and the white woods such as spruce are preferred.

How Much Timber is there in the Woodland?

The accurate measurement of timber volume is technically demanding and outside the scope of this book. This section concentrates on straightforward methods that will allow a woodland owner to obtain a good estimate of volume and to ensure that if timber is to be sold, the buyer is offering a fair deal.

Trees are usually measured by cubic volume, although small, low-value thinnings may be measured by weight. Low-value hardwoods sold for firewood may use the traditional measure of a cord. The accuracy required will be dictated largely by the value of the timber being sold and the time available to carry out the measurements.

The common types of measure used for timber are:

- Cubic metre. Used for conifer timber and most low-value thinnings. One cubic metre of hardwood weighs approximately 1 tonne (1,000kg), and of softwood approximately 0.75 tonne. 1 cubic metre = 27.74 Hoppus feet.
- Hoppus foot. Still used by merchants for the sale of high-value broadleaved timber, the logs are usually measured felled. 1 Hoppus foot = 0.036 cubic metres.
- Tonnes green (wet) weight. Usually used for shortwood (pulp) and sold in 2- or 3-metre lengths.
- Stacked volume. A stack of cut timber measuring 1 cubic metre in size will have a volume of approximately 0.6 solid cubic metres.
- Cord. This is a traditional unit of measurement often used for coppice or firewood, and measured as a stack of timber 8 × 4 × 4ft, equivalent to 128 cubic feet of wood and air.
- Length.
- Number of pieces.

Basic Tools Required for Measurement

A number of basic specialist tools will be needed and are available from forestry suppliers. More advanced equipment may also be purchased if it can be justified by the size of the woodland, or if a substantial amount of timber is being thinned, felled or sold.

1. Girth (diameter) tapes, metric (and Hoppus, if required). These are graduated to measure diameter directly from the measurement of the circumference of the tree or log.
2. Hypsometer or clinometer. A tool that measures tree height directly, by sighting the tree from a known distance away. A number of different types are sold, most of which are based on a damped pendulum.

More expensive versions use lasers but are not always accurate in dense woodland.

3. Metre tape. A standard 25m or 50m tape.
4. Metric (and Hoppus if required) conversion tables.
5. A copy of *Timber Measurement – A Field Guide*, FC Booklet 49, HMSO.

Tree Height

There are a number of basic methods that rely on rough assessments, and more accurate methods using optical instruments designed specifically for measuring tree height. One of each is explained here. The timber height in broadleaves, which is required for an assessment of volume, is measured to the point at which the main trunk divides into the branches forming the crown. This is much lower than the tree height.

1. Hold a pencil at arm's length. Close one eye and align the tip of the pencil with the top of the tree. Then, without moving the pencil, adjust the position of the thumb so that it is level with the base of the tree. Now rotate the pencil in an arc until it is in line with the ground and note the position corresponding with the tip of the pen-

Measuring the height of a tree.

cil. The tree height is equal to the distance from this point to the base of the tree.

2. Using a hypsometer, sight the base of the tree and take a reading, which on level ground should be zero. Then sight the top of the tree, or the timber height, and take another reading. On level ground the tree height will be the difference between the two readings, which should be simply the second reading. On sloping ground, if the base of the tree is below you, add the two readings; if the base is above you subtract the lower reading from the higher one.

Diameter

If the tree has been felled, the diameter of the cut logs can simply be measured with a ruler. However, trees are seldom circular and an average of two measurements should be taken. Also, the mid-diameter is often required, and this will entail the use of a girth tape around the mid-point of the log. Timber or trees less than 7cm diameter are not usually measured.

The basal diameter or 'diameter at breast height' (dbh) is measured at 1.3m above ground level, to take account of the buttresses at the base of the tree. If the ground is sloping, the measurement is made on the upper side of the tree.

In small woodlands, it is common practice to measure all the trees, either for thinning or for felling. If this is not practical, it may be necessary to take samples throughout the wood or stand. The easiest approach is to base the sample on either a square plot of 10 × 10m, or a circular plot with a radius of 5.64m. Both contain 0.01 of a hectare.

The Volume of a Standing Tree

A tree is a complex mixture of geometric shapes, but is simplified for practical field measurement. When assessing the standing volume of an individual conifer tree, allowance is made for a tendency to buttress at the base and to taper towards the top.

The following steps are required:

1. Measure the diameter (dbh) using a girth tape and halve it to give the radius (r).

2. Calculate the basal area (BA), of the tree at 1.3m above ground level using πr^2.
3. Measure the height of the tree in metres: in the case of conifers, to the top of the tree; in the caes of broadleaves to the position where the trunk spreads into the crown (the spring of the crown).
4. Apply a form factor to take into account taper, since a tree is not cylindrical. For mature conifers, use 0.5.
5. Multiply height by BA by the form factor to give the estimated volume in cubic metres: *Height (m) × BA (m²) × Form Factor = Volume m³*.

The Volume of a Felled Tree
Conifers may be sold either overbark (with the bark on) or underbark (with the bark off). When selling timber, it is important to be clear exactly which method is being used and to measure accordingly. In all cases, the same formula is used to calculate the volume.

Because the value of a broadleaved log may be very high, care must be taken to measure it accurately. Also, the logs may be graded into different quality classes, and will often be much shorter than is the case with conifers. Measurement is always overbark. Most of the value of a broadleaved (hardwood) log will be in the first 6m or so.

The volume is calculated as follows:

1. Measure the length of the log in metres (L).
2. Measure the diameter at the mid-point of the log in cm (dm). NOTE: If the log is longer than 15m, measure it in sections − shorter for broadleaves.
3. The volume (V) in m³ is then given using Huber's formula:

$$V = \frac{\pi d_m^{\,2}}{40000} \times L$$

The Volume of a Stand of Trees
There are many different methods that can be used, depending on the number of trees, the time available, the value of the stand, the reason for the measurement, and the accuracy required. In most situations, some form of sampling is carried out to enable a reliable estimate to be made at a realistic cost. The larger the area, or the greater the variability in the crop, the greater the intensity of sampling required. In some countries, an aerial survey, or even satellite remote sensing, may be used, particularly in remote regions.

There are three reasonably straightforward approaches for use in woodlands or stands of trees. The first is useful in very small woodlands, or where the individual trees are of high value. The second may be used with lower-value crops or where an estimation is required for thinning purposes, while the final approach is more technical but worth while in larger woodlands with a high proportion of even-aged conifers.

Measurement of Every Tree
This method is fairly straightforward. Every tree is measured standing for volume and the total volume is given by the sum of all the individual measurements. Care must be taken to ensure that trees are marked in some way so that no double-counting or missing out of trees occurs.

Using Representative Sample Plots
This commonly used method relies upon the selection of random plots that reflect the overall diversity of the stand of trees being measured. It is equally useful for conifers as for broadleaves, and the number of plots used will be determined by both the size of the area concerned and its variability.

An allowance has to be made for unplanted areas, including rides and poorly stocked areas. The final volume is given per hectare.

Tariff System
The tariff system is used for even-aged conifers. This is quite a complex system, and full details will be found in Forestry Commission Booklet 39.

Yield Class
It is quite likely that, if the woodland is managed for timber and discussions are held with professional foresters, mention will be made of the Yield Class (YC) system,

developed by the Forestry Commission in Britain for use in even-aged plantations. The Yield Class of a species is a measure of the long-term productivity of a stand of trees planted with that species. It is analogous to the idea of biomass, but measures only the timber component of a plantation. It depends upon such variables as climate, soil, provenance and silviculture.

It is used by foresters to assess future growth and production, to judge the best time to thin and to fell, and to help achieve the long-term sustainability of wood production central to well-managed commercial woodlands.

A species of YC 14 will, on average and throughout the rotation, produce 14 cubic metres of timber per hectare per year. Values for YC in Britain range from as low as 4 (poor-quality upland oak) to as high as 28 (high-quality Douglas fir on a fertile lowland site). Figures outside this range are also possible in exceptional circumstances and with less common species. It is not necessarily a measure of monetary value. A slow-growing, high-quality broadleaf stand of YC 8 may be more valuable than a fast-growing conifer stand of YC 18.

The predicted YC of a site for a particular species may be used when assessing grant aid support for the production of quality timber. This is the case in Wales where a supplement is available for certain species, including oak, ash, cherry, and Douglas fir, as long as certain silvicultural conditions are met.

Harvesting the Timber

Do I Need a Felling Licence?

If the woodland is being managed in accordance with a plan approved by the relevant forest authority, and the amount being felled is as stated in the plan, then a licence will not be required. Otherwise, one will be needed (*see* Chapter 12 for further details).

Felling

Nearly all felling is now carried out with chainsaws (motor manual) or, in the case of large-scale commercial operations, by purpose-built and expensive harvesting machines. Only in coppice woodland, or when cleaning a young stand, might hand tools be used. If you decide to use volunteers in your woodland, you should only supply them with hand tools, correctly sharpened and maintained, and provide them with the knowledge to use them correctly.

Felling trees with a chainsaw is potentially very dangerous and must be carried out by someone who has been trained and who carries the appropriate certification. Felling a tree in a woodland is far more dangerous than felling one situated in an open space, and the larger the tree the more skill required to fell it safely. In addition, a valuable timber tree can be rendered worthless if felled incorrectly.

Unless you have been properly trained, have attended and passed a five-day course, are confident in your abilities and have all the correct safety equipment, you should leave tree-felling to a competent contractor.

Even more dangerous is the situation found in areas of wind-throw, where trees are 'hung-up' in the crowns of other trees. Specialist courses are designed for these situations and, again, skilled contractors should be employed wherever this situation arises.

Harvesting Options

Once a decision has been made to fell some trees, it is necessary to think about how this will be done. For most owners, the choice will be between employing a contractor or selling the trees standing to a timber merchant. If the owner has the necessary skills, then felling and conversion on-site offers the best option for adding value to the trees (*see* Chapter 11).

Employing a Contractor
In many cases, the best option is to employ a good local contractor rather than one from outside the area. He or she will be fully trained, have the correct equipment, and will know the area well. If you can build up

a close working relationship, you will be able to articulate your vision for the woodland and explain your management objectives and reasons for ownership. There are many very professional and knowledgeable contractors, and a number of the trade associations listed in Useful Addresses hold registers listing their details and specialisms.

Selling Standing to a Timber Merchant
This is probably the easiest way to sell your timber, since the merchant will carry out the whole operation, employing their own contractors and organizing haulage. In most cases, it will not give you the best return, but for high-quality broadleaved timber, where there is some risk in assessing the standing value and in the felling, it might be the better option.

Extracting the Timber
Once felled, the timber needs to be extracted from the woodland, and this should usually be done very soon after felling in case the timber degrades. If the timber has been sold to a contractor or timber merchant, they will extract it, but you should ensure that any contract includes penalties for non-removal and appropriate time-scales for site clearance.

Timber is unwieldy and, in small woodlands or when dealing with large logs, it can be difficult to extract it without doing a lot of damage.

The extraction of timber calls for careful planning in order to:

• Minimize disruption to the site.
• Avoid damage to the remaining trees.
• Avoid damage to the soils and watercourses.
• Minimize the effects on wildlife habitats.
• Suit the site conditions and the availability of machinery.

The most common methods used in British woodlands are:

Tractor Skidding
The debranched, tree-length timber is usually winched up against a butt plate on a tractor, and then dragged along the ground to a suitable loading bay. It is then either cut to length at the loading bay or transported in tree lengths from the site.

If the timber is not suspended, it may dig into the ground and cause safety problems. Furthermore, the timber may get damaged and dirty, affecting the price obtained. This method may also cause a lot of damage to the soil and vegetation, as well as to the rides and trees adjacent to the harvesting site.

Tractor Forwarding
The cut lengths of timber are loaded on to a trailer, which is then moved to a suitable loading bay. This forwarding is usually done with a purpose-built combination tractor and trailer, with a crane and grapple mounted on the trailer. This system is more efficient than skidding, and usually more economical for distances over about 200m. Less damage is done to the environment and to the timber.

On very sensitive sites, low-pressure tyres and/or the use of 'brash mats' will help to reduce damage to the soil and vegetation.

When extracting very large timber, especially broadleaves, forwarding may not be an option as the weight of the timber is likely to exceed the safe working load (SWL) of the crane.

Horse Extraction
Horses were once the main method of timber extraction in Britain. By the 1950s they had been largely replaced by tractors, but there is now a renewed demand for horse logging, particularly on ecologically sensitive sites or in high-quality broadleaved woodland where trees are closely spaced. A number of owners, including the Forestry Commission, now specify the use of horses on certain sensitive sites and may in some cases pay a premium for this.

Small-scale Machines
A number of modifications may be made to general-purpose machinery to enable smaller lengths and volumes of timber to be extracted. For example, an all-terrain cycle

ABOVE: A farm tractor being used with a self-loading trailer to extract logs from a woodland.

LEFT: Chris Seymour and his horse Maddie extract young conifers from a site being returned to native woodland under a PAWS restoration scheme. The use of a horse here has helped prevent damage to the remaining ground flora and the seed bank in the soil. (Photo: Ted Wilson)

with a trailer is capable of transporting pieces of timber of up to 3m in length. Some purpose-built harvesting machines, imported from Europe and specifically designed for small woodlands, are now on the market.

On-site Conversion

In small woods, where an owner wishes to make use of the timber on-site, or perhaps where the cost of extracting a few large pieces of timber is not economically viable, it may be worth considering the use of a portable mill to convert the timber on-site. This approach is discussed in more detail in Chapter 11.

Specialist Systems

If timber needs to be extracted from the sides of steep valleys, inaccessible terrain or other situations beyond the capabilities of the methods described above, then more specialized systems may be required. These might include skylines, cable cranes or even helicopters, all of which are expensive and can be justified only in exceptional circumstances.

Generating an Income from Woodland

While many people buy and own woodland purely for 'life-style' reasons and have no wish to make a return on capital, others either need to ensure that they 'break even' or, ideally, earn some income from it. Even where regular income is not needed, woodland maintenance may become a drain on resources.

When timber prices were much higher in real terms than they are now, and there was generous tax relief, many owners made a reasonable return on their investment. This is no longer the case. In addition, over the last ten years or so there has been a shift away from grant-aiding timber growing towards grants for public benefits.

All these factors now make the 'woodland economy' quite complex and subject not just to market forces but also to the whims of politicians and policy makers. This makes decision making and planning particularly difficult when dealing with the long time-scales involved in woodland management. A useful analogy is with farming: the changes to woodland grants and support are equivalent to a farmer having to review the choice of crop about every three weeks!

Woodland owners have a number of potential sources of income to support their objectives:

- Sale of goods, including timber, added-value products and non-timber forest products.
- Sale of services, including recreation and sport.
- Grant aid: public money for public good, including tree planting, the provision of access and enhancing biodiversity.
- Business development grants to support woodland-related enterprises.
- Payments to offset loss of income such as the conversion of productive farmland to woodland.

Increasingly, many of the values associated with woodland are termed 'non-market benefits', meaning that, although the benefits are enjoyed by, say, the public, money is not actually earned by the woodland owner. A good example might be within a National Park, where woodland plays an important part in the landscape and contributes substantially to the experience of the visitors. Tourists might spend a lot of money in the local economy, but the owners of the woodlands earn nothing from them directly. A study of south-west England in 2002 showed that woodlands contributed between £300 and £375 million to the economy annually from tourism, sport and recreation alone. The value of some of these non-market benefits is slowly filtering down to owners in the form of grants for such things as providing public access, but the sums involved are still quite small.

The aim of this chapter is to look at some of the ways that an owner might generate income directly or indirectly from the woodland. It includes timber production but looks at other possibilities as well. The advice of rural agencies should be sought as many incentives are regional or local and change regularly.

For many owners, timber production remains an important factor in managing woodland. However, there has been a distinct shift over recent years towards using more of the timber on-site and adding value prior to sale. Increasingly, owners are looking at ways of converting the raw material into products that have a higher intrinsic value and that can help support the costs of management. In some cases, this means that a reasonable return can be made, while in others the added-value timber products simply reduce the costs of bought-in materials and hence the costs of maintaining and managing the woodland.

Timber tends to be a low-value commodity until it is converted to other uses. While some of these remain highly industrialized, such as paper and fibreboard production, others may use quite low-intensity means of production. In the case of the green-wood crafts, the value is added almost solely by the skill and manual dexterity of the craftsperson.

This chapter considers the following potential sources of income. (Grant aid is discussed in Chapter 12.)

• Timber and added-value products.
• Non-wood forest products.
• Reintroducing animals to woodland.
• Biomass crops.
• Tourism and recreation: case study.

Timber and Added-value Products

Types of Felled and Converted Timber

Chapter 10 considered the felling and harvesting choices. If a decision has been taken to add value rather than sell to a timber merchant, there are a number of options available.

Once timber has been felled, it usually needs to be sawn into planks for a specific end-use. The exceptions to this are when the logs are:

• To be peeled or sliced for veneer.
• To be used 'in the round', either green or seasoned.
• Squared for use as beams, either green or seasoned.
• To be pulped.
• Cleft.

A log is usually sawn in one of two ways, 'through and through' or 'quarter sawn'. The former is easier to carry out with relatively simple machinery; the latter produces fewer planks but an enhanced grain pattern and higher value for use in decorative furniture.

Adding Value

Conversion and Utilization of Timber On-site

Timber prices, with a few exceptions, have been falling over the last decade. If timber is needed for use in the woodland or on the estate, it makes sense to convert this on-site and to add value to the raw material. An allowance is made under the felling-licence rules (*see* Chapter 12) to enable woodland owners to cut timber for their own use on a quarterly cycle.

Simple conversion of smaller-diameter material does not need to entail a large expenditure. Over the last few years, a number of machines designed for small woodlands have been introduced to the market, many of which have been imported from Scandinavia where there is a long history of adding value on-site.

Certain timbers may be 'cleft' along the grain, producing very strong wood in which the direction of cleaving follows the fibre, rather than cutting across them as in the case of sawing. Small-diameter material may be cleft easily when green. The National Trust has a machine that cleaves large oak logs for use in the renovation of their properties.

The Conversion of Timber by a Contractor

It may be possible to employ a contractor to convert the timber on-site for either a daily rate or a price per cubic metre. Alternatively, timber can be taken to a mill for conversion and brought back to the site. This might be worth while if there are a few valuable logs and a use has been identified for them. However, larger logs are expensive to transport and handle, and the owner takes all the risk if, on sawing, the timber is of poor quality.

The converted timber may also be sold from the woodland, perhaps as part of a business. The owners in the case study at the end of this chapter are experimenting with the production of candlesticks from low-grade softwoods.

Seasoning
This is the process by which water is removed from the timber, either passively by air drying, or actively in some type of kiln. Air drying is slow and the timber can only be dried to the moisture level of the ambient air, around 12 per cent moisture content (MC). With kiln drying, the moisture level may be set much lower and, if selling timber for use in a centrally heated house, this may typically be 6 per cent MC.

If space and time permits, air drying may be viable. The timber should be properly stacked, with space for the air to circulate between the planks.

Solar-drying kilns, in which the energy of the sun is used to warm up the air and to speed up the drying, are now available. Some use simple polytunnels similar to those used in horticulture, while others are purpose-designed buildings for larger quantities of timber. By using a mixture of air drying followed by kiln drying, it is possible to get seasoned hardwood planks to 6 per cent MC in four to eight months.

The major differences between the properties of green and seasoned sawn timber are summarized in Table 31. There has recently been a renewed interest in the use of green timber for the construction of residential properties, championed for example in the Channel 4 television series 'Grand Designs'.

Timber Quality

What do we mean by timber quality? Trees and timber come in all shapes and sizes, and the uses to which they are put are to some

English oak sawn 'through and through' and ready to season. The sawn boards are separated with wooden stickers made from a softwood such as larch to prevent any staining or damage to the timber. (Photo: Edward Mills)

extent dictated by the timber itself. It is now possible to take very low-grade conifer timber and to 'engineer' it into higher-value laminated beams making use of high technology and advanced glues and resins. Conversely, a coppice craftsman can take some 'low-grade' oak or ash and 'bodge' it into a piece of high-value furniture with hand tools and a high degree of skill.

Despite the above, there is still some agreement on what constitutes quality timber, and good-quality timber will fetch a better price than poor-quality timber. As in other walks of life, quality commands a premium and, although timbers do come in and go out of fashion, there is a continuing demand for high-quality timber.

Broadleaved timber increases in value as it gets larger and, in general, a merchant will demand as long and as large a log as possible. Conifer timber reaches a peak in value at around 1 cubic metre in volume. A log should ideally be straight, have a low rate of taper and be free of knots or any signs of decay or damage. The log should not have any nails or bits of fencing in the wood, nor should any splits or 'shake' be visible.

Table 31: Properties of green and seasoned sawn timber

Property	Green timber	Air-dried sawn	Kiln-dried sawn
Environmental credentials	Excellent. The lack of any processing means minimal energy use	Excellent. Air drying ensures minimal fossil-fuel consumption	Very good. Some energy use in drying and transport. Compared with other building products, both renewable and sustainable
Availability	Specialist suppliers, or direct from wood with selection of trees standing	Some merchants specializing in hardwoods	Widely available, but much of it imported
Ease of working	Ideal for conversion and manufacture with hand tools, but shrinks over time	Harder than green so needs machinery to manufacture	As air-dried
Strength	Cleft is, size for size, the strongest. Enables use of smaller-diameter materials	Sawing cuts across fibres and reduces strength	As for air-dried sawn
Bending	Pliable and easier to bend, esp. for ash, beech, elm and yew	Difficult	Very difficult
Energy used	Minimal	Minimal but slightly higher with some solar kilns	High usage
Suitability	Requires specialist skills for construction	External use. Can air dry only to 12% MC	Dimensionally stable indoors. Meets 6% MC for internal use if required

The Great Oak Hall at Westonbirt Arboretum, manufactured from green English oak sourced from local trees and the arboretum itself. The medieval construction method uses traditional techniques involving dowels and wedges.

Table 32: Properties of the commonly grown broadleaves (hardwoods)

Species	General properties	Common defects, constraints, comments	Main commercial markets in Britain	Niche markets
Alder	Medium density. Permeable to preservatives. Reddish-brown	Often of poor form and in small sizes. Dries well and quite quickly	None	Turnery, charcoal, toys, soles of wooden clogs, brush-backs
Ash	High resistance to shock. Permeable to preservatives. White to light brown	May be grown too fast. The dark heartwood is called olive ash. Dries quite quickly with few defects	High-quality sawn timber, sports goods, decorative veneers, boat building, vehicle frames	Hurley sticks. Excellent firewood
Beech	Wide range of uses. Dense timber; machines and works well. Not durable outdoors. White to pale brown	Dries rapidly but may distort or crack. Fine-grained	Furniture, flooring, joinery, veneer	Charcoal, turnery, tool handles. If steamed, turns pinkish colour. Excellent firewood if seasoned
Birch	Pale timber of moderate density. Permeable to preservatives. Light brown to white	Mainly in small sizes. Veneer popular in Scandinavia. May distort on drying	None	Turnery, furniture, small carvings, besom brooms
Cherry	Resistant to preservatives. Moderate strength. Heartwood a rich, light brown	Wood turns orange if worked 'green'	Furniture, veneer, joinery	Turnery
Hornbeam	Very hard and dense. Permeable to preservatives	Generally in small sizes from neglected coppice	None	Turnery, charcoal, wood carving. Excellent firewood
Oak	Dense and very durable heartwood. Sapwood needs preservative. Light to dark brown	Dries slowly and may split or 'check'	Furniture, decorative veneers, flooring, fencing, marine uses	Cleft fencing, turnery, bark for tanning, sawdust for food smoking

(continued overleaf)

Table 32: Properties of the commonly grown broadleaves (hardwoods)
(continued)

Species	General properties	Common defects, constraints, comments	Main commercial markets in Britain	Niche markets
Poplar	Low density, it resists abrasion. Does not splinter. Tough for its weight. Sapwood permeable	Plantations established for matchstick production in the 1950s	Flooring	Food storage and pallets. Toys and turnery
Sweet chestnut	Similar to oak but with less sapwood	Used in France in a similar way to oak in Britain	Subject to 'shake', so large timber seldom on the market	Cleft fencing, external joinery, turnery
Sycamore	Very white timber with good working properties. Permeable to preservatives. White to yellowish-white	May darken and stain if kiln dried at too high a temperature. Air dry to start, standing on end. May be dyed grey (harewood)	Furniture, decorative veneer, kitchen utensils	Turnery. The figured timber (ripple grain) is highly sought-after for veneer
Walnut (English)	Very variable in colour. Heartwood is moderately durable	More figured than American imports. For highest value, roots should be left on bole	Furniture and decorative veneer	Bespoke joinery, turnery, gun and rifle stocks

Timber Properties

Tables 32 and 33 summarize the properties of the more common timbers sold from British woodlands. Many of these timbers are suitable for use on-site, either for general maintenance or for construction.

Firewood

Wood is becoming increasingly sought-after as a fuel, particularly if used in modern, high-efficiency systems. It is a renewable source of energy, being carbon neutral and producing low levels of sulphur and ash. The establishment of an area of land on a firewood rotation might be worth considering, especially if the woodland is close to the heating system. In general, it is better to use broadleaved species, as they have the added advantage of coppicing and many derelict woods may serve as a useful source of firewood.

Green-energy grants are now available for the installation of energy-efficient wood-burning systems, and it may also be possible to obtain grant aid towards firewood-processing equipment. Other advantages include self-sufficiency, freedom from VAT and the conservation benefits that come from an actively managed coppice rotation.

Adding Value to the Raw Material

Raw logs are only the start of a process of adding value as the timber is processed into manufactured goods. The series of operations is called the 'wood chain'. At each stage in the wood chain, value is added by doing something to the timber that makes it more

Table 33: Properties of the commonly grown conifers (softwoods)

Species	General properties	Common defects, constraints, comments	Main commercial markets in Britain
Western red cedar	Low density and low strength. Resistant to fungi	Lightweight. Corrodes steel	Greenhouses and sheds. Weather-boarding. General joinery and fencing
Douglas fir	Heartwood resistant to decay. Sapwood needs preservative	Large-diameter material available	High-quality sawn timber, flooring, load-bearing beams. Plywood. General joinery and fencing (needs preservative). Gates. Flag poles
Western hemlock	Wide range of uses. White timber with few knots	Cannot be used outdoors.	Pulp and particle-board. Joinery, internal cladding, timber framing and flooring
Larch	Durable and hard. Heartwood resistant to decay	The three larches are similar in properties	Boat building (high-quality EL) and fencing
Scots pine	Heartwood is resinous. Preservative treatment if used outdoors	Reddish colour, resin bleeding	Joinery, flooring and construction, furniture
Norway spruce	Clean, white timber. Works well. Sapwood takes preservative well	Dimensionally stable so used indoors	Construction and general joinery. Sold imported as 'Baltic whitewood'. Pulp
Sitka spruce	Similar to Norway spruce	High-yielding species	Construction, particle-board, pulp

'saleable', or which puts it into a higher value category. Selling timber standing or at roadside does not allow the woodland owner to profit from the added-value potential of timber that may have taken a hundred years or more to grow.

Another reason to consider adding value relates to timber quality. While it is relatively easy to find a buyer who will pay a good price for high-quality timber, poor-quality timber often fails to find a buyer.

A number of low- and medium-cost methods of adding value are now available to owners of woodland. The following section explains three different approaches.

Chainsaw Mill

A chainsaw mill is an attachment that can be fitted to most professional chainsaws and, by means of an alloy guide system, allows a log to be cut 'through and through'. Some versions use just one chainsaw, while others are designed to run with one at each end.

They are very versatile and have a number of clear advantages over other approaches, namely:

- Low capital cost, or reasonable hire rates.
- Fast set-up times and ease of use.
- Lightweight, and may be carried to otherwise inaccessible locations.

- Small numbers of trees may be converted, which might otherwise be left in the wood.
- Larger trees that may be difficult or expensive to extract may be utilized.
- Planks of varying size and thickness can be cut.

However, they do have a number of disadvantages; these include the relatively large volume of timber lost as sawdust due to the wide cut (kerf), and the dimensional inaccuracy of the planks.

Mobile Sawmill

Mobile sawmills are now quite common and may be bought or hired. A number of technological developments have led to more accurate sawing, and the use of lightweight alloys allows some mills to be operated by just one person. Many of the smaller estate sawmills have closed and in some parts of Britain it is now quite difficult to find somewhere to saw small numbers of logs.

The main advantages of a mobile mill over a static mill are:

- Transport costs are reduced as the mill is brought to the timber.
- May be used in remote locations where infrastructure is limited.
- Sawn materials can be cut to the owner's own specification for use on-site or locally.
- The timber can be sawn close to where it is to be stored or dried, thus reducing the costs of transporting waste or unwanted material.
- Small volumes can be processed on-site when it would not be economic to transport less than full loads of timber.

There are a number of disadvantages, however, and these relate primarily to the technology used. If large volumes are available close to a modern sawmill, it may prove more cost-effective to use this method, but this is not usually the case with smaller woodlands. Factors to consider in advance of hiring a mobile mill include:

- The daily hire rate will need to be supplemented by costing-in the additional labour and equipment needed to off-load cut material and lift large logs.
- Quoted outputs are often very optimistic and assume perfect conditions and no down-time.
- Site selection and logistics are critical to ensure optimum use of the mill.
- Space is required to sort and stack the milled timber.
- The skill level of the operator and expertise on similar jobs with similar species.
- It is difficult to mill thin boards accurately using mobile saws, particularly if the timber is of poor quality.
- Mills are designed for different diameters and lengths of log.

Green-wood Crafts

Over the last few years, there has been a renaissance in the use of 'green-wood', and in the re-emergence of the traditional woodland skills and techniques such as bodging, weaving and steam bending. In addition, a demand has been created for locally produced charcoal, utensils and furniture made in predominantly broadleaved woodlands with low-impact manufacturing techniques.

A number of books are now available that detail these skills and celebrate the lifestyles

A chainsaw mill being used to plank a short length of Scots pine timber that might otherwise be used as firewood. (Photo: Neville Elstone)

they sustain. With the possible emergence of a low-carbon economy and pricing based on the embedded energy of manufactured products, there may come a time when such approaches lead to a wholesale reappraisal of traditional techniques of management and manufacture.

Non-timber Forest Products

In many countries throughout the world, non-timber forest products (NTFPs) are a major source of income for forest dwellers and local communities. Examples include natural honey, Brazil-nuts, cork, ginseng, truffles and rattan. In Europe, many families collect wild mushrooms and berries on a regular basis and, of course, truffle hunting is well developed and very lucrative in France and Italy (there are over 100,000 registered truffle hunters in Italy alone).

In Britain, the collection and marketing of these products is not yet well developed, but a number of woodland owners are beginning to see the opportunities.

The following categories of NTFPs are considered to have the most potential for British conditions:

- Edible goods. These include wild fungi, high-quality preserves and beverages.
- Game.
- Herbal medicines.
- Decorative products.
- Aromatics.
- Pharmaceuticals.

Of these, the two best-developed are edible goods and game.

Edible Goods

Fungi
Probably the best-developed market is the trade in wild fungi. This has grown considerably over the last ten years, with sales direct to restaurants, London markets and even export to Europe.

The most commonly sold fungi include:

'Woodmizer' mobile sawmill operating on a farm. The mill uses a narrow bandsaw that can just be seen in front of the operator. Behind the machine are sawn planks ready for seasoning. (Photo: Neville Elstone)

- Chanterelle.
- Cep.
- Chicken-of-the-woods.
- Hedgehog mushroom.
- Oyster mushroom.
- Wood blewit.

While many of these are wild, increasing attention is being given to the cultivation of fungi by inoculation. One company, Gourmet Woodland Mushrooms based in Pickering, North Yorkshire, specializes in selling kits to enable woodland owners to grow a variety of both native and exotic mushrooms.

Truffles
In recent years, the price paid for truffles has overtaken gold, with some fetching prices well in excess of this. The Black Perigord truffle (*Tuber melanosporum*) lives underground where it has a symbiotic relationship with the roots of a number of tree species, notably oak. Research is currently underway on the inoculation of native oaks with truffle spores at locations in the south of England.

CASE STUDY:
Low Bridge End Farm, Cumbria

Graham and Sarah Chaplin-Brice live at Low Bridge End with their family and have, over the last ten years or so, developed a tourism business based partly on woodland established in the early 1980s with forestry grants.

The farm is small: some 20 hectares of which 8 hectares are woodland and the rest poor-quality grazing and riparian (streamside) habitat. It is situated within the Lake District National Park and is typical of many small farm holdings in the uplands. Located in St John's-in-the-Vale, in an area of outstanding landscape and ecological interest, the land is too poor to make an adequate income from farming alone.

The woodland was established on previously wooded land cleared after the Second World War. The new planting was typical of the time, with close commercial spacing, little open space and a mix of conifers, mainly larch, and some broadleaves. The woods also contain one of the largest silver birch trees in Cumbria and a fine specimen of the common walnut, about 140 years old. The woodland is on steep ground, which makes extraction of timber difficult and expensive.

The farm has been in the family for nearly a hundred years and is now benefiting from its tourism developments with the following key objectives:

1. To maintain the farm as a viable enterprise in order to keep it in the family for future generations – stewardship.
2. To make the enterprise as environmentally friendly as possible.
3. To enhance the natural beauty of the farm.

Graham and Sarah make extensive use of a range of grants to enable them to move towards achieving their objectives, and the woodland plays an important part in this. The venture has also been a catalyst for their son, William, to set up a woodland conservation contracting business with support from a number of rural agencies.

The farm has a public footpath adjacent to the woodland, and an estimated 12,000 people use it every year. The proximity of the woodland to the footpath and the management that has been done in it, help to meet the diversification and free-public-access agenda, and so 'tick boxes' with rural grant-aiding bodies. On the site there is also a tea garden, camping barn and self-catering business, all of which support each other in some way.

The presence of woodland has contributed an added value to the enterprise by making the following possible:

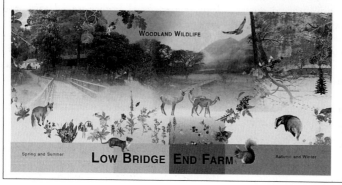

A postcard used by the owners to market the farm in tourist offices and through mailshots. The design features woodland and wildlife interest seen on the farm throughout the year, and the production costs were grant aided. Design by the East Cumbria Countryside Project.

- Construction of a woodland trail and printing of leaflets.
- Construction and management of viewpoints with interpretation displays.
- Free woodland information centre: this adds value to the visitor's experience.
- Woodland wildlife: difficult to quantify in terms of income, but it adds to the overall experience of the visitors.
- Leaflets downloadable from the website, www.campingbarn.com, which has about 10,000 'hits' annually.
- Business advice through a 'Forest Futures' project run by Cumbria Woodlands, aimed at helping to develop woodland-related businesses.
- Craft products using low-grade wood and marketed through the tea garden.

The farm has a very high wildlife interest. Otters and salmon use the river, while kingfishers and woodpeckers are seen regularly by visitors.

The following are some of the lessons learned by the owners:

- Each and every potential woodland business is unique and there is no single solution to success.
- Woodland may contribute many intangible benefits to a local enterprise, and these need to be linked to existing rural initiatives, often in creative ways.
- The presence of woodland may contribute significantly to the wildlife of the area and boost tourism and public access.
- An entrepreneurial approach is needed to maximize grant and income opportunities and to think laterally about the contribution woodland can make to a rural business.

Game

Although the management of woodland for game is quite common, and large numbers of people enjoy shooting on a recreational basis, the sale of game as a commercial venture is restricted to venison, with pheasant and other game-birds sold locally as a by-product of either syndicates or commercial shoots.

Venison is a healthy meat, low in cholesterol and reared under free-range and organic conditions. Most venison sold in Britain is farmed, although attempts have been made to market venison from wild upland deer. Looked at objectively, the market should be healthy and prices high enough to make it a commercial venture. However,

- There has been a decline in the sale of red meats.
- Until venison becomes more popular, it is unlikely to be stocked in supermarkets.
- Exports are to Europe where high quality is appreciated.
- The market is fragmented and economies of scale are not apparent.

With the total British deer population for the six species now approaching an estimated one million animals, there is an urgent need for a co-ordinated control programme aimed at reducing the population to more sustainable levels. If this could include a marketing and distribution strategy at a regional level, then venison sales may prove profitable for the woodland owner.

Reintroducing Animals to Woodland

Over the last few years a number of woodland owners have experimented with the introduction of either semi-wild or domesticated animals. Some of these, such as the wild boar, have been native in the past while others are domesticated animals which in the wild are forest dwellers. The introductions have been for food, to support woodland management and for eco-tourism ventures.

Wild Boar (Sus scrofa scrofa)

The wild boar was originally native to Britain where it numbered some one million during the Mesolithic period. At that time, only the red deer was a more common large mammal. The last wild populations were hunted to extinction by the end of the 13th century, and the populations reared for hunting were last seen here over 300 years ago.

The wild boar is a large, nocturnal and secretive woodland mammal. Adults may weigh over 150kg and live for twenty to thirty years. They have been farmed commercially in Britain for some years, and a number have been established in fenced woodland for meat production and eco-tourism ventures. Escapees from farms have established a number of breeding populations in southern England, and the absence of natural predators, such as the wolf and lynx, means that these populations may increase quite rapidly. They have no legal protection and may be controlled at any time. They are common throughout Europe, where they feed on, among other things, beech mast, acorns and chestnuts, and they are actively hunted in woodland. This helps maintain a viable, healthy and sustainable population.

There are conflicting views on their value in woodlands. They have a very positive effect on soil disturbance, leading to improved seedling regeneration and better control of woody weeds. However, their rooting habit may affect the distribution and abundance of plants such as the bluebell, and the survival of a number of rarer woodland orchids.

Pigs

At one time, pigs were a common sight in woodlands, and the right to 'pannage' goes back centuries. Pigs were originally woodland animals and their behaviour reflects this.

Pigs feed on the mast of beech and oak, and acorn-fed meat is in demand again. A number of research sites have been established where pigs have been introduced into established broadleaved woodland. Pigs are natural scarifiers in that their rooting behaviour helps to improve the ground and soil conditions in advance of natural regeneration.

Chickens

A novel experiment is currently underway by the Northmoor Trust in Oxfordshire to assess the suitability of woodland as a habit for commercially reared poultry. Initial results from the integration of free-range poultry with trees in an organic farming system show benefits to both trees and animals. The trees benefit from fertilizer inputs and reduced weeding, while the poultry gain from better welfare, with the shelter reducing predation.

Cattle

The revival in interest in traditional wood pasture systems, together with developments in agroforestry, point the way for a greater role for cattle in woodlands. The changes to the CAP, with subsidies paid for environmental benefits and products, together with a move away from intensive management systems, means that greater interest is likely to be paid to novel approaches to farming and forestry.

Biomass

Following concerns about the increasing use of fossil fuels, reflected in agreements on reducing or stabilizing the emissions of carbon dioxide, there have been various grants and incentives aimed at using non-fossil fuels for energy generation.

A number of woodland owners have considered the use of timber, possibly alongside other sources of energy, as a means of making use of these grants. The advent of more efficient wood burners makes such an approach to timber utilization, particularly for lower-grade materials, a real possibility. Furthermore, research into short-rotation coppice (SRC) grown on a two- to five-year rotation has shown excellent growth and yield on better soils.

At the time of writing, an Energy Crops Scheme is in place in England, offering grants of £1000 per hectare for SRC willow or poplar if at least 3 hectares is planted. There has to be an end-use for the crop, and this could be:

• A biomass power plant.
• A community energy scheme (CHP).
• Heat for a small business or (own) home.

CHAPTER 12

Buying and Owning a Woodland

This chapter is concerned with buying, or looking to buy, a woodland and with the practical implications of owning and managing one. It includes information on current legislation, health and safety and other related issues.

Buying Woodland

Over the last ten years, there has been a large increase in the number of people buying small woodlands. This has resulted in an active market with prices increasing far faster than is the case for larger and more 'commercial' woodlands. There has also been a tendency for larger woodlands to be subdivided, making buying more affordable, but perhaps not always in the best interests of the woodland itself. There has been a marked decline in the conversion of woodland to other uses, and in the replacement of broadleaved species with conifers. As with houses, the market for individuals buying smaller woodlands can be summed up as 'location, location, location'. The use of the internet for trading, and articles in consumer and style magazines have all helped to keep the market buoyant.

Many buyers are looking for broadleaved woodland within a few hours' drive of home, ideally with good access, some older trees and a stream or lake. In many cases, a substantial premium will be paid for smaller woodlands, reflecting a desire for ownership without a high level of maintenance. Some-

times the purchase might be part of a 'lifestyle choice' and, with larger woodlands, some desire to produce goods or services.

There is also an increasing interest from community groups in buying woodland for economic, social and cultural reasons. Such purchases may in the coming years alter the pattern of woodland ownership, which in some regions is concentrated in the hands of a few wealthy landowners. The Land Reform Act passed in Scotland in 2003 makes provision for this.

Charitable trusts, notably the Woodland Trust, have also been very active in purchasing woodland, often supported by donations and the use of lottery and other funding. These purchases often tend to be larger than those of individuals but, in some cases, a number of different interests will be bidding for the same woodland, pushing prices above typical market values.

Market Values

In some regions of Britain, woodland has increased in price sixfold in the last ten years. In comparison with many other purchases, woodland provides something tangible and long-lived. A small freehold woodland can just about be purchased for the price of a family motor car. With the increase in residential property values over the last few years, more and more people are converting some of their equity into trees.

Across Britain, prices vary enormously from one area to another (there may be as

173

much as a twenty-fold difference in the price per hectare). The large variations reflect the diverse nature of the woodlands sold and the importance of such factors as species, access, historic and landscape value, and the presence of sought-after features such as streams and lakes. Many woodlands change hands without coming on the open market, so it is always worth while making your interest known locally.

Commercial woodlands purchased for timber and/or investment reasons typically sell for a lower average price per hectare. They will tend to be larger and often more remote from urban centres. In addition, they tend to be valued and marketed by crop age and yield class, reflecting the importance of investment return and the time-scale involved.

Points to Consider
For many people, the purchase of a woodland is the fulfilment of a dream, and often the decision will be emotional rather than objective. Many owners will simply 'have the right feeling' about the woodland, and a combination of available capital and location might tip the balance. In the case of community groups or trusts, the purchase might be a response to a threat to the woodland, or it might be strategic or economic.

Whatever the reasons, there are a few points worth considering and a number of questions to ask before making an offer.

1. The local planning environment. What does the strategic plan tell you about future aspirations for the area? What might happen in relation to urban developments and road building?
2. Access. How easy will it be to get into the woodland, particularly in winter? What about access for larger vehicles if timber is to be extracted? Is there space to store timber prior to sale? Could the public visit the site easily?
3. Services. What is in the woodland and what is within easy reach? What are the likely costs of providing basic services such as water and electricity?

4. Liabilities. What might you be responsible for? For example, there might be mine workings, quarries and rights of way through the woodland.
5. If it is being sold leasehold, what rights are being retained by the freeholder?
6. Boundaries and maintenance. Whose responsibility are they? What condition are they in?
7. Statutory designations. Are there any affecting the woodland itself or is it within a larger designated area such as a National Park?
8. Watercourses, including streams, wells and springs. Are there any abstraction issues?
9. Could the woodland be developed for shooting, fishing and game? Are there any restrictions that may hinder future developments of this type?

Owning a Woodland

For many people, the simple enjoyment of wandering through their woodland in different seasons is enough justification for owning it. However, for many others an understanding and appreciation of the tree species, their ecology and silviculture, together with a desire to produce goods or services, will lead on to a more active role in the management of the woodland.

This might entail straightforward tasks utilizing quite simple tools, or it may involve more specialized expertise and equipment. In the majority of cases, some element of training will be required, and there may be statutory implications concerned with the use of herbicides and chainsaws. It might also be necessary to employ skilled contractors or to seek professional advice. In some cases, the development of woodland-related businesses, such as paint-balling and orienteering, might require advice from rural development specialists.

This section is concerned with a number of these ownership issues including:

• Advice from across the 'pond'.
• Living in your woodland.

- Rights and responsibilities.
- Sale of timber and employment of contractors.
- Felling licences.
- Health & Safety and training.
- Insurance.
- Professional advice.
- Grant aid.

Advice from across the 'Pond'

Hans Morsbach, whose excellent book, *Common Sense Forestry*, is written with American woodland owners much in mind, has a useful list of what he calls his 'Ten Commandments of Stewardship'. They are reproduced here, slightly edited, with his kind permission. Like all commandments, you may choose those that best fit your needs.

1. Enjoy your woodland.
2. Buy near. One key to enjoying your woodland is buying one that is quick and easy to get to.
3. Do not expect to make money. If this is what you want, place hope in appreciating land values.
4. Don't buy more land than you can manage. Your pleasure is more likely to come from observing and working your land than from its size.
5. Do not spend too much time, effort, and money on your trees.
6. Be kind to the environment.
7. Consult experts ... but remember who is boss. Go with your instincts if necessary.
8. Favour 'merchandisable' trees
9. Repress your tidying instincts. Remember that nature recycles more efficiently than you do.
10. Be a good citizen and activist.

These points apply equally to the private woodland owner in Britain and elsewhere. It is worth stressing the importance of a clear vision for your woodland, even if it may conflict with the prevailing trends.

Living in Your Woodland

For many woodland owners, the opportunity to live in it is often part of the dream and life-style choice. Having spent some time in it, and seen the effects of management taking shape, the option of living there, even for a short period, can seem quite natural and even sensible. However, in practice, obtaining planning permission for permanent residential use is extremely difficult. This applies not only to a building but also to caravans, yurts or temporary shelters.

In the few cases where permission has been granted, this has been justified by a need for residence based upon a woodland business integral to the production of timber products.

The only exceptions are for 'seasonal' forestry workers and an allowance of up to twenty-eight days per year for up to three caravans in a woodland exceeding 2 hectares. With the increasing pressure for residential development in the 'Green Belt', and calls for a relaxation of the rules on woodlands to allow traditional crafts to flourish, changes to the current situation could be a possibility.

Rights and Responsibilities

Land law is a complex subject in Britain, partly because the land has been settled for so long and partly because we live on a small island with many other people. This complexity is compounded by the fact that the law often differs across Britain and devolution is making it even more complex still. This section is designed simply to highlight the more important constraints that may affect a woodland owner in Britain.

For further detailed information on rights and responsibilities in the countryside, contact:

England: Countryside Commission.
Wales: Countryside Council for Wales.
Scotland: Scottish Natural Heritage.

Rights of Way

There are a number of different types of rights of way that might be present either in or adjacent to the woodland. Some of these are statutory rights, while others are common-law rights acquired over time, usually by local people. Some of these carry specific obligations to ensure the safe passage of people, horses or even vehicles. In summary, they include:

1. Definitive Public Rights of Way (DPROW) (England and Wales). These permit public access along designated routes at all times. Closure of a DPROW, for example for harvesting, requires public notices to be advertised and alternative routes to be provided for specified periods of time. The public access may be for: pedestrians (footpath), horses (bridleway), or all traffic (byways or 'green lanes'). Definitive maps are published and available for consultation at local planning offices. They are shown in green on the OS 1:25,000 Explorer maps.
2. Countryside and Rights of Way Act (2000). The CROW Act in England and Wales provides for public right of access on mountain, moor, heath and down (MMHD), and on registered common land.
3. Rights of way in Scotland. Access legislation in Scotland is currently undergoing review following the Land Reform (Scotland) Act 2003, under which there will be a Statutory Right of Responsible Access. Scottish Natural Heritage (SNH) has the Statutory duty to produce a Scottish Outdoor Access Code.
4. Private rights of way. In many rural areas, individuals or groups of people may have certain rights of access over woodland, perhaps to access adjacent land or property.
5. Permissive rights of way. These are quite common on large landed estates, and allow access in the same way as a DPROW but may be closed more easily by the owner. It is usual for an owner to close the route once a year and to erect appropriate signs.
6. Wayleaves and Easements. These are specific rights granted to utility companies to allow access over land for underground services and overhead power lines. It gives them rights of access to maintain the services in exchange for annual payments. There are strict controls on working with trees near services.

Occupier's Liability Acts
An owner has a legal duty under the Acts to ensure that any visitor to the woodland is reasonably safe for the purpose for which they are there. Certain caveats apply, depending upon the particular circumstances and the 'business' status of the woodland. Regular inspections are advised and hazards should be fenced off. You should seek legal advice with regard to the particular circumstances that might apply in your woodland.

Rights in Woodland
The close cultural links between woodland and rural people are perhaps best highlighted by the many rights that still exist in some areas for local people to take certain produce from woodland. Many of these are still valuable rights, and woodland properties may be sold with some of these specifically excluded from the sale. These may include:

• Firewood (traditionally called 'estovers').
• Sporting.
• Game.
• Minerals.
• Peat ('turbary').

Statutory Designations
The two more common designations likely to affect woodland are:

1. Tree Preservation Order. This might apply to the whole woodland, part of the woodland or to individual trees within it. A TPO comes under planning legislation and restricts the felling, lopping or uprooting of protected trees unless prior permission has been granted by the planning authority. A woodland already under a Forestry Commission approved management plan will not have a TPO placed upon it, although if a TPO is already in force at the time of approval it will remain.
2. Sites of Special Scientific Interest (SSSI). These are designated under the Wildlife and Countryside Act 1981 and are designed to protect those sites of the highest nature conservation value, either nationally or regionally. Any woodland

so designated will have a list of potentially damaging operations attached to it, and permission will have to be obtained to carry out any work listed. Advice should be sought from the local office of English Nature, Scottish Natural Heritage or the Countryside Council for Wales.

Others that may apply are listed in Table 10, Chapter 6.

Sale of Timber

Tenders and Contracts for the Sale of Standing Timber
Once a decision has been made to sell some of the trees, it will be necessary to apply to the Forestry Commission for a felling licence (*see* below), unless the felling has already been agreed as part of an approved management plan under a grant scheme.

An 'invitation to tender' should be sent to a number of reputable local contractors and this should include the following:

- Location: including national grid reference and a good-quality map.
- Area to be thinned or felled in hectares.
- Timing: when the operation is to start and to finish.
- Trees to be sold: detail how the trees will be marked and the boundaries indicated.
- Trees to be sold: the assessment of the volume may be done as detailed in Chapter 10 or carried out professionally. In either case, it must be clearly stated how the volume has been assessed.
- Inspection: when the site may be inspected and whom to contact to arrange a visit.
- Constraints: anything that may affect the operation, including conservation interests, designations or rights of way.
- Access: indicate on the map the main access routes and any other internal access issues.
- Deadline for receipt of tender, with a clear indication of postal address and the addressee.
- A note to the effect that you will not be bound to accept the lowest or any tender.

Once the contractor has been selected, a legally binding contract should be drawn up detailing the sale.

Employment of Contractors
There are many excellent contractors with a vast range of skills and expertise in woodland management. In many cases, it will be far more cost-effective, but possibly less fun, to employ a contractor to carry out specific tasks within a reasonable time-frame.

Because a lot of woodland work is weather-dependant, it often makes sense to complete an operation when the ground conditions are right. Try to prevent the work stretching into the following year, or interfering with the breeding seasons of the woodland mammals and birds.

For a number of reasons, it is often preferable to build up a relationship with a local contractor who will have a good knowledge of local conditions, woodland types and current markets.

Certification of Small Woods
The concept of woodland certification has its origins in the concerns voiced by the international forest and environmental community at the destruction of the tropical rainforests during the late 1980s and early 1990s. Put simply, the hope was that by 'labelling' timber as having come from well-managed forests, a market would develop for such timber and the consumer would put pressure on merchants to supply it. This would then lead to better and more 'sustainable' management of forests worldwide, but particularly in the tropics.

In practice, such schemes have done little to halt rainforest destruction, but have led to a growing demand for certified wood sourced from temperate regions. In some cases, it is now necessary to gain certification in order to sell timber in the market. For larger growers and companies, the costs of certification can be absorbed quite easily, but for owners of small woods the costs can be significant. As a result, a number of new approaches – specifically for small-woodland owners aiming for certification – are being adopted or trialled.

Among the more common certification schemes and standards in current use in Britain, are:

- UK Woodland Assurance Standard (UKWAS).
- Programme for the Endorsement of Forest Certification (PEFC).
- Forest Stewardship Council (FSC).
- 'Woodmark', run by the Soil Association and endorsed by the FSC.

Felling Licences

To fell trees in a woodland that is not under an approved management plan and not protected by a TPO, you have to apply to the Forestry Commission for a licence. The main exceptions to this requirement are:

- If you are felling less than 5 cubic metres per calendar quarter, of which 2 cubic metres or less is to be sold.
- Trees which are dead, dying or dangerous.
- Trees in a garden, orchard or public open space.
- If, in the case of thinnings, the trees are below 10cm dbh, coppice below 15cm dbh and any small trees under 8cm dbh.
- If required for felling under statutory provisions, for example to keep a utilities wayleave clear, or under approved planning consent.

Health & Safety and Training

Certificates of Competence

Figures produced by the Health and Safety Executive (HSE) show that forestry work involving chainsaws is one of the more dangerous activities. In addition, timber harvesting might use high-risk machinery, while the application of chemicals requires certain types of protection. The HSE now recognize the differing requirements of full-time contractors and occasional users in, for example, the use of chainsaws.

It is a legal requirement that people are adequately trained and competent to do their job safely. The responsibility for providing relevant training rests with the employer or self-employed person. However, the responsibility for deciding the level of training and competence required for a particular worksite falls to the person commissioning the work.

For certain forestry and arboricultural operations, independent assessment is necessary to confirm that training has been fully understood and appropriate skills developed. Nationally recognized certificates of competence are awarded for a wide range of operations, including chainsaws, brush cutters, herbicides, chippers and harvesting machinery.

Professional chainsaw operators need an accredited NPTC Certificate of Competence in the relevant unit or units (*see* AFAG 805). Those working outside forestry and wishing to fell trees of up to 20cm diameter need to obtain a Certificate of Basic Training. Occasional users wishing to fell trees over 20cm diameter must also hold an NPTC Certificate of Competence.

AFAG Guides

The HSE produce a number of leaflets written by the Arboricultural and Forestry Advisory Group (AFAG). These detail the Health and Safety current requirements relevant to the most common woodland operations, including the application of pesticides, the use of chainsaws and felling small trees. Although it is not compulsory to abide by the guides, their recommendations carry significant authority and, if an accident occurs, you would be expected to have taken notice of the contents.

The guides may be used as part of the risk assessment process, and detail the protective equipment needed for each operation.

In common with many H&S publications, the current versions are available on-line at www.hse.gov.uk/pubns/forindex.html.

Some of those more relevant to woodland operations include:

AFAG 202: Application of pesticides by hand-held equipment.
AFAG 203: Clearing saw.
AFAG 805: Training and certification (certificates of competence).

INDG 214: First aid at work. Your questions answered.

INDG 294: Managing Health and Safety in forestry.

INDG 317: Chainsaws at work.

INDG 345: Health & Safety training. What you need to know.

Regulations

If you employ staff, are self-employed or manage or control operations in a woodland, you will be expected to comply with a number of Regulations designed to ensure safety in the workplace. It is your duty to ensure that you keep up to date on the current HSE requirements.

Detailed information sheets on the following regulations are available from the HSE (*see* Useful Addresses).

- Provision and Use of Work Equipment Regulations 1998 (PUWER). HSE information sheet No.27.
- Lifting Operations and Lifting Equipment Regulations 1998 (LOLER). HSE information sheet No. 29.
- Manual Handling Operations Regulations 1992.

Risk Assessments

It is a legal requirement for an owner and/or employer to carry out a risk assessment if:

- The public has access to the woodland.
- You invite people into the woodland.
- You employ people in the woodland.

The HSE website has a number of guides to carrying out risk assessment, available to download free of charge.

Insurance

Two types of insurance are recommended for woodland owners:

1. Public liability. This covers claims by third parties for injury or damage sustained in the woodland.
2. Employers' liability. It is a legal requirement to hold insurance of this type if you employ staff, either directly or as subcontractors. It covers liability for damages and injury arising out of the course of their employment.

Further Insurance

Depending on the nature of the woodland and/or the business venture, insurance may be taken out for the following: wind-blow, fire and equipment.

Professional Woodland Advice

The Institute of Chartered Foresters maintains a list of approved consultants, many of whom specialize in woodland management. Also, the Forestry Commission's woodland officers are employed partly to support private owners, and there are a number of regional and local initiatives specifically set up to provide advice and assistance.

Grant Aid

Grants are given to woodland owners to help support certain national or regional objectives and priorities. These grants tend to reflect both political demands and, increasingly, the requirement to meet international obligations on such things as sustainable woodland management and climate change. As a result the grant packages are subject to continual review and modification. In the past, the objectives set for grant aid tended to remain the same for many years, to the extent that there are still woodland grants in operation today, for example Dedication Schemes, that date from the 1940s. With the long time-scales involved in managing woodland, some grant-aid stability is desirable but, in reality, is probably unlikely.

In Britain, the principal sources of grant aid are the England Woodland Grant Scheme (EWGS) in England, the Better Woodlands for Wales (BWW) in Wales, and the Scottish Forestry Grants Scheme (SFGS) in Scotland, all administered by the Forestry Commission. If you apply for grant aid, the application will be put on a public register for consultation and comments. In addition, the relevant statutory authorities will be notified of your proposals. In both cases, a time limit, usually twenty-eight days, will be set for receipt of responses. You may be asked to modify your proposals if objections are raised.

Grants are discretionary and, increasingly, the sums are allocated on a point-scoring system, so it is often difficult to know in advance whether an application will be successful. The proposed 'one-stop-shop' approach for rural grants should help owners maximize the grant aid available in future.

The changes being made to the Common Agricultural Policy (CAP), with the decoupling of subsidies from production, will inevitably have an effect on woodland grant support, either directly through Forestry Commission schemes or indirectly through links with agri-environment payments. If your woodland is within an agricultural holding you should seek expert advice on the objectives likely to maximize support for woodland management. However, you may decide to forgo grant support to achieve other objectives that are more important to you and to the woodland in the longer term.

At the time of writing, a woodland management grant may be applied for to meet some or all of the following 'activities that support woodland sustainability':

- Permissive access.
- Cultural heritage.
- Archaeological and historic features within woodland.
- Veteran trees and the deadwood resource.
- Management of open space.
- Soil protection.
- Pest control.
- Silvicultural operations to improve the stand, including pruning and thinning.
- Monitoring and mapping.
- Invasive species control.

The Regional Dimension
Devolution and the move towards more regional decision-making will continue to have a major effect on woodland policy making. Whereas in the past there was a common approach to grant aid and support for woodlands across Britain, today different regions might promote quite different objectives for local woodlands. For example, the priorities for woodland in the south-east of England, where the pressures for recreation and access are high, may be quite different to those in the Highlands of Scotland. These differences are being expressed in the Regional Forestry Frameworks currently in preparation for the English regions. They will be used in future to help allocate funds on the basis of local and regional need.

Glossary

afforestation Planting trees on unwooded land.

agro-forestry Growing trees on land also used for the production of crops or livestock.

ancient semi-natural woodland Ancient woodland composed of locally native species and which maintains itself by natural regeneration and/or by vegetative reproduction.

ancient woodland Woodland that has remained uncleared since at least AD 1600 in England and Wales, and since AD 1750 in Scotland.

ancient woodland indicators Species that are likely to be found only (or in most cases) in ancient woodland.

arboriculture The growing and tending of trees as individuals, as distinct from silviculture.

Atlantic period An episode of warm weather, which in Britain lasted from about 7,500 to 5,000 years ago.

basal area The area of the cross-section of a tree stem, including the bark, generally at breast height.

bast The inner living part of the bark which conducts sap down to the roots from the leaves.

beating-up The replacement of trees lost in young plantations, usually only for the first few years.

biodiversity (biological diversity) The variety and abundance of life forms, processes, functions and structures, including the relative complexity of species, communities, gene pools, and ecosystems at spatial scales that range from local through regional to global.

biomass Plant crops grown for fuel. The entire amount of living organisms in a particular habitat, usually measured in kilograms per hectare.

bole The main stem or trunk of the tree.

boreal forest Sometimes also called the Taiga, it is the world's largest forest biome, stretching around the northern hemisphere. In Europe, it includes the Scottish Highlands and is composed primarily of dominant conifer species together with some broadleaves, including birch, aspen, alder and goat willow.

brashing The removal of the dead side branches of conifer trees to about 2m above ground – to allow access, but sometimes for visual or protection reasons.

breast height A standard height from ground level for recording diameter, girth, or basal area of a tree, generally 1.3m.

broadleaf A tree with broad, flat leaves. Nearly always deciduous in Britain, and sometimes referred to as hardwood.

brown earth A fertile soil capable of growing a wide range of different tree species. Rich in organic matter, generally deep and with a rich variety of soil organisms.

bryophytes Mosses and liverworts.

butt The largest end of the tree or log.

cambium The thin layer of growing cells just beneath the bark of a tree.

canopy The foliar cover in a forest stand, consisting of one or several layers.

cant An area of coppice harvested on a regular cycle.

carr Waterlogged woodland, usually dominated by common alder.

clear-fell An area over 0.25 hectares in which all the trees are cut down.

clone A tree or trees propagated vegetatively from a single individual, all of which are genetically identical.

compartment A distinct subdivision of a woodland suitable as a basis for long-term management and record-keeping.

conifer A tree bearing cones and having seeds unenclosed. The leaves are needle- or scale-like and most found in Britain are evergreen.

Continental (as applied to climate) Clear distinctions between seasons, with hot summers and cold winters.

continuous cover The use of a silvicultural system in which the canopy of trees is maintained without clear-felling.

coppice A tree or shrub repeatedly cut down close to the ground. It may also refer to a wood (copse) that has been coppiced, usually on a cycle of between eight and twenty-five years.

crown The spreading branches and foliage of a tree. In woodland, this will be narrower than if the tree is grown in the open.

cultivars Cultivated varieties.

dominant Trees with crowns extending above the general level of the main canopy of even-aged stands or, in uneven-aged stands, above the crowns of the tree's immediate neighbours, and receiving full light from above and partly from the sides.

epicormic shoots Shoots sprouting from adventitious or dormant buds just below the bark on the main stem.

even-aged stand A stand of trees containing a single age class in which the range of tree ages is usually less than 20 per cent of the rotation.

Fertile Crescent Possibly the earliest centre of food production in the world, it flourished about 9,000 years ago in what is now the Middle East.

flush The first spurt of growth after dormancy when the buds burst into leaf. An area of land into which nutrient-rich water flows.

forest Originally any area of land owned by the Crown and managed for large game under Forest Law. Now generally refers to larger commercial plantations, but also to natural pinewoods, the New Forest in Hampshire and to the National Forest (farm and forest) in the Midlands.

fragmentation The process, natural or through clearance, of reducing the size and connectivity of stands that compose a forest or landscape.

frost hollow A low-lying region where cold air collects, causing damage to the shoots or leaves of trees in late spring or early summer. May also occur if a belt of trees prevents cold air moving down a slope.

genotype The genetic constitution of an organism in terms of its hereditary characteristics, as distinguished from its physical appearance (phenotype).

granny pine A term used in Scotland to denote a veteran Scots pine of large girth and crown.

green tonne A weight measurement of freshly felled timber before any drying has occurred.

habitat The place where an animal or plant naturally or normally lives and develops.

Habitat Action Plan (HAP) A plan that identifies the management required to maintain or improve a habitat with high conservation status. HAPs fall within the UK Biodiversity Action Plan (BAP).

heartwood The inner core of a tree that no longer conducts sap. When felled generally more durable than sapwood.

hectare An area of land equal to 10,000 square metres. (1 hectare = 2.471 acres.)

high forest Woodland composed of single-stemmed trees with no coppice present and managed sustainably on long rotations, often for the production of timber.

iron pan An impermeable layer of soil, formed where iron compounds have been washed down. Prevents free drainage but may be broken mechanically. Often found under sandy soils.

locally native Species present after the post-glacial colonization but naturally restricted to a particular locality.

lower-impact silvicultural systems (LISS) Systems such as group selection and minimum intervention that promote species and structural diversity, usually in conifer plantations on wind-firm sites.

Lyme's disease A disease caused by infection from a micro-organism (*Borrelia burghdorferi*), itself transmitted by a bite from the wood tick, a blood-sucking parasite normally of deer. The wood tick is found in many areas, particularly in woodland where deer are common. A tick will settle anywhere on a human body, but prefers warm, moist and dark places such as the crotch or armpits. Symptoms include those associated with flu, including sickness, drowsiness and lethargy.

mast Seed that is produced as a heavy crop in some years.

monoculture A stand of a single species, generally even-aged.

mycorrhizae The symbiotic association between certain fungi and plant roots which enhances the uptake of water and mineral nutrients.

native species A species considered to have naturally colonized part or parts of the British Isles before the formation of the English Channel.

natural regeneration The regeneration of woodland by natural means without planting or sowing.

non-intervention The management of woods when they are left to develop without human intervention. May also be referred to as 'areas of minimum intervention'.

nurse tree A tree, either naturally occurring or introduced, used to nurture, improve the survival or improve the form of a more desirable tree or crop when young by protecting it from frost, sun, or wind.

old growth A forest that has developed free from any large-scale disturbance over an extended time period, and that contains large, old trees, large variations in tree size and spacing, and both standing and fallen deadwood.

origin The original natural genetic source of a species.

overbark The volume of wood including the bark, measured standing or felled.

pannage The practice of turning pigs out into woodlands in autumn.

perambulation A legal document defining a piece of land by describing its boundaries, from which comes the practice of walking the 'bounds'.

phenotype The visible expression of a trait in an individual resulting from the interaction of the individual's genotype and its environment.

plantations on ancient woodland sites (PAWS) Any woodland that has been planted on the site of an ancient woodland.

pollard A tree that has been repeatedly cut 2–4m above ground level to produce a crop of small-diameter material for harvesting.

primary woodland In Britain, woodland from the last glaciation which has never been cleared.

provenance The region where a tree comes from, or where the seed is collected from.

refugia Isolated areas to which vegetation retreated during the last ice age and which acted as seed sources for the succession that took place when the climate warmed up again.

restocking The practice of replanting a site after felling.

retention (long-term) An area left beyond its normal economic rotation age, usually to provide habitat and landscape diversity, and in which it is intended to allow the trees to reach biological maturity.

ride Areas left unplanted between stands of trees to allow access. Often managed to provide open and edge habitats.

ring-barking The practice of removing completely the bark of a living tree all around the trunk, thereby severing all the conducting tissues. This may be done to stimulate seed production as an aid to natural regeneration, or to create standing deadwood to increase biodiversity.

riparian zone The land immediately adjacent to a watercourse.

rotation In even-aged systems, the period between establishment and final felling.

roundwood Logs and small branches.

sawlogs Logs of at least 14cm top diameter capable of being sawn into planks or boards.

scarification Mechanical removal of competing vegetation and/or disturbance of the soil surface, designed to enhance natural regeneration.

secondary woodland Woodland resulting from natural succession or planting on land that had been previously cleared of woodland at some stage in the past (*see also* primary woodland).

semi–natural woodland Woodland composed primarily of species native to the site and which has arisen as a result of natural regeneration rather than planting.

shade tolerance The relative capacity of a plant to become established and grow beneath overtopping vegetation.

shake Timber defect, especially in oak and sweet chestnut, where stress cracks, caused by such factors as growth on certain soils, felling and drying, reduce the value of a log.

shelterwood A method of regenerating an even–aged stand in which a new age class develops beneath the moderated microclimate provided by the residual trees.

silviculture A planned process whereby a stand is tended, harvested, and re-established. The system name is based on the number of age classes.

snag A standing dead tree.

short rotation coppice (SRC) Coppice, usually of willow or poplar clones, established at high density and grown on a rotation of two to five years for biomass energy production.

stand A contiguous group of trees sufficiently uniform in age/class distribution, composition, and structure, and growing on a site of sufficiently uniform quality, to be a distinguishable unit.

standing volume The volume of a tree or stand measured before felling and usually expressed in cubic metres overbark.

stewardship Caring for land and associated resources in a manner that enables their passing on to future generations in a healthy condition.

succession A series of dynamic changes by which organisms succeed one another through a series of plant community (seral) stages, leading to potential natural community or climax.

sustainability The capacity of forests, ranging from stands to ecosystems, to maintain their health, productivity, diversity, and overall integrity, in the long run, in the context of human activity and use.

symbiotic A relationship between two organisms where both benefit.

thinning A cultural treatment made to reduce the stand density of trees primarily to improve growth, enhance forest health, or to recover potential mortality.

transformation The process by which the management of even–aged stands is altered in order to achieve greater within-stand structural and species diversity.

underwood The woody component of the shrub layer (often applied to coppice). Also used to denote the cut wood.

veneer A thin or very thin layer of wood produced by peeling or slicing a log. Used either for decorative purposes, or for engineered products such as plywood.

vernal Plants adapted to flower in early spring when light levels are high and before the canopy trees come into leaf.

veteran tree A tree that, by virtue of its great age, size or condition, is of exceptional value culturally, in the landscape or for wildlife.

virgin woodland Wholly natural woodland that flourished before human influence affected the structure and composition. In Britain, this last occurred during the Atlantic period before Neolithic man arrived.

'waterhouse' pile A log pile specifically retained for invertebrates.

wildwood The type of woodland that is presumed to have occurred in Britain after the retreat of the ice sheet and before human intervention.

wind–firm Usually referring to edge trees that will remain stable in strong winds.

wind–throw The uprooting of trees by very high winds.

woodland Defined as land with a canopy cover of trees of at least twenty per cent, or having the potential to reach this. It may include felled areas and internal open space.

wood pasture Grazed woodland with open-grown and often pollarded veteran trees at various densities.

Further Reading

There is a wealth of published information about trees and woodlands, written for both the non-specialist and for professional foresters and academics. Increasingly the most up-to-date research and advice is often published first on the web, and many technical guides are available to download free of charge. The websites of the major providers of this type of technical information are included in the list of useful addresses.

Many of the following books will be found useful for anyone wishing to learn more about trees and woodland, particularly in the temperate regions. A number of excellent books are currently out of print but, because the timescales involved in managing woodland are so long, they often remain very useful and relevant and are worth seeking out. Out of print titles may be found in second-hand bookshops specializing in natural history and ecology or borrowed from public libraries. They may also be obtained through specialist out-of-print search services.

Agate, Elizabeth (ed.), *Woodlands: A Practical Handbook*, BTCV, 2002.

Broad, Ken, *Caring for Small Woods*, Earthscan, 1998.

Budiansky, Stephen, *Nature's Keepers*, Weidenfeld & Nicolson, 1995.

Edlin, Herbert, *British Woodland Trees*, Batsford, 1944.

Edlin, Herbert, *Wildlife of Wood and Forest*, Hutchinson, 1960.

Harris, Esmond, *et. al.*, *Oak: A Natural History*, Windgather Press, 2003.

Harris, Esmond and Jeanette, *Wildlife Conservation in Managed Woodlands and Forests*, Research Studies Press, 2003.

Law, Ben, *The Woodland Way*, Permanent Publications, 2001.

Leopold, Aldo, *A Sand County Almanac*, Oxford University Press, 1949 (paperback reprint 1989).

Mabey, Richard, *The Common Ground*, Hutchinson, 1980.

Marren, Peter, *The Wild Woods. A Regional Guide to Britain's Ancient Woodland*, David and Charles, 1992.

Miles, Archie, *Silva: The Tree in Britain*, Ebury Press, 1999.

Mitchell, Alan, *et. al.*, *Field Guide to the Trees of Britain and Northern Europe*, Collins, 1992.

Mitchell, Alan, *Trees of Britain and Northern Europe*, Collins, 1982.

More, David and Johnston, Owen, *Collins Tree Guide*, Collins, 2004.

More, David and White, John, *Cassell's Trees of Britain and Northern Europe*, Cassell, 2003.

Morsbach, Hans, *Common Sense Forestry*, Chelsea Green, 2002.

Mutch, William, *Tall Trees and Small Woods*, Mainstream Publishing, 1998

Pakenham, Thomas, *Meetings With Remarkable Trees*, Weidenfeld & Nicolson, 1996.

Perlin, John, *A Forest Journey: The Role of Wood in the Development of Civilization*, Harvard University Press, 1991.

Peterken, George, *Natural Woodland*, Cambridge University Press, 1996.

Rackham, Oliver, *Ancient Woodland: Its History, Vegetation and Uses in England*, Castlepoint Press, 2003.

Rackham, Oliver, *Trees and Woodland in the British Landscape*, Weidenfeld and Nicholson, 2001.

Read, Helen and Frater, Mark, *Woodland Habitats*, Routledge, 1999.

Stokes, Jon, *et. al.*, *The Heritage Trees: Britain and Northern Ireland*, Constable and Robinson, 2004.

Tapper, Stephen (ed), *A Question of Balance: Game Animals and their Role in the Countryside*, The Game Conservancy Trust, 1999.

Thomas, Peter, *Trees: Their Natural History*, Cambridge University Press, 2000.

Williams, Hugh, *Create a Farm Woodland*, free from the National Forest Company, 2003.

Worster, Donald, *Nature's Economy*, Cambridge University Press, 1994.

Forestry Commission Publications

(Those marked ★ may be downloaded free of charge from: www.forestry.gov.uk/publications)

Anon, *Forest Mensuration – Management Handbook* (previously Booklet 39), 1975 (reprint 2005).

Anon, *Introduction to the UK Woodland Assurance Standard*, 2003. ★

Anon, *The Management of Semi-natural Woodlands – Practice Guide Numbers 1–8*, 2003.★

Anon, *The UK Forest Standard*, 2004. ★

Anon, *Timber Measurement – Management Handbook* (previously Booklet 49), 1983.

Evans, Julian, *Silviculture of Broadleaved Woodland, Bulletin 62*, 1984.★

Harmer, Ralph, *The Silviculture and Management of Coppice Woodlands – Management Handbook*, 2003.

Kerr, Gary, *Growing Broadleaves for Timber – Management Handbook*, 1993.

Mason, Bill, *Managing the Pinewoods of Scotland – Management Handbook*, 2004.

Quine, Chris, *et. al.* (Eds), *Managing Woodlands and their Mammals*, 2004.

Willoughby, Ian, *et. al.*, *Creating New Broadleaved Woodlands by Direct Seeding, Practice Guide*, 2004. ★

Willoughby, Ian, *Reducing Pesticide Use in Forestry – Practice Guide*, 2004. ★

Humphrey, Jonathan, *Restoration of Native Woodland on Ancient Woodland Sites – Practice Guide*, 2003. ★

Useful Addresses

Ancient Tree Forum:
www.woodland-trust.org.uk/ancient-tree-forum

British and Irish Hardwood Improvement Programme (BIHIP)
www.bhip.org.uk

British Deer Society
Fordingbridge
Hampshire SP6 1EF
www.bds.org.uk

British Trust for Conservation Volunteers
(BTCV)
163 Balby Road
Doncaster
South Yorkshire DN4 0RH
www.btcv.org

British Trust for Ornithology
The Nunnery
Thetford
Norfolk IP24 2PL
www.bto.org.uk

Coppice Association North West (CANW)
www.coppicenorthwest.org.uk

Countryside Agency
John Dower House
Crescent Place
Cheltenham
Gloucestershire GL50 3RA
www.countryside.gov.uk

Countryside Council for Wales
Headquarters:
Maes-y-Ffynnon,
Penrhosgarnedd, Bangor,
Gwynedd LL57 2DW
www.ccw.gov.uk

The Deer Initiative
PO Box 2196
Wrexham LL14 6YH
www.thedeerinitiative.co.uk

Department of Agriculture and Rural Development (DARDNI):
www.dardni.gov.uk

Department for Environment Food and Rural Affairs (DEFRA)
Information Resource Centre
Lower Ground Floor
Ergon House
c/o Nobel House
17 Smith Square
London SW1P 3JR
Help line: 08459 335577
www.defra.gsi.gov.uk

Deer Commission for Scotland
Knowsley
82 Fairfield Road
Inverness IV3 5LH
www.dcs.gov.uk

English Nature
Northminster House
Peterborough, PE1 1UA
www.english-nature.org.uk
(From January 2007, part of a larger
agency, Natural England, which will also
include parts of the Countryside Agency
and DEFRA .)

Forest Research
Alice Holt Lodge
Farnham
Surrey GU10 4LH
AND
Northern Research Station
Roslin
Midlothian EH25 9ST
www.forestresearch.co.uk

Forest Stewardship Council (FSC)
Unit D
Station Buildings
Llanidloes
Powys SY18 6EB
www.fsc-uk.info

Forestry Commission HQ
Silvan House
231 Corstorphine Road
Edinburgh EH12 7AT
www.forestry.gov.uk

FC Publications Section
PO Box 25
Wetherby
West Yorkshire LS23 7EW
0870 121 4180

Forestry Contracting Association (FCA)
Dalfling
Inverurie AB51 5LA
www.fcauk.com

Forestry and Timber Association (FTA)
5 Dublin Street Lane South
Edinburgh EH1 3PX
www.forestryandtimber.org

Game Conservancy Trust
Fordingbridge
Hampshire SP6 1EF
www.gct.org.uk

Health and Safety Executive (HSE)
HSE Information Services
Caerphilly Business Park
Caerphilly CF83 3GG
www.hse.gov.uk

HSE Books
PO Box 1999
Sudbury
Suffolk CO10 2WA
www.hsebooks.co.uk

Institute of Chartered Foresters
7A St Colme Street
Edinburgh EH3 6AA
www.charteredforesters.org

Lantra Awards
Lantra House
Stoneleigh Park
Stoneleigh
Warwickshire CV8 2LG
www.lantra.co.uk

The Mammal Society
2B Inworth Street
London SW11 3EP
www.mammal.org.uk

National Forest Company
Enterprise Glade
BatchLane
Moira
Swadlincote
Derbyshire DE12 6BD
www.nationalforest.org

National Proficiency Tests Council (NPTC)
Stoneleigh Park
National Agricultural Centre
Stoneleigh
Warwickshire CV8 2LG
www.nptc.org.uk

National School of Forestry
University of Central Lancashire
Penrith
Cumbria CA11 0AH
www.forestry.org.uk

Northern Ireland Forest Service
Dundonald House
Upper Newtownards Road
Belfast BT4 3SB
www.forestserviceni.gov.uk

Northmoor Trust
Little Wittenham
Abingdon
Oxfordshire OX14 4RA
www.northmoortrust.co.uk

Ordnance Survey
www.ordnancesurvey.co.uk

*Programme for the Endorsement of Forest
Certification (PEFC)*
www.pefc.co.uk

Ramblers Association
2nd Floor, Camelford House
87-90 Albert Embankment
London SE1 7TW
www.ramblers.org.uk

*Royal Forestry Society of England, Wales and
Northern Ireland*
102 High Street
Tring
Hertfordshire HP23 4AF
www.rfs.org.uk

Royal Scottish Forestry Society
RSFS Offices
Hagg-on-Esk
Canonbie
Dumfrieshire DG14 0XE
www.rsfs.org

Royal Society for the Protection of Birds (RSPB)
The Lodge
Sandy
Bedfordshire SG19 2DL
www.rspb.org.uk

Scottish Natural Heritage (SNH)
12 Hope Terrace
Edinburgh EH9 2AS
www.snh.org.uk

Small Woods Association,
The Old Bakery
Pontesbury
Shropshire SY5 0RR,
www.smallwoods.org.uk

Soil Association (Woodmark)
Bristol House
40–56 Victoria Street
Bristol BS1 6BY
www.soilassociation.org.uk

Summerfield Books
www.summerfieldbooks.com

Tree Aid
www.treeaid.org.uk

Tree Council
71 Newcomen Street
London SE1 1YT
www.treecouncil.org.uk

Tree Help Line
Alice Holt Lodge
Wrecclesham
Farnham
Surrey GU10 4LH
Tel: 09065 161147

The Vincent Wildlife Trust
3 & 4 Bronsil Courtyard
Eastnor
Hertfordshire HR8 1EP
www.vwt.org.uk

Woodland Heritage:
www.woodlandheritage.org.uk

The Woodland Trust
Autumn Park
Dysart Road
Grantham
Lincolnshire NG31 6LL
www.woodland-trust.org.uk

Index

Metric/Imperial conversion factors

Metric		Imperial	Metric		Imperial
1 centimetre	=	0.394 inches	1 cubic centimetre	=	0.061 cubic inches
1 metre	=	3.281 feet	1 cubic metre	=	35.310 cubic feet
1 kilometre	=	0.621 miles			
			1 gram	=	0.035 ounces
1 sq. centimetre	=	0.155 square inches	1 kilogram	=	2.205 pounds
1 sq. metre	=	10.760 square feet	1 tonne	=	0.984 tons
1 hectare	=	2.471 acres			
			1 litre	=	1.76 pints
					(35.211 fl. ounces)

Centigrade to Fahrenheit:
Centigrade × 9 ÷ 5 + 32 = Fahrenheit